GRANITE AND RAINBOW

BOOKS BY VIRGINIA WOOLF

The Voyage Out, 1915

Night and Day, 1919

Kew Gardens, 1919

Monday or Tuesday, 1921

Jacob's Room, 1922

The Common Reader: *First Series,* 1925

Mrs. Dalloway, 1925

To the Lighthouse, 1927

Orlando, 1928

A Room of One's Own, 1929

The Waves, 1931

Letter to a Young Poet, 1932

The Common Reader: *Second Series,* 1932

Flush, 1933

The Years, 1937

Three Guineas, 1938

Roger Fry: *A Biography,* 1940

Between the Acts, 1941

The Death of the Moth and Other Essays, 1942

A Haunted House and Other Essays, 1944

The Moment and Other Essays, 1947

The Captain's Deathbed and Other Essays, 1950

A Writer's Diary, 1954

Virginia Woolf and Lytton Strachey: Letters, 1956

Granite and Rainbow, 1958

Contemporary Writers, 1965

Collected Essays *(4 vols.),* 1967

Mrs. Dalloway's Party, 1973

GRANITE
AND RAINBOW

Essays by

VIRGINIA WOOLF

A HARVEST BOOK

HARCOURT BRACE JOVANOVICH

NEW YORK AND LONDON

Printed in the United States of America

Library of Congress Cataloging in Publication Data
Woolf, Virginia Stephen, 1882-1941.
    Granite and rainbow.
    (A Harvest book ; HB 318)
    1. Fiction—History and criticism—Addresses,
essays, lectures.   2. Biography (as a literary form)
—History and criticism—Addresses, essays, lectures.
I. Title.
 [PN3324.W6 1975]   809.3   75-6782
ISBN 0-15-636475-1

First Harvest edition 1975
B   C   D   E   F   G   H   I   J

CONTENTS

6 CONTENTS

EDITORIAL NOTE

VIRGINIA WOOLF published during her life two volumes of collected essays: *The Common Reader*, First and Second Series. After her death I took steps to gather together her essays which had not been included in those volumes. There were a considerable number of them; most of them had been published in journals, but a few had never been published. They proved sufficient to fill three posthumous volumes: *The Death of the Moth*, 1942; *The Moment*, 1947, and *The Captain's Death Bed*, 1950. I included in those volumes only those essays which seemed to me of the same order of excellence as those which she herself had chosen to reprint in *The Common Reader*. When I published *The Captain's Death Bed*, I thought that I had been able to identify all the essays which had appeared in journals and I wrote in the Editorial Note to that volume that it would be the last book of collected essays, since I had now included in the posthumous volumes all her essays, with a few unimportant exceptions.

I was mistaken about this, for those who had searched the records, including myself, had overlooked a considerable number of essays of the same kind and of the same merit as those published in the five volumes. There were several reasons for this. Virginia Woolf only spasmodically kept copies of essays and reviews written by her for journals and there was often no record of their publication among her papers. This accounted for the fact that the existence of the long essay, *Phases of Fiction*, published in *The Bookman* in 1929, was forgotten. Another difficulty was that so many of her essays appeared anonymously in papers like the *Times Literary Supplement*, and a further complication, not noticed by the searchers, was that in some cases they had been written under her maiden name, Virginia Stephen. The discovery of the essays now published was due to the zeal and intelligence of Miss B. L. Kirkpatrick and Dr. Mary Lyon. Miss Kirkpatrick has devoted infinite pains to the preparation of her *Bibliography of Virginia Woolf.* Dr. Lyon is Director of Graduate Residence of Radcliffe College, Cambridge, Mass., and teacher of a literature course at Harvard University. She is writing a book on *Virginia Woolf as Critic,* and came to England on a visit in order to do some research on her subject. She took much trouble to determine what had or had not been published and re-published. Without the work of Miss Kirkpatrick and Dr. Mary Lyon I should never have found the essays now published in this volume. The journals in which they first appeared are given by me in footnotes to the essays.

LEONARD WOOLF

PART I
THE ART OF FICTION

The Narrow Bridge of Art[1]

FAR the greater number of critics turn their backs upon the present and gaze steadily into the past. Wisely, no doubt, they make no comment upon what is being actually written at the moment; they leave that duty to the race of reviewers whose very title seems to imply transiency in themselves and in the objects they survey. But one has sometimes asked oneself, must the duty of the critic always be to the past, must his gaze always be fixed backward? Could he not sometimes turn round and, shading his eyes in the manner of Robinson Crusoe on the desert island, look into the future and trace on its mist the faint lines of the land which some day perhaps we may reach? The truth of such speculations can never be proved, of course, but in an age like ours there is a great temptation to indulge in them. For it is an age clearly when we are not fast anchored where we are; things are moving round us; we are moving ourselves. Is it not the critic's duty to tell us, or to guess at least, where we are going?

Obviously the inquiry must narrow itself very strictly, but it might perhaps be possible in a short space to take one instance of dissatisfaction and difficulty, and, having examined into that, we might be the better able to guess the direction in which, when we have surmounted it, we shall go.

Nobody indeed can read much modern literature without being aware that some dissatisfaction, some difficulty, is lying in our way. On all sides writers are attempting what they cannot achieve, are forcing the form they use to contain a meaning which is strange to it. Many reasons might be given, but here let us select only one, and that is the failure of poetry to serve us as it has served so many generations of our fathers. Poetry is not lending her services to us nearly as

[1] *New York Herald Tribune*, August 14, 1927.

11

freely as she did to them. The great channel of expression which has carried away so much energy, so much genius, seems to have narrowed itself or to have turned aside.

That is true only within certain limits of course; our age is rich in lyric poetry; no age perhaps has been richer. But for our generation and the generation that is coming the lyric cry of ecstasy or despair, which is so intense, so personal, and so limited, is not enough. The mind is full of monstrous, hybrid, unmanageable emotions. That the age of the earth is 3,000,000,000 years; that human life lasts but a second; that the capacity of the human mind is nevertheless boundless; that life is infinitely beautiful yet repulsive; that one's fellow creatures are adorable but disgusting; that science and religion have between them destroyed belief; that all bonds of union seem broken, yet some control must exist—it is in this atmosphere of doubt and conflict that writers have now to create, and the fine fabric of a lyric is no more fitted to contain this point of view than a rose leaf to envelop the rugged immensity of a rock.

But when we ask ourselves what has in the past served to express such an attitude as this—an attitude which is full of contrast and collision; an attitude which seems to demand the conflict of one character upon another, and at the same time to stand in need of some general shaping power, some conception which lends the whole harmony and force, we must reply that there was a form once, and it was not the form of lyric poetry; it was the form of the drama, of the poetic drama of the Elizabethan age. And that is the one form which seems dead beyond all possibility of resurrection to-day.

For if we look at the state of the poetic play we must have grave doubts that any force on earth can now revive it. It has been practised and is still practised by writers of the highest genius and ambition. Since the death of Dryden every great poet it seems has had his fling. Wordsworth and Coleridge, Shelley and Keats, Tennyson, Swinburne, and Browning (to name the dead only) have all written poetic plays, but none has succeeded. Of all the plays they wrote, probably only Swinburne's *Atalanta* and Shelley's *Prometheus* are still read, and they less frequently than other works by the same writers. All the rest have climbed to the top shelves of our bookcases, put their heads under their wings, and gone to sleep. No one will willingly disturb those slumbers.

Yet it is tempting to try to find some explanation of this failure in case it should throw light upon the future which we are considering. The reason why poets can no longer write poetic plays lies somewhere perhaps in this direction.

There is a vague, mysterious thing called an attitude toward life. We all know people—if we turn from literature to life for a moment—who are at loggerheads with existence; unhappy people who never get what they want; are baffled, complaining, who stand at an uncomfortable angle whence they see everything askew. There are others again who, though they appear perfectly content, seem to have lost all touch with reality. They lavish all their affections upon little dogs and old china. They take interest in nothing but the vicissitudes of their own health and the ups and downs of social snobbery. There are, however, others who strike us, why precisely it would be difficult to say, as being by nature or circumstances in a position where they can use their faculties to the full upon things that are of importance. They are not necessarily happy or successful, but there is a zest in their presence, an interest in their doings. They seem alive all over. This may be partly the result of circumstances —they have been born into surroundings that suit them— but much more is the result of some happy balance of qualities in themselves so that they see things not at an awkward angle, all askew; nor distorted through a mist; but four square, in proportion; they grasp something hard; when they come into action they cut real ice.

A writer too has in the same way an attitude toward life, though it is a different life from the other. They too can stand at an uncomfortable angle; can be baffled, frustrated, unable to get at what they want as writers. This is true, for example, of the novels of George Gissing. Then, again, they can retire to the suburbs and lavish their interest upon pet dogs and duchesses—prettinesses, sentimentalities, snobberies, and this is true of some of our most highly successful novelists. But there are others who seem by nature or circumstances so placed that they can use their faculties freely upon important things. It is not that they write quickly or easily, or become at once successful or celebrated. One is rather trying to analyse a quality which is present in most of the great ages of literature and is most marked in the work of Elizabethan dramatists. They seem to have an attitude toward life, a position which allows them to move their limbs freely; a view which, though made up of all sorts of different things, falls into the right perspective for their purposes.

In part, of course, this was the result of circumstances. The public appetite, not for books, but for the drama, the smallness of the towns, the distance which separated people, the ignorance in which even the educated then lived, all made it natural for the Elizabethan imagination to fill itself with lions and unicorns, dukes and duchesses, violence and mystery. This was reinforced by something which we cannot explain so simply, but which we can certainly feel. They had an attitude toward life which made them able to express themselves freely and fully. Shakespeare's plays are not the work of a baffled and frustrated mind; they are the perfectly elastic envelope of his thought. Without a hitch he turns from philosophy to a drunken brawl; from love songs to an argument; from simply merriment to profound speculation. And it is true of all the Elizabethan dramatists that though they may bore us—and they do—they never make us feel that they are afraid or self-conscious, or that there is anything hindering, hampering, inhibiting the full current of their minds.

Yet our first thought when we open a modern poetic play —and this applies to much modern poetry—is that the writer is not at his ease. He is afraid, he is forced, he is self-conscious. And with what good reason! we may exclaim, for which of us is perfectly at his ease with a man in a toga called Xenocrates, or with a woman in a blanket called Eudoxa? Yet for some reason the modern poetic play is always about

Xenocrates and not about Mr. Robinson; it is about Thessaly and not about Charing Cross Road. When the Elizabethans laid their scenes in foreign parts and made their heroes and heroines princes and princesses they only shifted the scene from one side to the other of a very thin veil. It was a natural device which gave depth and distance to their figures. But the country remained English; and the Bohemian prince was the same person as the English noble. Our modern poetic playwrights, however, seem to seek the veil of the past and of distance for a different reason. They want not a veil that heightens but a curtain that conceals; they lay their scene in the past because they are afraid of the present. They are aware that if they tried to express the thoughts, the visions, the sympathies and antipathies which are actually turning and tumbling in their brains in this year of grace 1927 the poetic decencies would be violated; they could only stammer and stumble and perhaps have to sit down or to leave the room. The Elizabethans had an attitude which allowed them complete freedom; the modern playwright has either no attitude at all, or one so strained that it cramps his limbs and distorts his vision. He has therefore to take refuge with Xenocrates, who says nothing or only what blank verse can with decency say.

But can we explain ourselves a little more fully? What has changed, what has happened, what has put the writer now at such an angle that he cannot pour his mind straight into the old channels of English poetry? Some sort of answer may be suggested by a walk through the streets of any large town. The long avenue of brick is cut up into boxes, each of which is inhabited by a different human being who has put locks on his doors and bolts on his windows to ensure some privacy, yet is linked to his fellows by wires which pass overhead, by waves of sound which pour through the roof and speak aloud to him of battles and murders and strikes and revolutions all over the world. And if we go in and talk to him we shall find that he is a wary, secretive, suspicious animal, extremely self-conscious, extremely careful not to give himself away. Indeed, there is nothing in modern life which forces him to do it. There is no violence in private life; we are polite, tolerant, agreeable, when we meet. War even is conducted by companies and communities rather than by individuals. Duelling is extinct. The marriage bond can stretch indefinitely without snapping. The ordinary person is calmer, smoother, more self-contained than he used to be.

But again we should find if we took a walk with our friend that he is extremely alive to everything—to ugliness, sordidity, beauty, amusement. He follows every thought careless where it may lead him. He discusses openly what used never to be mentioned even privately. And this very freedom and curiosity are perhaps the cause of what appears to be his most marked characteristic—the strange way in which things that have no apparent connection are associated in his mind. Feelings which used to come single and separate do so no longer. Beauty is part ugliness; amusement part disgust; pleasure part pain. Emotions which used to enter the mind whole are now broken up on the threshold.

For example: It is a spring night, the moon is up, the nightingale singing, the willows bending over the river. Yes, but at the same time a diseased old woman is picking over her greasy rags on a hideous iron bench. She and the spring enter his mind together; they blend but do not mix. The two emotions, so incongruously coupled, bite and kick at each other in unison. But the emotion which Keats felt when he heard the song of the nightingale is one and entire, though it passes from joy in beauty to sorrow at the unhappiness of human fate. He makes no contrast. In his poem sorrow is the shadow which accompanies beauty. In the modern mind beauty is accompanied not by its shadow but by its opposite. The modern poet talks of the nightingale who sings 'jug jug to dirty ears'. There trips along by the side of our modern beauty some mocking spirit which sneers at beauty for being beautiful; which turns the looking-glass and shows us that the other side of her cheek is pitted and deformed. It is as if the modern mind, wishing always to verify its emotions, had lost the power of accepting anything simply for what it is. Undoubtedly this sceptical and testing spirit has led to a great freshening and quickening of soul. There is a candour, an honesty in modern writing which is salutary if not supremely delightful. Modern literature, which had grown a little sultry and scented with Oscar Wilde and Walter Pater, revived instantly from her nineteenth-century languor when Samuel Butler and Bernard Shaw began to burn their feathers and apply their salts to her nose. She awoke; she sat up; she sneezed. Naturally, the poets were frightened away.

For of course poetry has always been overwhelmingly on the side of beauty. She has always insisted on certain rights, such as rhyme, metre, poetic diction. She has never been used for the common purpose of life. Prose has taken all the dirty work on to her own shoulders; has answered letters, paid bills, written articles, made speeches, served the needs of businessmen, shopkeepers, lawyers, soldiers, peasants.

Poetry has remained aloof in the possession of her priests. She has perhaps paid the penalty for this seclusion by becoming a little stiff. Her presence with all her apparatus—her veils, her garlands, her memories, her associations—affects us the moment she speaks. Thus when we ask poetry to express this discord, this incongruity, this sneer, this contrast, this curiosity, the quick, queer emotions which are bred in small separate rooms, the wide, general ideas which civilization teaches, she cannot move quickly enough, simply enough, or broadly enough to do it. Her accent is too marked; her manner too emphatic. She gives us instead lovely lyric cries of passion; with a majestic sweep of her arm she bids us take refuge in the past; but she does not keep pace with the mind and fling herself subtly, quickly, passionately into its various sufferings and joys. Byron in *Don Juan* pointed the way; he showed how flexible an instrument poetry might become, but none has followed his example or put his tool to further use. We remain without a poetic play.

Thus we are brought to reflect whether poetry is capable of the task which we are now setting her. It may be that the emotions here sketched in such rude outline and imputed to the modern mind submit more readily to prose than to poetry. It may be possible that prose is going to take over—has, indeed, already taken over—some of the duties which were once discharged by poetry.

If, then, we are daring and risk ridicule and try to see in what direction we who seem to be moving so fast are going, we may guess that we are going in the direction of prose and that in ten or fifteen years' time prose will be used for purposes for which prose has never been used before. That cannibal, the novel, which has devoured so many forms of art will by then have devoured even more. We shall be forced to invent new names for the different books which masquerade under this one heading. And it is possible that there will be among the so-called novels one which we shall scarcely know how to christen. It will be written in prose, but in prose which has many of the characteristics of poetry. It will have something of the exaltation of poetry, but much of the ordinariness of prose. It will be dramatic, and yet not a play. It will be read, not acted. By what name we are to call it is not a matter of very great importance. What is important is that this book which we see on the horizon may serve to express some of those feelings which seem at the moment to be balked by poetry pure and simple and to find the drama equally inhospitable to them. Let us try, then, to come to closer terms with it and to imagine what may be its scope and nature.

In the first place, one may guess that it will differ from the novel as we know it now chiefly in that it will stand further back from life. It will give, as poetry does, the outline rather than the detail. It will make little use of the marvellous fact-recording power, which is one of the attributes of fiction. It will tell us very little about the houses, incomes, occupations of its characters; it will have little kinship with the sociological novel or the novel of environment. With these limitations it will express the feeling and ideas of the characters closely and vividly, but from a different angle. It will resemble poetry in this that it will give not only or mainly people's relations to each other and their activities together, as the novel has hitherto done, but it will give the relation of the mind to general ideas and its soliloquy in solitude. For under the dominion of the novel we have scrutinized one part of the mind closely and left another unexplored. We have come to forget that a large and important part of life consists in our emotions toward such things as roses and nightingales, the dawn, the sunset, life, death, and fate; we forget that we spend much time sleeping, dreaming, thinking, reading, alone; we are not entirely occupied in personal relations; all our energies are not absorbed in making our livings. The psychological novelist has been too prone to limit psychology to the psychology of personal intercourse; we long sometimes to escape from the incessant, the remorseless analysis of falling into love and falling out of love, of what Tom feels for Judith and Judith does or does not altogether feel for Tom. We long for some more impersonal relationship. We long for ideas, for dreams, for imaginations, for poetry.

And it is one of the glories of the Elizabethan dramatists that they give us this. The poet is always able to transcend the particularity of Hamlet's relation to Ophelia and to give us his questioning not of his own personal lot alone but of the state and being of all human life. In *Measure for Measure*, for example, passages of extreme psychological subtlety are mingled with profound reflections, tremendous imaginations. Yet it is worth noticing that if Shakespeare gives us this profundity, this psychology, at the same time Shakespeare makes no attempt to give us certain other things. The plays are of no use whatever as 'applied sociology'. If we had to depend upon them for a knowledge of the social and economic conditions of Elizabethan life, we should be hopelessly at sea.

In these respects then the novel or the variety of the novel which will be written in time to come will take on some of the attributes of poetry. It will give the relations of man to nature, to fate; his imagination; his dreams. But it will also give the sneer, the contrast, the question, the closeness and complexity of life. It will take the mould of that queer conglomeration of incongruous things—the modern mind. Therefore it will clasp to its breast the precious prerogatives of the democratic art of prose; its freedom, its fearlessness, its flexibility. For prose is so humble that it can go anywhere; no place is too low, too sordid, or too mean for it to enter. It is infinitely patient, too, humbly acquisitive. It can lick up with its long glutinous tongue the most minute fragments of fact and mass them into the most subtle labyrinths, and listen silently at doors behind which only a murmur, only a whisper, is to be heard. With all the suppleness of a tool which is in constant use it can follow the windings and record the changes which are typical of the modern mind. To this, with Proust and Dostoevsky behind us, we must agree.

But can prose, we may ask, adequate though it is to deal with the common and the complex—can prose say the simple things which are so tremendous? Give the sudden emotions which are so surprising? Can it chant the elegy, or hymn the love, or shriek in terror, or praise the rose, the nightingale, or the beauty of the night? Can it leap at one spring at the heart of its subject as the poet does? I think not. That is the penalty it pays for having dispensed with the incantation and the mystery, with rhyme and metre. It is true that prose writers are daring; they are constantly forcing their instrument to make the attempt. But one has always a feeling of discomfort in the presence of the purple patch or the prose poem. The objection to the purple patch, however, is not that it is purple but that it is a patch. Recall for instance Meredith's 'Diversion on a Penny Whistle' in *Richard Feveral*. How awkwardly, how emphatically, with a broken poetic metre it begins: 'Golden lie the meadows; golden run the streams; red-gold is on the pine-stems. The sun is coming down to earth and walks the fields and the waters.' Or recall the famous description of the storm at the end of Charlotte Brontë's *Villette*. These passages are eloquent, lyrical, splendid; they read very well cut out and stuck in an anthology; but in the context of the novel they make us uncomfortable. For both Meredith and Charlotte

Brontë called themselves novelists; they stood close up to life; they led us to expect the rhythm, the observation, and the perspective of poetry. We feel the jerk and the effort; we are half woken from that trance of consent and illusion in which our submission to the power of the writer's imagination is most complete.

But let us now consider another book, which though written in prose and by way of being called a novel, adopts from the start a different attitude, a different rhythm, which stands back from life, and leads us to expect a different perspective—*Tristram Shandy*. It is a book full of poetry, but we never notice it; it is a book stained deep purple, which is yet never patchy. Here though the mood is changing always, there is no jerk, no jolt in that change to waken us from the depths of consent and belief. In the same breath Sterne laughs, sneers, cuts some indecent ribaldry, and passes on to a passage like this:

> Time wastes too fast: every letter I trace tells me with what rapidity life follows my pen; the days and hours of it more precious—my dear Jenny—than the rubies about thy neck, are flying over our heads like light clouds of a windy day, never to return more; everything presses on —whilst thou are twisting that lock—see! it grows gray; and every time I kiss thy hand to bid adieu, and every absence which follows it, are preludes to that eternal separation which we are shortly to make.—Heaven have mercy upon us both!
>
> CHAP. IX
>
> Now, for what the world thinks of that ejaculation—I would not give a groat.

And he goes on to my Uncle Toby, the Corporal, Mrs. Shandy, and the rest of them.

There, one sees, is poetry changing easily and naturally into prose, prose into poetry. Standing a little aloof, Sterne lays his hands lightly upon imagination, wit, fantasy; and reaching high up among the branches where these things grow, naturally and no doubt willingly forfeits his right to the more substantial vegetables that grow on the ground.

21

For, unfortunately, it seems true that some renunciation is inevitable. You cannot cross the narrow bridge of art carrying all its tools in your hands. Some you must leave behind, or you will drop them in midstream or, what is worse, overbalance and be drowned yourself.

So, then, this unnamed variety of the novel will be written standing back from life, because in that way a larger view is to be obtained of some important features of it; it will be written in prose, because prose, if you free it from the beast-of-burden work which so many novelists necessarily lay upon it, of carrying loads of details, bushels of fact—prose thus treated will show itself capable of rising high from the ground, not in one dart, but in sweeps and circles, and of keeping at the same time in touch with the amusements and idiosyncrasies of human character in daily life.

There remains, however, a further question. Can prose be dramatic? It is obvious, of course, that Shaw and Ibsen have used prose dramatically with the highest success, but they have been faithful to the dramatic form. This form one may prophesy is not the one which the poetic dramatist of the future will find fit for his needs. A prose play is too rigid, too limited, too emphatic for his purposes. It lets slip between its meshes half the things that he wants to say. He cannot compress into dialogue all the comment, all the analysis, all the richness that he wants to give. Yet he covets the explosive emotional effect of the drama; he wants to draw blood from his readers, and not merely to stroke and tickle their intellectual susceptibilities. The looseness and freedom of *Tristram Shandy*, wonderfully though they encircle and float off such characters as Uncle Toby and Corporal Trim, do not attempt to range and marshal these people in dramatic contrast together. Therefore it will be necessary for the writer of this exacting book to bring to bear upon his tumultuous and contradictory emotions the generalizing and simplifying power of a strict and logical imagination. Tumult is vile; confusion is hateful; everything in a work of art should be mastered and ordered. His effort will be to generalize and split up. Instead of enumerating details he will mould blocks. His characters thus will have a dramatic power which the minutely realized characters of contemporary fiction often sacrifice in the interests of psychology. And then, though this is scarcely visible, so far distant it lies on the rim of the horizon—one can imagine that he will have extended the scope of his interest so as to dramatize some of those influences which play so large a part in life, yet have so far escaped the novelist—the power of music, the stimulus of sight, the effect on us of the shape of trees or the play of colour, the emotions bred in us by crowds, the obscure terrors and hatreds which come so irrationally in certain places or from certain people, the delight of movement, the intoxication of wine. Every moment is the centre and meeting-place of an extraordinary number of perceptions which have not yet been expressed. Life is always and inevitably much richer than we who try to express it.

But it needs no great gift of prophecy to be certain that whoever attempts to do what is outlined above will have need of all his courage. Prose is not going to learn a new step at the bidding of the first comer. Yet if the signs of the times are worth anything the need of fresh developments is being felt. It is certain that there are scattered about in England, France, and America writers who are trying to work themselves free from a bondage which has become irksome to them; writers who are trying to readjust their attitude so that they may once more stand easily and naturally in a position where their powers have full play upon important things. And it is when a book strikes us as the result of that attitude rather than by its beauty or its brilliancy that we know that it has in it the seeds of an enduring existence.

Hours in a Library[1]

LET us begin by clearing up the old confusion between the man who loves learning and the man who loves reading, and point out that there is no connexion whatever between the two. A learned man is a sedentary, concentrated solitary enthusiast, who searches through books to discover some particular grain of truth upon which he has set his heart. If the passion for reading conquers him, his gains dwindle and vanish between his fingers. A reader, on the other hand, must check the desire for learning at the outset; if knowledge sticks to him well and good, but to go in pursuit of it, to read on a system, to become a specialist or an authority, is very apt to kill what it suits us to consider the more humane passion for pure and disinterested reading.

In spite of all this we can easily conjure up a picture which does service for the bookish man and raises a smile at his expense. We conceive a pale, attenuated figure in a dressing-gown, lost in speculation, unable to lift a kettle from the hob, or address a lady without blushing, ignorant of the daily news, though versed in the catalogues of the second-hand booksellers, in whose dark premises he spends the hours of sunlight—a delightful character, no doubt, in his crabbed simplicity, but not in the least resembling that other to whom we would direct attention. For the true reader is essentially young. He is a man of intense curiosity; of ideas; open minded and communicative, to whom reading is more of the nature of brisk exercise in the open air than of sheltered study; he trudges the high road, he climbs higher and higher upon the hills until the atmosphere is almost too fine to breathe in; to him it is not a sedentary pursuit at all.

[1] *Times Literary Supplement*, November 30, 1916.

But, apart from general statements, it would not be hard to prove by an assembly of facts that the great season for reading is the season between the ages of eighteen and twenty-four. The bare list of what is read then fills the heart of older people with despair. It is not only that we read so many books, but that we had such books to read. If we wish to refresh our memories, let us take down one of those old notebooks which we have all, at one time or another, had a passion for beginning. Most of the pages are blank, it is true; but at the beginning we shall find a certain number very beautifully covered with a strikingly legible hand-writing. Here we have written down the names of great writers in their order of merit; here we have copied out fine passages from the classics; here are lists of books to be read; and here, most interesting of all, lists of books that have actually been read, as the reader testifies with some youthful vanity by a dash of red ink. We will quote a list of the books that some one read in a past January at the age of twenty, most of them probably for the first time. 1. *Rhoda Fleming*, 2. *The Shaving of Shagpat*. 3. *Tom Jones*. 4. *The Laodicean*. 5. Dewey's *Psychology*. 6. *The Book of Job*. 7. Webbe's *Discourse of Poesie*. 8. *The Duchess of Malfi*. 9. *The Revenger's Tragedy*. And so he goes on from month to month, until, as such lists will, it suddenly stops in the month of June. But if we follow the reader through his months it is clear that he can have done practically nothing but read. Elizabethan literature is gone through with some thoroughness; he read a great deal of Webster, Browning, Shelley, Spenser, and Congreve; Peacock he read from start to finish; and most of Jane Austen's novels two or three times over. He read the whole of Meredith, the whole of Ibsen, and a little of Bernard Shaw. We may be fairly certain, too, that the time not spent in reading was spent in some stupendous argument in which the Greeks were pitted against the moderns, romance against realism, Racine against Shakespeare, until the lights were seen to have grown pale in the dawn.

The old lists are there to make us smile and perhaps to sigh a little, but we would give much to recall also the mood in which this orgy of reading was done. Happily, this reader was no prodigy, and with a little thought we can most of us recall the stages at least of our own initiation. The books we read in childhood, having purloined them from some shelf supposed to be inaccessible, have something of the unreality and awfulness of a stolen sight of the dawn coming over quiet fields when the household is asleep. Peeping between the curtains we see strange shapes of misty trees which we hardly recognize, though we may remember them all our lives; for children have a strange premonition of what is to come. But the later reading of which the above list is an example is quite a different matter. For the first time, perhaps, all restrictions have been removed, we can read what we like; libraries are at our command, and, best of all, friends who find themselves in the same position. For days upon end we do nothing but read. It is a time of extraordinary excitement and exaltation. We seem to rush about recognizing heroes. There is a sort of wonderment in our minds that we ourselves are really doing this, and mixed with it an absurd arrogance and desire to show our familiarity with the greatest human beings who have ever lived in the world. The passion for knowledge is then at its keenest, or at least most confident, and we have, too, an intense singleness of mind which the great writers gratify by making it appear that they are at one with us in their estimate of what is good in life. And as it is necessary to hold one's own against some one who has adopted Pope, let us say, instead of Sir Thomas Browne, for a hero, we conceive a deep affection for these men, and feel that we know them not as other people know them, but privately by ourselves. We are fighting under their leadership, and almost in the light of their eyes. So we haunt the old bookshops and drag home folios and quartos, Euripides in wooden boards, and Voltaire in eighty-nine volumes octavo.

But these lists are curious documents, in that they seem to include scarcely any of the contemporary writers. Meredith and Hardy and Henry James were of course alive when this reader came to them, but they were already accepted among the classics. There is no man of his own generation who influences him as Carlyle, or Tennyson, or Ruskin influenced the young of their day. And this we believe to be very characteristic of youth, for unless there is some admitted giant he will have nothing to do with the smaller men, although they deal with the world he lives in. He will rather go back to the classics, and consort entirely with minds of the very first order. For the time being he holds himself aloof from all the activities of men, and, looking at them from a distance, judges them with superb severity.

Indeed, one of the signs of passing youth is the birth of a sense of fellowship with other human beings as we take our place among them. We should like to think that we keep our standard as high as ever; but we certainly take more interest in the writings of our contemporaries and pardon their lack of inspiration for the sake of something that brings them nearer to us. It is even arguable that we get actually more from the living, although they may be much inferior, than from the dead. In the first place there can be no secret vanity in reading our contemporaries, and the kind of admiration which they inspire is extremely warm and genuine because in order to give way to our belief in them we have often to sacrifice some very respectable prejudice which does us credit. We have also to find our own reasons for what we like and dislike, which acts as a spur to our attention, and is the best way of proving that we have read the classics with understanding.

Thus to stand in a great bookshop crammed with books so new that their pages almost stick together, and the gilt on their backs is still fresh, has an excitement no less delightful than the old excitement of the second-hand bookstall. It is not perhaps so exalted. But the old hunger to know what the immortals thought has given place to a far more tolerant curiosity to know what our own generation is thinking. What do living men and women feel, what are their houses like and what clothes do they wear, what money have they and what food do they eat, what do they love and hate, what do they see of the surrounding world, and what is the dream that fills the spaces of their active lives? They tell us all these things in their books. In them we can see as much both of the mind and of the body of our time as we have eyes for seeing.

When such a spirit of curiosity has fully taken hold of us, the dust will soon lie thick upon the classics unless some necessity forces us to read them. For the living voices are, after all, the ones we understand the best. We can treat them as we treat our equals; they are guessing our riddles, and, what is perhaps more important, we understand their jokes. And we soon develop another taste, unsatisfied by the great —not a valuable taste, perhaps, but certainly a very pleasant possession—the taste for bad books. Without committing the indiscretion of naming names we know which authors can be trusted to produce yearly (for happily they are prolific) a novel, a book of poems or essays, which affords us indescribable pleasure. We owe a great deal to bad books; indeed, we come to count their authors and their heroes among those figures who play so large a part in our silent life. Something of the same sort happens in the case of the memoir writers and autobiographers, who have created almost a fresh branch of literature in our age. They are not all of them important people, but strangely enough, only the most important, the dukes and the statesmen, are ever really dull. The men and women who set out, with no excuse except perhaps that they saw the Duke of Wellington once, to confide to us their opinions, their quarrels, their aspirations, and their diseases, generally end by becoming, for the time at least, actors in those private dramas with which we beguile our solitary walks and our sleepless hours. Refine all this out of our consciousness and we should be poor indeed. And then there are the books of facts and history, books about bees and wasps and industries and gold mines and Empresses and diplomatic intrigues, about rivers and savages, trade unions, and Acts of Parliament, which we always read and always, alas! forget. Perhaps we are not making out a good case for a bookshop when we have to confess that it gratifies so many desires which have apparently nothing to do with literature. But let us remember that here we have a literature in the making. From these new books our children will select the one or two by which we shall be known for ever. Here, if we could recognize it, lies some poem, or novel, or history which will stand up and speak with other ages about our age when we lie prone and silent as the crowd of Shakespeare's day is silent and lives for us only in the pages of his poetry.

This we believe to be true; and yet it is oddly difficult in the case of new books to know which are the real books and what it is that they are telling us, and which are the stuffed books which will come to pieces when they have lain about for a year or two. We can see that there are many books, and we are frequently told that every one can write nowadays. That may be true; yet we do not doubt that at the heart of this immense volubility, this flood and foam of language, this irreticence and vulgarity and triviality, there lies the heat of some great passion which only needs the accident of a brain more happily turned than the rest to issue in a shape which will last from age to age. It should be our delight to watch this turmoil, to do battle with the ideas and visions of our own time, to seize what we can use, to kill what we consider worthless, and above all to realize that we must be generous to the people who are giving shape as best they can to the ideas within them. No age of literature is so little submissive to authority as ours, so free from the dominion of the great; none seems so wayward with its gift of reverence, or so volatile in its experiments. It may well seem, even to the attentive, that there is no trace of school or aim in the work of our poets and novelists. But the pessimist is inevitable, and he shall not persuade us that our literature is dead, or prevent us from feeling how true and vivid a beauty flashes out as the young writers draw together to form their new vision, the ancient words of the most beautiful of living languages. Whatever we may have learnt from reading the classics we need now in order to judge the work of our contemporaries, for whenever there is life in them they will be casting their net out over some unknown abyss to snare new shapes, and we must throw our imaginations after them if we are to accept with understanding the strange gifts they bring back to us.

But if we need all our knowledge of the old writers in order to follow what the new writers are attempting, it is certainly true that we come from adventuring among new books with a far keener eye for the old. It seems that we should now be able to surprise their secrets; to look deep down into their work and see the parts come together, because we have watched the making of new books, and with eyes clear of prejudice can judge more truly what it is that they are doing, and what is good and what bad. We shall find, probably, that some of the great are less venerable than we thought them. Indeed, they are not so accomplished or so profound as some of our own time. But if in one or two cases this seems to be true, a kind of humiliation mixed with joy overcomes us in front of others. Take Shakespeare, or Milton, or Sir Thomas Browne. Our little knowledge of how things are done does not avail us much here, but it does lend an added zest to our enjoyment. Did we ever in our youngest days feel such amazement at their achievement as that which fills us now that we have sifted myriads of words and gone along uncharted ways in search of new forms for our new sensations? New books may be more stimulating and in some ways more suggestive than the old, but they do not give us that absolute certainty of delight which breathes through us when we come back again to *Comus*, or *Lycidas*, *Urn Burial*, or *Antony and Cleopatra*. Far be it from us to hazard any theory as to the nature of art. It may be that we shall never know more about it than we know by nature, and our longer experience of it teaches us this only—that of all our pleasures those we get from the great artists are indisputably among the best; and more we may not know. But, advancing no theory, we shall find one or two qualities in such works as these which we can hardly expect to find in books made within the span of our lifetime. Age itself may have an alchemy of its own. But this is true: you can read them as often as you will without finding that they have yielded any virtue and left a meaningless husk of words; and

there is a complete finality about them. No cloud of suggestions hangs about them teasing us with a multitude of
irrelevant ideas. But all our faculties are summoned to the
task, as in the great moments of our own experience; and
some consecration descends upon us from their hands which
we return to life, feeling it more keenly and understanding
it more deeply than before.

Impassioned Prose[1]

WHEN he was still a boy, his own discrimination led De Quincey to doubt whether 'his natural vocation lay towards poetry'. He wrote poetry, eloquently and profusely, and his poetry was praised; but even so he decided that he was no poet, and the sixteen volumes of his collected works are written entirely in prose. After the fashion of his time, he wrote on many subjects—on political economy, on philosophy, on history; he wrote essays and biographies and confessions and memoirs. But as we stand before the long row of his books and make, as we are bound to make after all these years, our own selection, the whole mass and range of these sixteen volumes seems to reduce itself to one sombre level in which hang a few splendid stars. He dwells in our memory because he could make phrases like 'trepidations of innumerable fugitives', because he could compose scenes like that of the laurelled coach driving into the midnight market-place, because he could tell stories like that of the phantom woodcutter heard by his brother on the desert island. And, if we examine our choice and give a reason for it, we have to confess that, prose writer though he is, it is for his poetry that we read him and not for his prose.

What could be more damaging, to him as writer, to us as readers, than this confession? For if the critics agree on any point it is on this, that nothing is more reprehensible than for a prose writer to write like a poet. Poetry is poetry and prose is prose—how often have we not heard that! Poetry has one mission and prose another. Prose, Mr. Binyon wrote the other day, 'is a medium primarily addressed to the intelligence, poetry to feeling and imagination'. And again, 'the poetical prose has but a bastard kind of beauty, easily

[1] *Times Literary Supplement*, September 16, 1926.

appearing overdressed'. It is impossible not to admit, in part at least, the truth of these remarks. Memory supplies but too many instances of discomfort, of anguish, when in the midst of sober prose suddenly the temperature rises, the rhythm changes, we go up with a lurch, come down with a bang, and wake, roused and angry. But memory supplies also a number of passages—in Browne, in Landor, in Carlyle, in Ruskin, in Emily Brontë—where there is no such jerk, no such sense (for this perhaps is at the root of our discomfort) of something unfused, unwrought, incongruous, and casting ridicule upon the rest. The prose writer has subdued his army of facts; he has brought them all under the same laws of perspective. They work upon our minds as poetry works upon them. We are not woken; we reach the next point—and it may well be highly commonplace— without any sense of strain.

But, unfortunately for those who would wish to see a great many more things said in prose than are now thought proper, we live under the rule of the novelists. If we talk of prose we mean in fact prose fiction. And of all writers the novelist has his hands fullest of facts. Smith gets up, shaves, has his breakfast, taps his egg, reads *The Times*. How can we ask the panting, the perspiring, the industrious scribe with all this on his hands to modulate beautifully off into rhapsodies about Time and Death and what the hunters are doing at the Antipodes? It would upset the whole proportions of his day. It would cast grave doubt upon his veracity. Moreover, the greatest of his order seem deliberately to prefer a method which is the antithesis of prose poetry. A shrug of the shoulders, a turn of the head, a few words spoken in a hurry at a moment of crisis—that is all. But the train has been laid so deep beneath page after page and chapter after chapter that the single word when it is spoken is enough to start an explosion. We have so lived and thought with these men and women that they need only raise a finger and it seems to reach the skies. To elaborate that gesture would be to spoil it. The whole tendency therefore of fiction is against prose poetry. The lesser novelists are not going to take risks which the greater deliberately avoid. They trust that, if only the egg is real and the kettle boils, stars and nightingales will somehow be thrown in by the imagination of the reader. And therefore all that side of the mind which is exposed in solitude they ignore. They ignore its thoughts, its rhapsodies, its dreams, with the result that the people of fiction bursting with energy on one side are atrophied on the other; while prose itself, so long in service to this drastic master, has suffered the same deformity, and will be fit, after another hundred years of such discipline, to write nothing but the immortal works of Bradshaw and Baedeker.

But happily there are in every age some writers who puzzle the critics, who refuse to go in with the herd. They stand obstinately across the boundary lines, and do a greater service by enlarging and fertilizing and influencing than by their actual achievement, which, indeed, is often too eccentric to be satisfactory. Browning did a service of this kind to poetry. Peacock and Samuel Butler have both had an influence upon novelists which is out of all proportion to their own popularity. And one of De Quincey's claims to our gratitude, one of his main holds upon our interest, is that he was an exception and a solitary. He made a class for himself. He widened the choice for others. Faced with the usual problem of what to write, since write he must, he decided that with all his poetic sensibility he was not a poet. He lacked the fire and the concentration. Nor, again, was he a novelist. With immense powers of language at his command, he was incapable of a sustained and passionate interest in the affairs of other people. It was his disease, he said, 'to meditate too much and to observe too little'. He would follow a poor family who went marketing on a Saturday night, sympathetically, but at a distance. He was intimate with no one. Then, again, he had an extraordinary gift for the dead languages, and a passion for acquiring knowledge of all kinds. Yet there was some quality in him which forbade him to shut himself up alone with his books, as such gifts seemed to indicate. The truth was

that he dreamed—he was always dreaming. The faculty
was his long before he took to eating opium. When
he was a child he stood by his sister's dead body and
suddenly

> a vault seemed to open in the zenith of the far blue sky, a
> shaft which ran up for ever. I, in spirit, rose as on billows
> that also ran up the shaft for ever; and the billows seemed
> to pursue the throne of God; but that also ran before us
> and fled away continually.

The visions were of extreme vividness; they made life seem
a little dull in comparison; they extended it, they completed
it. But in what form was he to express this that was the most
real part of his own existence? There was none ready made
to his hand. He invented, as he claimed, 'modes of impas-
sioned prose'. With immense elaboration and art he formed
a style in which to express these 'visionary scenes derived
from the world of dreams'. For such prose there were no
precedents, he believed; and he begged the reader to remember 'the perilous difficulty' of an attempt where 'a single
false note, a single word in a wrong key, ruins the whole
music'.

Added to that 'perilous difficulty' was another which is
often forced upon the reader's attention. A prose writer may
dream dreams and see visions, but they cannot be allowed to
lie scattered, single, solitary upon the page. So spaced out
they die. For prose has neither the intensity nor the self-
sufficiency of poetry. It rises slowly off the ground; it must
be connected on this side and on that. There must be some
medium in which its ardours and ecstasies can float without
incongruity, from which they receive support and impetus.
Here was a difficulty which De Quincey often faced and
often failed to solve. Many of his most tiresome and dis-
figuring faults are the result of the dilemma into which his
genius plunged him. There was something in the story before
him which kindled his interest and quickened his powers.
For example, the Spanish Military Nun, as she descends
half starved and frozen from the Andes, sees before her a
belt of trees which promises safety. As if De Quincey had

himself reached that shelter and could breathe in safety, he broadens out—

Oh! verdure of dark olive foliage, offered suddenly to fainting eyes, as if by some winged patriarchal herald of wrath relenting—solitary Arab's tent, rising with saintly signals of peace in the dreadful desert, must Kate indeed die even yet, whilst she sees but cannot reach you? Outpost on the frontier of man's dominions, standing within life, but looking out upon everlasting death, wilt thou hold up the anguish of thy mocking invitation only to betray?

Alas, how easy it is to rise, how dangerous to fall! He has Kate on his hands; he is half-way through with her story; he must rouse himself, he must collect himself, he must descend from these happy heights to the levels of ordinary existence. And, again and again, it is in returning to earth that De Quincey is undone. How is he to bridge the horrid transition? How is he to turn from an angel with wings of flame and eyes of fire to a gentleman in black who talks sense? Sometimes he makes a joke—it is generally painful. Sometimes he tells a story—it is always irrelevant. Most often he spreads himself out in a waste of verbosity, where any interest that there may have been peters out dismally and loses itself in the sand. We can read no more.

It is tempting to say that De Quincey failed because he was not a novelist. He ought to have left Kate alone; he had not a novelist's sense of character and action. To a critic such formulas are helpful; unfortunately, they are often false. For in fact, De Quincey can convey character admirably; he is a master of the art of narrative once he has succeeded (and the condition is indispensable for all writers) in adjusting the perspective to suit his own eyesight. It was a sight, it is true, that required a most curious rearrangement of the landscape. Nothing must come too close. A veil must be drawn over the multitudinous disorder of human affairs. It must always be possible, without distressing the reader, to allude to a girl as 'a prepossessing young female'. A mist must lie upon the human face. The hills must be higher and the distances bluer than they are in the world we know. He required, too, endless leisure and ample elbow-room. He wanted time to soliloquize and loiter; here to pick up some trifle and bestow upon it all his powers of analysis and decoration; here to brush aside such patient discrimination and widen and enlarge and amplify until nothing remains but the level sands and the immense sea. He wanted a subject that would allow him all possible freedom and yet possess enough emotional warmth to curb his inborn verbosity.

He found it, naturally, in himself. He was a born auto-biographer. If the *Opium Eater* remains his masterpiece, a longer and less perfect book, the *Autobiographic Sketches*, runs it very close. For here it is fitting that he should stand a little apart, should look back, under cover of his raised hand, at scenes which had almost melted into the past. His enemy, the hard fact, became cloudlike and supple under his hands. He was under no obligation to recite 'the old hackneyed roll-call, chronologically arranged, of inevitable facts in a man's life'. It was his object to record impressions, to render states of mind without particularizing the features of the precise person who had experienced them. A serene and lovely light lies over the whole of that distant prospect of his childhood. The house, the fields, the garden, even the neighbouring town of Manchester, all seem to exist, but far away on some island separated from us by a veil of blue. On this background, where no detail is accurately rendered, the little group of children and parents, the little island of home and garden, are all distinctly visible and yet as if they moved and had their being behind a veil. Upon the opening chapters rests the solemnity of a splendid summer's day, whose radiance, long since sunk, has something awful in it, in whose profound stillness sounds strangely reverberate—the sounds of hooves on the far-away high road, the sound of words like 'palm', the sound of that 'solemn wind, the saddest that ear ever heard', which was for ever to haunt the mind of the little boy who now heard it for the first time. Nor, so long as he keeps within the circle of the past, is it necessary that he should face the disagreeable necessity of waking. About the reality of childhood still hung some of the charm of illusion. If the peace is broken, it is by an apparition like that of the mad dog which passes and pauses with something of the terror of a dream. If he needs variety, he finds it in describing with a whimsical humour perfectly suited to the subject the raptures and miseries of childhood. He mocks; he dilates; he makes the very small very great; then he describes the war with the mill hands, the brothers' imaginary kingdoms, his brother's boast that he could walk upon the ceiling like a fly, with admirable particularity. He can rise easily and fall naturally here. Here too, given his own memories to work upon, he can exercise his extraordinary powers of description. He was never exact; he disliked glitter and emphasis; he sacrificed the showy triumphs of the art; but he had to perfection the gift of composition. Scenes come together under his hands like congregations of clouds which gently join and slowly disperse or hang solemnly still. So displayed before us we see the coaches gathering at the post office in all their splendour; the lady in the carriage to whom the news of victory brings only sorrow; the couple surprised on the road at midnight by the thunder of the mail coach and the threat of death; Lamb asleep in his chair; Ann disappearing for ever into the dark London night. All these scenes have something of the soundlessness and the lustre of dreams. They swim up to the surface, they sink down again into the depths. They have, into the bargain, the strange power of growing in our minds, so that it is always a surprise to come upon them again and see what, in the interval, our minds have done to alter and expand.

Meanwhile, all these scenes compose an autobiography of a kind, but of a kind which is so unusual that one is forced to ask what one has learnt from it about De Quincey in the end. Of facts, scarcely anything. One has been told only what De Quincey wished us to know; and even that has been chosen for the sake of some adventitious quality—as that it fitted in here, or was the right colour to go there— never for its truth. But nevertheless there grows upon us a curious sense of intimacy. It is an intimacy with the mind, and not with the body; yet we cannot help figuring to ourselves, as the rush of eloquence flows, the fragile little body, the fluttering hands, the glowing eyes, the alabaster cheeks, the glass of opium on the table. We can guess that no one so gifted with silver speech, so prone to plunge into reverie and awe, held his own imperturbably among his fellows. We can guess at his evasion and unpunctualities; at the hordes of old papers that littered his room; at the courtesy which excused his inability to abide by the ordinary rules of life; at the overmastering desire that possessed him to wander and dream on the hills alone; at the seasons of gloom and irritability with which he paid for that exquisite fineness of ear that tuned each word to harmony and set each paragraph flowing and following like the waves of the sea. All this we know or guess. But it is odd to reflect how little, after all, we have been admitted to intimacy. In spite of the fact that he talks of confessions and calls the work by which he set most store *Suspiria de Profundis*, he is always self-possessed, secretive, and composed. His confession is not that he has sinned but that he has dreamed. Hence it comes about that his most perfect passages are not lyrical but descriptive. They are not cries of anguish which admit us to closeness and sympathy; they are descriptions of states of mind in which, often, time is miraculously prolonged and space miraculously expanded. When in the *Suspiria de Profundis* he tries to rise straight from the ground and to achieve in a few pages without prelude or sequence his own peculiar effects of majesty and distance, his force is not sufficient to bear him the whole distance. There juts up a comment upon the rules of Eton, a note to remind us that this refers to the tobacco States of North America, in the midst of 'Levana and Our Ladies of Sorrow', which puts their sweet-tongued phrases sadly out of countenance.

But if he was not a lyric writer, he was undoubtedly a descriptive writer, a reflective writer, who with only prose at his command—an instrument hedged about with restrictions, debased by a thousand common uses—made his way into precincts which are terribly difficult to approach. The breakfast table, he seems to say, is only a temporary apparition which we can think into non-existence, or invest with such associations that even its mahogany legs have their charm. To sit cheek by jowl with our fellows cramped up together is distasteful, indeed repulsive. But draw a little apart, see people in groups, as outlines, and they become at once memorable and full of beauty. Then it is not the actual sight or sound itself that matters, but the reverberations that it makes as it travels through our minds. These are often to be found far away, strangely transformed; but it is only by gathering up and putting together these echoes and fragments that we arrive at the true nature of our experience. So thinking, he altered slightly the ordinary relationships. He shifted the values of familiar things. And this he did in prose, which makes us wonder whether, then, it is quite so limited as the critics say, and ask further whether the prose writer, the novelist, might not capture fuller and finer truths than are now his aim if he ventured into those shadowy regions where De Quincey has been before him.

Life and the Novelist[1]

THE novelist—it is his distinction and his danger—is terribly exposed to life. Other artists, partially at least, withdraw; they shut themselves up for weeks alone with a dish of apples and a paint-box, or a roll of music paper and a piano. When they emerge it is to forget and distract themselves. But the novelist never forgets and is seldom distracted. He fills his glass and lights his cigarette, he enjoys presumably all the pleasures of talk and table, but always with a sense that he is being stimulated and played upon by the subject-matter of his art. Taste, sound, movement, a few words here, a gesture there, a man coming in, a woman going out, even the motor that passes in the street or the beggar who shuffles along the pavement, and all the reds and blues and lights and shades of the scene claim his attention and rouse his curiosity. He can no more cease to receive impressions than a fish in mid-ocean can cease to let the water rush through his gills.

But if this sensibility is one of the conditions of the novelist's life, it is obvious that all writers whose books survive have known how to master it and make it serve their purposes. They have finished the wine and paid the bill and gone off, alone, into some solitary room where, with toil and pause, in agony (like Flaubert), with struggle and rush, tumultuously (like Dostoevsky) they have mastered their perceptions, hardened them, and changed them into the fabrics of their art.

So drastic is the process of selection that in its final state we can often find no trace of the actual scene upon which the chapter was based. For in that solitary room, whose door the critics are for ever trying to unlock, processes of the strangest kind are gone through. Life is subjected to a

[1] *New York Herald Tribune*, November 7, 1926.

thousand disciplines and exercises. It is curbed; it is killed. It is mixed with this, stiffened with that, brought into contrast with something else; so that when we get our scene at a café a year later the surface signs by which we remembered it have disappeared. There emerges from the mist something stark, something formidable and enduring, the bone and substance upon which our rush of indiscriminating emotion was founded.

Of these two processes, the first—to receive impressions—is undoubtedly the easier, the simpler, and the pleasanter. And it is quite possible, provided one is gifted with a sufficiently receptive temperament and a vocabulary rich enough to meet its demands, to make a book out of this preliminary emotion alone. Three-quarters of the novels that appear to-day are concocted of experience to which no discipline, except the mild curb of grammar and the occasional rigours of chapter divisions, has been applied. Is Miss Stern's *A Deputy Was King* another example of this class of writing, has she taken her material away with her into solitude, or is it neither one nor the other, but an incongruous mixture of soft and hard, transient and enduring?

A Deputy Was King continues the story of the Rakonitz family which was begun some years ago in *The Matriarch*. It is a welcome reappearance, for the Rakonitz family is a gifted and cosmopolitan family with the admirable quality, so rare now in English fiction, of belonging to no particular sect. No parish boundary contains them. They overflow the continent. They are to be found in Italy and Austria, in Paris and Bohemia. If they lodge temporarily in some London studio they are not condemning themselves thereby to wear forever the livery of Chelsea, or Bloomsbury, or Kensington. Abundantly nourished on a diet of rich meats and rare wines, expensively but exquisitely clothed, enviably though inexplicably flush of ready money, no restraint of class or convention lies upon them, if we except the year 1921; it is essential that they should be up to date. They dance, they marry, they live with this man or with that;

they bask in the Italian sun; they swarm in and out of each other's houses and studios, gossiping, quarrelling, making it up again. For, after all, besides the constraint of fashion, they lie, consciously or unconsciously, under the bond of family. They have that Jewish tenacity of affection which common hardship has bred in an outcast race. Hence, in spite of their surface gregariousness, they are fundamentally loyal to each other underneath. Toni and Val and Loraine may quarrel and tear each other asunder publicly, but in private the Rakonitz women are indissolubly united. The present instalment of the family history, which, though it introduces the Goddards and relates the marriage of Toni and Giles Goddard, is really the history of a family, and not of an episode, pauses, for the time presumably, in an Italian villa provided with seventeen bedrooms, so that uncles, aunts, cousins can all come to lodge there. For Toni God-dard, with all her fashion and modernity, would rather shelter uncles and aunts than entertain emperors, and a second cousin whom she has not seen since she was a child is a prize above rubies.

From such materials surely a good novel might be made— that is what one catches oneself saying, before a hundred pages are finished. And this voice, which is not altogether our own, but the voice of that dissentient spirit which may split off and take a line of its own as we read, should be cross-examined instantly, lest its hints should spoil the pleasure of the whole. What, then, does it mean by insinuat-ing this doubtful, grudging sentiment in the midst of our general well-being? Hitherto nothing has interfered with our enjoyment. Short of being a Rakonitz oneself, of actually taking part in one of those 'diamonded evenings', dancing, drinking, flirting with the snow upon the roof and the gramophone braying out 'It's moonlight in Kalua', short of seeing Betty and Colin 'slightly grotesque advancing . . . in full panoply; velvet spread like a huge inverted cup round Betty's feet, as she minced over the pure, sparkling strip of snow, the absurd tangle of plumes on Colin's helmet'— short of taking hold of all this glitter and fantasy with one's own fingers and thumbs, what is better than Miss Sterne's report of it?

The grudging voice will concede that it is all very brilliant; will admit that a hundred pages have flashed by like a hedge seen from an express train; but will reiterate that for all that something is wrong. A man can elope with a woman without our noticing it. That is a proof that there are no values. There is no shape for these apparitions. Scene melts into scene; person into person. People rise out of a fog of talk, and sink back into talk again. They are soft and shapeless with words. There is no grasping them.

The charge has substance in it, because it is true, when we consider it, that Giles Goddard can run off with Loraine, and it is to us as if somebody had got up and gone out of the room—a matter of no importance. We have been letting ourselves bask in appearances. All this representation of the movement of life has sapped our imaginative power. We have sat receptive and watched, with our eyes rather than with our minds, as we do at the cinema, what passes on the screen in front of us. When we want to use what we have learnt about one of the characters to urge them through some crisis we realize that we have no steam up; no energy at our disposal. How they dressed, what they ate, the slang they used—we know all that; but not what they are. For what we know about these people has been given us (with one exception) by following the methods of life. The characters are built up by observing the incoherence, the fresh natural sequences of a person who, wishing to tell the story of a friend's life in talk, breaks off a thousand times to bring in something fresh, to add something forgotten, so that in the end, though one may feel that one has been in the presence of life, the particular life in question remains vague. This hand-to-mouth method, this ladling out of sentences which have the dripping brilliance of words that live upon real lips, is admirable for one purpose, disastrous for another. All is fluent and graphic; but no character or situation emerges cleanly. Bits of extraneous matter are left sticking to the edges. For all their brilliancy the scenes are clouded;

the crises are blurred. A passage of description will make both the merit and the defect of the method clear. Miss Sterne wants us to realize the beauty of a Chinese coat.

Gazing at it, you might think you had never seen embroidery before, for it was the very climax of all that was brilliant and exotic. The flower-petals were worked in a flaming pattern round the broad bands of kingfisher blue embroidery; and again round each oval plaque that was woven of a silvery heron with a long green beak, and behind his outstretched wings a rainbow. All among the silver arabesques, butterflies were delicately poised, golden butterflies and black butterflies, and butterflies that were gold and black. The closer you looked the more there was to see; intricate markings on the butterfly wings, purple and grass-green and apricot . . .

As if we had not enough to see already, she goes on to add how there were tiny stamens springing from every flower, and circles ringing the eye of each separate stork, until the Chinese coat wobbles before our eyes and merges in one brilliant blur.

The same method applied to people has the same result. Quality is added to quality, fact to fact, until we cease to discriminate and our interest is suffocated under a plethora of words. For it is true of every object—coat or human being—that the more one looks the more there is to see. The writer's task is to take one thing and let it stand for twenty: a task of danger and difficulty; but only so is the reader relieved of the swarm and confusion of life and branded effectively with the particular aspect which the writer wishes him to see. That Miss Sterne has other tools at her disposal, and could use them if she liked, is hinted now and again, and is revealed for a moment in the brief chapter describing the death of the matriarch, Anastasia Rakonitz. Here suddenly the flow of words seems to darken and thicken. We are aware of something beneath the surface, something left unsaid for us to find out for ourselves and think over. The two pages in which we are told how the old woman died asking for gooseliver sausage and a tortoise-shell comb, short though they are, hold, to my thinking, twice the substance of any other thirty pages in the book.

These remarks bring me back to the question with which I started: the relation of the novelist to life and what it should be. That he is terribly exposed to life *A Deputy Was King* proves once more. He can sit and watch life and make his book out of the very foam and effervescence of his emotions; or he can put his glass down, retire to his room and subject his trophy to those mysterious processes by which life becomes, like the Chinese coat, able to stand by itself—a sort of impersonal miracle. But in either case he is faced by a problem which does not afflict the workers in any other arts to the same extent. Stridently, clamorously, life is forever pleading that she is the proper end of fiction and that the more he sees of her and catches of her the better his book will be. She does not add, however, that she is grossly impure; and that the side she flaunts uppermost is often, for the novelist, of no value whatever. Appearance and movement are the lures she trails to entice him after her, as if these were her essence, and by catching them he gained his goal. So believing, he rushes feverishly in her wake, ascertains what fox-trot is being played at the Embassy, what skirt is being worn in Bond Street, worms and winds his way into the last flings of topical slang, and imitates to perfection the last toss of colloquial jargon. He becomes terrified more than anything of falling behind the times: his chief concern is that the thing described shall be fresh from the shell with the down on its head.

This kind of work requires great dexterity and nimbleness, and gratifies a real desire. To know the outside of one's age, its dresses and its dances and its catchwords, has an interest and even a value which the spiritual adventures of a curate, or the aspirations of a high-minded schoolmistress, solemn as they are, for the most part lack. It might well be claimed, too, that to deal with the crowded dance of modern life so as to produce the illusion of reality needs far higher literary skill than to write a serious essay upon the poetry of John Donne or the novels of M. Proust. The novelist, then, who is a slave to life and concocts his books out of the froth of the moment is doing something difficult, something which pleases, something which, if you have a mind that way, may even instruct. But his work passes as the year 1921 passes, as fox-trots pass, and in three years' time looks as dowdy and dull as any other fashion which has served its turn and gone its way.

On the other hand, to retire to one's study in fear of life is equally fatal. It is true that plausible imitations of Addison, say, can be manufactured in the quiet there, but they are as brittle as plaster and as insipid. To survive, each sentence must have, at its heart, a little spark of fire, and this, whatever the risk, the novelist must pluck with his own hands from the blaze. His state then is a precarious one. He must expose himself to life; he must risk the danger of being led away and tricked by her deceitfulness; he must seize her treasure from her and let her trash run to waste. But at a certain moment he must leave the company and withdraw, alone, to that mysterious room where his body is hardened and fashioned into permanence by processes which, if they elude the critic, hold for him so profound a fascination.

On Rereading Meredith[1]

THIS new study [2] of Meredith is not a text-book to be held in one hand while in the other you hold *The Shaving of Shagpat* or *Modern Love*; it is addressed to those who have so far solved the difficulties of the Master that they wish to make up their minds as to his final position in English literature. The book should do much to crystallize opinion upon Meredith, if only because it will induce many people to read him again. For Mr. Crees has written in a spirit of enthusiasm which makes it easy to do so. He summons Diana and Willoughby Patterne and Richard Feverel from the shelves where they have fallen a little silent lately and in a moment the air is full of high-pitched, resonant voices, speaking the unmistakable language of metaphor, epigram, and fantastic poetic dialogue. Some readers, to judge from our own case, will feel a momentary qualm, as at meeting after the lapse of years some hero so ardently admired once that his eccentricities and foibles are now scarcely tolerable; they seem to preserve too well the faults of our own youth. Further, in the presence of so faithful an admirer as Mr. Crees we may be reminded of some intervening disloyalties. It was not Thackeray or Dickens or George Eliot who seriously tempted us from our allegiance; but can we say the same of the great Russians? Oddly enough, when Mr. Crees is taking Meredith's measure by comparing him with his contemporaries he makes no mention of Turgenev, Tolstoy, or Dostoevsky. But it was *Fathers and Sons*, *War and Peace*, *Crime and Punishment* that seduced multitudes of the faithful and, worse still, seemed for the time to reduce Meredith to an insular hero bred and cherished for the delight of connoisseurs in some sheltered corner of a Victorian hothouse.

[1] *Times Literary Supplement*, July 25, 1918.
[2] *George Meredith: A Study of his Works and Personality*, by J. H. E. Crees.

48

The Russians might well overcome us, for they seemed to possess an entirely new conception of the novel and one that was larger, saner, and much more profound than ours. It was one that allowed human life in all its width and depth, with every shade of feeling and subtlety of thought, to flow into their pages without the distortion of personal eccentricity or mannerism. Life was too serious to be juggled with. It was too important to be manipulated. Could any English novel survive in the furnace of that overpowering sincerity? For some time the verdict seemed to go tacitly against Meredith. His fine phrases, his perpetual imagery, the superabundant individuality which so much resembled an overweening egotism seemed to be the very stuff to perish in that uncompromising flame. Perhaps some of us went as far as to believe that the process had already been accomplished and that it was useless to open books in which you would find nothing but charred bones and masses of contorted wire. The poems, *Modern Love*, *Love in the Valley*, and some of the shorter pieces survived the ordeal more successfully and did perhaps keep alive that latent enthusiasm upon which Mr. Crees now blows with the highest praise that it is possible to bestow upon literature. He does not scruple to compare Meredith with Shakespeare. Shakespeare alone, he says, could have written the 'Diversion Played upon a Penny Whistle' in Richard Feverel. Meredith 'illustrates better than any since Shakespeare that impetuous mental energy which Matthew Arnold deemed the source of our literary greatness'. One might even infer from some statements that Meredith was the undisputed equal of the greatest of poets. 'No man has ever been endowed with richer gifts.' He was the possessor of 'in some ways the most consummate intellect that has ever been devoted to literature'. These, moreover, are not the irresponsible flings of a momentary enthusiasm but the considered opinion of a man who writes with ability and critical insight and has reached his superlatives by intelligible degrees of appreciation. We should perhaps alter his scale by putting Donne in the place of Shakespeare; but however we may regulate our superlatives he creates the right mood for reading Meredith again.

The right mood for reading Meredith should have a large proportion of enthusiasm in it, for Meredith aims at, and when he is successful has his dwelling in, the very heart of the emotions. There, indeed, we have one of the chief differences between him and the Russians. They accumulate; they accept ugliness; they seek to understand; they penetrate further and further into the human soul with their terrible power of sustained insight and their undeviating reverence for truth. But Meredith takes truth by storm; he takes it with a phrase, and his best phrases are not mere phrases but are compact of many different observations, fused into one and flashed out in a line of brilliant light. It is by such phrases that we get to know his characters. They come to mind at once in thinking of them. Sir Willoughby 'has a leg'. Clara Middleton 'carries youth like a flag'. Vernon Whitford is 'Phoebus Apollo turned fasting Friar'; every one who has read the novels holds a store of such phrases in his memory. But the same process is applied not only to single characters but to large and complicated situations where a number of different states of mind are represented. Here, too, he wishes to crush the truth out in a series of metaphors or a string of epigrams with as little resort to dull fact as may be. Then, indeed, the effort is prodigious, and the confusion often chaotic. But the failure arises from the enormous scope of his ambition. Let us suppose that he has to describe a tea party; he will begin by destroying everything by which it is easy to recognize a tea party—chairs, tables, cups, and the rest; he will represent the scene merely by a ring on a finger and a plume passing the window. But into the ring and plume he puts such passion and character and such penetrating rays of vision play about the denuded room that we seem to be in possession of all the details as if a painstaking realist had described each one of them separately. To have produced this effect as often as Meredith has done so is an enormous feat. That is the way, as one trusts at such moments, that the art of fiction will develop. For such beauty and such high emotional excitement it is well worth while to exchange the solidity which is the result of knowing the day of the week, how the ladies are dressed, and by what series of credible events the great crisis was accomplished. But the doubt will suggest itself whether we are not sacrificing something of greater importance than mere solidity. We have gained moments of astonishing intensity; we have gained a high level of sustained beauty; but perhaps the beauty is lacking in some quality that makes it a satisfying beauty? 'My love', Meredith wrote, 'is for epical subjects—nor for cobwebs in a putrid corner, though I know the fascination of unravelling them.' He avoids ugliness as he avoids dullness. 'Sheer realism', he wrote, 'is at best the breeder of the dungfly.' Sheer romance breeds an insect more diaphanous, but it tends perhaps to be even more heartless than the dungfly. A touch of realism—or is it a touch of something more akin to sympathy?—would have kept the Meredith hero from being the honourable but tedious gentleman that, with deference to Mr. Crees, we have always found him. It would have charged the high mountain air of his books with the greater variety of clouds.

But, for good or for ill, Meredith has the habit of nobleness ingrained in him. No modern writer, for example, has so completely ignored the colloquial turns of speech and cast his dialogue in sentences that could without impropriety have been spoken by Queen Elizabeth in person. 'Out of my sight, I say!' 'I went to him of my own will to run from your heartlessness, mother—that I call mother!' are two examples found upon turning two pages of *The Tragic Comedians*. That is his natural pitch, although we may guess that the long indifference of the public increased his tendency to the strained and the artificial. For this, among other reasons, it is easy to complain that his world is an aristocratic world, strictly bounded, thinly populated, a little hard-hearted, and not to be entered by the poor, the vulgar, the stupid, or that very common and interesting individual who is a mixture of all three.

And yet there can be no doubt that, even judged by his novels alone, Meredith remains a great writer. The doubt is rather whether he can be called a great novelist; whether, indeed, anyone to whom the technique of novel writing had so much that was repulsive in it can excel compared with those who are writing, not against the grain, but with it. He struggles to escape, and the chapters of amazing but fruitless energy which he produces in his struggle to escape are the true obstacles to the enjoyment of Meredith. What, we ask, is he struggling against? What is he striving for? Was he, perhaps, a dramatist born out of due time—an Elizabethan sometimes, and sometimes, as the last chapters of *The Egoist* suggest, a dramatist of the Restoration? Like a dramatist, he flouts probability, disdains coherency, and lives from one high moment to the next. His dialogue often seems to crave the relief of blank verse. And for all his analytic industry in the dissection of character, he creates not the living men and women who justify modern fiction, but superb conceptions who have more of the general than of the particular in them. There is a large and beautiful conception of womanhood in Diana rather than a single woman; there is the fervour of romantic love in Richard Feverel, but the faces of the lovers are dim in the rosy light. In this lies both the strength and the weakness of his books, but, if the weakness is at all of the kind we have indicated, the strength is of a nature to counterbalance it. His English power of imagination, with its immense audacity and fertility, his superb mastery of the great emotions of courage and love, his power of summoning nature into sympathy with man and of merging him in her vastness, his glory in all fine living and thinking—these are the qualities that give his conceptions their size and universality. In these respects we must recognize his true descent from the greatest of English writers and his enjoyment of qualities that are expressed nowhere save in the masterpieces of our literature.

The Anatomy of Fiction[1]

SOMETIMES at country fairs you may have seen a professor on a platform exhorting the peasants to come up and buy his wonder-working pills. Whatever their disease, whether of body or mind, he has a name for it and a cure; and if they hang back in doubt he whips out a diagram and points with a stick at different parts of the human anatomy, and gabbles so quickly such long Latin words that first one shyly stumbles forward and then another, and takes his bolus and carries it away and unwraps it secretly and swallows it in hope. 'The young aspirant to the art of fiction who knows himself to be an incipient realist', Mr. Hamilton vociferates from his platform,[2] and the incipient realists advance and receive—for the professor is generous—five pills together with nine suggestions for home treatment. In other words they are given five 'review questions' to answer, and are advised to read nine books or parts of books. '1. Define the difference between realism and romance. 2. What are the advantages and disadvantages of the realistic method? 3. What are the advantages and disadvantages of the romantic method?'—that is the kind of thing they work out at home, and with such success that a 'revised and enlarged edition' of the book has been issued on the tenth anniversary of the first publication. In America, evidently, Mr. Hamilton is considered a very good professor, and has no doubt a bundle of testimonials to the miraculous nature of his cures. But let us consider: Mr. Hamilton is not a professor; we are not credulous ploughboys; and fiction is not a disease.

In England we have been in the habit of saying that fiction is an art. We are not taught to write novels; dissua-

[1] *The Athenaeum*, May 16, 1919.
[2] *Materials and Methods of Fiction*, by Clayton Hamilton. With an Introduction by Brander Matthews.

sion is our most usual incentive; and though perhaps the critics have 'deduced and formulated the general principles of the art of fiction', they have done their work as a good housemaid does hers; they have tidied up after the party is over. Criticism seldom or never applies to the problems of the present moment. On the other hand, any good novelist, whether he be dead or alive, has something to say about them, though it is said very indirectly, differently to different people, and differently at different stages of the same person's development. Thus, if anything is essential, it is essential to do your reading with your own eyes. But, to tell the truth, Mr. Hamilton has sickened us of the didactic style. Nothing appears to be essential save perhaps an elementary knowledge of the A.B.C., and it is pleasant to remember that Henry James, when he took to dictation, dispensed even with that. Still, if you have a natural taste for books it is probable that after reading *Emma*, to take an instance, some reflections upon the art of Jane Austen may occur to you— how exquisitely one incident relieves another; how definitely, by not saying something, she says it; how surprising, therefore, her expressive phrases when they come. Between the sentences, apart from the story, a little shape of some kind builds itself up. But learning from books is a capricious business at best, and the teaching so vague and changeable that in the end, far from calling books either 'romantic' or 'realistic', you will be more inclined to think them, as you think people, very mixed, very distinct, very unlike one another. But this would never do for Mr. Hamilton. According to him every work of art can be taken to pieces, and those pieces can be named and numbered, divided and subdivided, and given their order of precedence, like the internal organs of a frog. Thus we learn how to put them together again—that is, according to Mr. Hamilton, we learn how to write. There is the complication, the major knot, and the explication; the inductive and the deductive methods; the kinetic and the static; the direct and the indirect with subdivisions of the same; connotation, annotation, personal equation, and denotation; logical sequence and chronological succession—all parts of the frog and all capable of further dissection. Take the case of 'emphasis' alone. There are eleven kinds of emphasis. Emphasis by terminal position, by initial position, by pause, by direct proportion, by inverse proportion, by iteration, by antithesis, by surprise, by suspense—are you tired already? But consider the Americans. They have written one story eleven times over, with a different kind of emphasis in each. Indeed, Mr. Hamilton's book teaches us a great deal about the Americans.

Still, as Mr. Hamilton uneasily perceives now and then, you may dissect your frog, but you cannot make it hop; there is, unfortunately, such a thing as life. Directions for imparting life to fiction are given, such as to 'train yourself rigorously never to be bored', and to cultivate 'a lively curiosity and a ready sympathy'. But it is evident that Mr. Hamilton does not like life, and, with such a tidy museum as his, who can blame him? He has found life very troublesome, and, if you come to consider it, rather unnecessary; for, after all, there are books. But Mr. Hamilton's views on life are so illuminating that they must be given in his own words:

> Perhaps in the actual world we should never bother to converse with illiterate provincial people; and yet we do not feel it a waste of time and energy to meet them in the pages of *Middlemarch*. For my own part, I have always, in actual life, avoided meeting the sort of people that appear in Thackeray's *Vanity Fair*; and yet I find it not only interesting but profitable to associate with them through the entire extent of a rather lengthy novel.

'Illiterate provincial people'—'interesting but profitable' —'waste of time and energy'—now after much wandering and painful toil we are on the right track at last. For long it seemed that nothing could reward the American people for having written eleven themes upon the eleven kinds of emphasis. But now we perceive dimly that there is something to be gained by the daily flagellation of the exhausted brain. It is not a title; it has nothing to do with pleasure or with literature; but it appears that Mr. Hamilton and his industrious band see far off upon the horizon a circle of superior enlightenment to which, if only they can keep on reading long enough, they may attain. Every book demolished is a milestone passed. Books in foreign languages count twice over. And a book like this is of the nature of a dissertation to be sent up to the supreme examiner, who may be, for any- thing we know, the ghost of Matthew Arnold. Will Mr. Hamilton be admitted? Can they have the heart to reject anyone so ardent, so dusty, so worthy, so out of breath? Alas! look at his quotations; consider his comments upon them:

> 'The murmuring of innumerable bees.' . . . The word innumerable, which denotes to the intellect merely 'in- capable of being numbered,' is, in this connection, made to suggest to the senses the murmuring of bees.

The credulous ploughboy could have told him more than that. It is not necessary to quote what he says about 'magic casements' and the 'iniquity of oblivion'. Is there not, upon page 208, a definition of style?

No; Mr. Hamilton will never be admitted; he and his disciples must toil for ever in the desert sand, and the circle of illumination will, we fear, grow fainter and farther upon their horizon. It is curious to find, after writing the above sentence, how little one is ashamed of being, where literature is concerned, an unmitigated snob.

Gothic Romance[1]

IT says much for Miss Birkhead's [2] natural good sense that
she has been able to keep her head where many people
would have lost theirs. She has read a great many books
without being suffocated. She has analysed a great many
plots without being nauseated. Her sense of literature has
not been extinguished by the waste-paper baskets full of old
novels so courageously heaped on top of it. For her 'attempt
to trace in outline the origin of the Gothic romance and the
tale of terror' has necessarily led her to grope in basements
and attics where the light is dim and the dust is thick. To
trace the course of one strand in the thick skein of our
literature is well worth doing. But perhaps Miss Birkhead
would have increased the interest of her work if she had
enlarged her scope to include some critical discussion of the
aesthetic value of shock and terror, and had ventured some
analysis of the taste which demands this particular stimulus.
But her narrative is quite readable enough to supply the
student with material for pushing the enquiry a little further.

Since it is held that Gothic romance was introduced by
Horace Walpole's *Castle of Otranto*, in the year 1764, there is
no need to confound it with the romance of Spenser or of
Shakespeare. It is a parasite, an artificial commodity, produced half in joke in reaction against the current style, or in
relief from it. If we run over the names of the most famous
of the Gothic romancers—Clara Reeve, Mrs. Radcliffe,
Monk Lewis, Charles Maturin, Sarah Wilkinson—we shall
smile at the absurdity of the visions which they conjure up.
We shall, perhaps, congratulate ourselves upon our improve-
ment. Yet since our ancestors bought two thousand copies of
Mrs. Bennett's *Beggar Girl and her Benefactors*, on the day of

[1] *Times Literary Supplement*, May 5, 1921.
[2] *The Tale of Terror: A Study of the Gothic Romance*, by Edith Birkhead.

publication, at a cost of thirty-six shillings for the seven volumes, there must have been something in the trash that was appetizing, or something in the appetites that was coarse. It is only polite to give our ancestors the benefit of the doubt. Let us try to put ourselves in their places. The books that formed part of the ordinary library in the year 1764 were, presumably, Johnson's *Vanity of Human Wishes*, Gray's Poems, Richardson's *Clarissa*, Addison's *Cato*, Pope's *Essay on Man*. No one could wish for a more distinguished company. At the same time, as literary critics are too little aware, a love of literature is often roused and for the first years nourished not by the good books, but by the bad. It will be an ill day when all the reading is done in libraries and none of it in tubes. In the eighteenth century there must have been a very large public which found no delight in the peculiar literary merits of the age; and if we reflect how long the days were and how empty of distraction, we need not be surprised to find a school of writers grown up in flat defiance of the prevailing masters. Horace Walpole, Clara Reeve, and Mrs. Radcliffe all turned their backs upon their time and plunged into the delightful obscurity of the Middle Ages, which were so much richer than the eighteenth century in castles, barons, moats, and murders.

What Horace Walpole began half in fun was continued seriously and with considerable power by Mrs. Radcliffe. That she had a conscience in the matter is evident from the pains she is at to explain her mysteries when they have done their work. The human body 'decayed and disfigured by worms, which were visible in the features and hands', turns out to be a waxen image credibly placed there in fulfilment of a vow. But there is little wonder that a novelist perpetually on the stretch first to invent mysteries and then to explain them had no leisure for the refinements of the art. 'Mrs. Radcliffe's heroines', says Miss Birkhead, 'resemble nothing more than a composite photograph in which all distinctive traits are merged into an expressionless type.' The same fault can be found with most books of sensation and adventure, and is, after all, inherent in the subject; for it is un-

likely that a lady confronted by a male body stark naked,
wreathed in worms, where she had looked, maybe, for a
pleasant landscape in oils, should do more than give a loud
cry and drop senseless. And women who give loud cries and
drop senseless do it in much the same way. That is one of the
reasons why it is extremely difficult to write a tale of terror
which continues to shock and does not first become insipid
and later ridiculous. Even Miss Wilkinson, who wrote that
'Adeline Barnett was fair as a lily, tall as the pine, her fine
dark eyes sparkling as diamonds, and she moved with the
majestic air of a goddess', had to ridicule her own favourite
style before she had done. Scott, Jane Austen, and Peacock
stooped from their heights to laugh at the absurdity of the
convention and drove it, at any rate, to take refuge underground. For it flourished subterraneously all through the
nineteenth century, and for sixpence you can buy to-day at
the bookstall the recognizable descendant of the *Mysteries of
Udolpho*. Nor is Adeline Barnett by any means defunct. She
is probably an earl's daughter at the present moment;
vicious, painted; in society. But if you call her Miss Wilkinson's Adeline she will have to answer none the less.

It would be a fine exercise in discrimination to decide the
precise point at which romance becomes Gothic and imagination moonshine. Coleridge's lines in *Kubla Khan* about the
woman wailing for her demon lover are a perfect example
of the successful use of emotion. The difficulty, as Miss Birkhead shows, is to know where to stop. Humour is com-
paratively easy to control; psychology is too toilsome to be
frequently overdone; but a gift for romance easily escapes
control and cruelly plunges its possessor into disrepute.
Maturin and Monk Lewis heaped up horrors until Mrs.
Radcliffe herself appeared calm and composed. And they
have paid the penalty. The skull-headed lady, the vampire
gentleman, the whole troop of monks and monsters who
once froze and terrified now gibber in some dark cupboard
of the servants' hall. In our day we flatter ourselves the
effect is produced by subtler means. It is at the ghosts
within us that we shudder, and not at the decaying bodies of

barons or the subterranean activities of ghouls. Yet the desire
to widen our boundaries, to feel excitement without danger,
and to escape as far as possible from the facts of life drive us
perpetually to trifle with the risky ingredients of the mysterious and the unknown. Science, as Miss Birkhead suggests, will modify the Gothic romance of the future with the
aeroplane and the telephone. Already the bolder of our
novelists have made use of psycho-analysis to startle and
dismay. And already such perils attend the use of the
abnormal in fiction—the younger generation has been
heard to complain that the horror of the *Turn of the Screw* is
altogether too tame and conventional to lift a hair of their
heads. But can we possibly say that Henry James was a
Goth?

The Supernatural in Fiction[1]

WHEN Miss Scarborough [2] describes the results of her inquiries into the supernatural in fiction as 'suggestive rather than exhaustive' we have only to add that in any discussion of the supernatural suggestion is perhaps more useful than an attempt at science. To mass together all sorts of cases of the supernatural in literature without much more system or theory than the indication of dates supplies leaves the reader free where freedom has a special value. Perhaps some psychological law lies hidden beneath the hundreds of stories about ghosts and abnormal states of mind (for stories about abnormal states of mind are included with those that are strictly supernatural) which are referred to in her pages; but in our twilight state it is better to guess than to assert, to feel than to classify our feelings. So much evidence of the delight which human nature takes in stories of the supernatural will inevitably lead one to ask what this interest implies both in the writer and in the reader.

In the first place, how are we to account for the strange human craving for the pleasure of feeling afraid which is so much involved in our love of ghost stories? It is pleasant to be afraid when we are conscious that we are in no kind of danger, and it is even more pleasant to be assured of the mind's capacity to penetrate those barriers which for twenty-three hours out of the twenty-four remain impassable. Crude fear, with its anticipation of physical pain or of terrifying uproar, is an undignified and demoralizing sensation, while the mastery of fear only produces a respectable mask of courage, which is of no great interest to ourselves, although it may impose upon others. But the fear which we get from reading ghost stories of the supernatural is a refined and spiritualized essence of fear. It is a fear

[1] *Times Literary Supplement*, January 31, 1918.
[2] *The Supernatural in Modern English Fiction*, by Dorothy Scarborough.

which we can examine and play with. Far from despising ourselves for being frightened by a ghost story we are proud of this proof of sensibility, and perhaps unconsciously welcome the chance for the licit gratification of certain instincts which we are wont to treat as outlaws. It is worth noticing that the craving for the supernatural in literature coincided in the eighteenth century with a period of rationalism in thought, as if the effect of damming the human instincts at one point causes them to overflow at another. Such instincts were certainly at full flood when the writings of Mrs. Radcliffe were their chosen channel. Her ghosts and ruins have long suffered the fate which so swiftly waits upon any exaggeration of the supernatural and substitutes our ridicule for our awe. But although we are quick to throw away imaginative symbols which have served our turn, the desire persists. Mrs. Radcliffe may vanish, but the craving for the supernatural survives. Some element of the supernatural is so constant in poetry that one has come to look upon it as part of the normal fabric of the art; but in poetry, being etherealized, it scarcely provokes any emotion so gross as fear. Nobody was ever afraid to walk down a dark passage after reading *The Ancient Mariner*, but rather inclined to venture out to meet whatever ghosts might deign to visit him. Probably some degree of reality is necessary in order to produce fear; and reality is best conveyed by prose. Certainly one of the finest ghost stories, Wandering Willie's Tale in *Redgauntlet*, gains immensely from the homely truth of the setting, to which the use of the Scotch dialect contributes. The hero is a real man, the country is as solid as can be; and suddenly in the midst of the green and gray landscape opens up the crimson transparency of Redgauntlet Castle with the dead sinners at their feasting.

The superb genius of Scott here achieves a triumph which should keep this story immortal however the fashion in the supernatural may change. Steenie Steenson is himself so real and his belief in the phantoms is so vivid that we draw our fear through our perception of his fear, the story itself being of a kind that has ceased to frighten us. In fact, the vision of the dead carousing would now be treated in a humorous, romantic or perhaps patriotic spirit, but scarcely with any hope of making our flesh creep. To do that the author must change his direction; he must seek to terrify us not by the ghosts of the dead, but by those ghosts which are living within ourselves. The great increase of the psychical ghost story in late years, to which Miss Scarborough bears witness, testifies to the fact that our sense of our own ghostliness has much quickened. A rational age is succeeded by one which seeks the supernatural in the soul of man, and the development of psychical research offers a basis of disputed fact for this desire to feed upon. Henry James, indeed, was of opinion before writing *The Turn of the Screw* that 'the good, the really effective and heart-shaking ghost stories (roughly so to term them) appeared all to have been told. . . . The new type, indeed, the mere modern "psychical case", washed clean of all queerness as by exposure to a flowing laboratory tap, . . . the new type clearly promised little.' Since *The Turn of the Screw*, however, and no doubt largely owing to that masterpiece, the new type has justified its existence by rousing, if not 'the dear old sacred terror', still a very effective modern representative. If you wish to guess what our ancestors felt when they read *The Mysteries of Udolpho* you cannot do better than read *The Turn of the Screw*.

Experiment proves that the new fear resembles the old in producing physical sensations as of erect hair, dilated pupils, rigid muscles, and an intensified perception of sound and movement. But what is it that we are afraid of? We are not afraid of ruins, or moonlight, or ghosts. Indeed, we should be relieved to find that Quint and Miss Jessel are ghosts, but they have neither the substance nor the independent existence of ghosts. The odious creatures are much closer to us than ghosts have ever been. The governess is not so much frightened of them as of the sudden extension of her own field of perception, which in this case widens to reveal to her the presence all about her of an unmentionable evil. The appearance of the figures is an illustration, not in itself specially alarming, of a state of mind which is profoundly mysterious and terrifying. It is a state of mind; even the external objects are made to testify to their subjection. The oncoming of the state is preceded not by the storms and howlings of the old romances, but by an absolute hush and lapse of nature which we feel to represent the ominous trance of her own mind. 'The rooks stopped cawing in the golden sky, and the friendly evening hour lost for the unspeakable minute all its voice.' The horror of the story comes from the force with which it makes us realize the power that our minds possess for such excursions into the darkness; when certain lights sink or certain barriers are lowered, the ghosts of the mind, untracked desires, indistinct intimations, are seen to be a large company.

In the hands of such masters as Scott and Henry James the supernatural is so wrought in with the natural that fear is kept from a dangerous exaggeration into simple disgust or disbelief verging upon ridicule. Mr. Kipling's stories *The Mark of the Beast* and *The Return of Imray* are powerful enough to repel one by their horror, but they are too violent to appeal to our sense of wonder. For it would be a mistake to suppose that supernatural fiction always seeks to produce fear, or that the best ghost stories are those which most accurately and medically describe abnormal states of mind. On the contrary, a vast amount of fiction both in prose and in verse now assures us that the world to which we shut our eyes is far more friendly and inviting, more beautiful by day and more holy by night, than the world which we persist in thinking the real world. The country is peopled with nymphs and dryads, and Pan, far from being dead, is at his pranks in all the villages of England. Much of this mythology is used not for its own sake, but for purposes of satire and allegory; but there exists a group of writers who have the sense of the unseen without such alloy. Such a sense may bring visions of fairies or phantoms, or it may lead to a quickened perception of the relations existing between men and plants, or houses and their inhabitants, or any one of those innumerable alliances which somehow or other we spin between ourselves and other objects in our passage.

Henry James's Ghost Stories[1]

IT is plain that Henry James was a good deal attracted by the ghost story, or, to speak more accurately, by the story of the supernatural. He wrote at least eight of them, and if we wish to see what led him to do so, and what opinion he had of his success, nothing is simpler than to read his own account in the preface to the volume containing *Altar of the Dead*. Yet perhaps we shall keep our own view more distinct if we neglect the preface. As the years go by certain qualities appear, and others disappear. We shall only muddle our own estimate if we try, dutifully, to make it square with the verdict which the author at the time passed on his own work. For example, what did Henry James say of *The Great Good Place*?

> There remains *The Great Good Place* (1900)—to the spirit of which, however, it strikes me that any gloss or comment would be a tactless challenge. It embodies a calculated effect, and to plunge into it, I find, even for a beguiled glance—a course I indeed recommend—is to have left all else outside.

And to us, in 1921, *The Great Good Place* is a failure. It is another example of the fact that when a writer is completely and even ecstatically conscious of success he has, as likely as not, written his worst. We ought, we feel, to be inside, and we remain coldly outside. Something has failed to work, and we are inclined to accuse the supernatural. The challenge may be tactless, but challenge it we must.

That *The Great Good Place* begins admirably, no one will deny. Without the waste of a word we find ourselves at once in the heart of a situation. The harassed celebrity, George Dane, is surrounded by unopened letters and unread books; telegrams arrive; invitations accumulate; and the things of

[1] *Times Literary Supplement*, December 22, 1921.

value lie hopelessly buried beneath the litter. Meanwhile, Brown the manservant announces that a strange young man has arrived to breakfast. Dane touches the young man's hand, and, at this culminating point of annoyance, lapses into a trance or wakes up in another world. He finds himself in a celestial rest-cure establishment. Far bells toll; flowers are fragrant; and after a time the inner life revives. But directly the change is accomplished we are aware that something is wrong with the story. The movement flags; the emotion is monotonous. The enchanter waves his wand and the cows go on grazing. All the characteristic phrases are there in waiting—the silver bowls, the melted hours—but there is no work for them to do. The story dwindles to a sweet soliloquy. Dane and the Brothers become angelic allegorical figures pacing a world that is like ours but smoother and emptier. As if he felt the need of something hard and objective the author invokes the name of the city of Bradford; but it is vain. *The Great Good Place* is an example of the sentimental use of the supernatural and for that reason no doubt Henry James would be likely to feel that he had been more than usually intimate and expressive.

The other stories will presently prove that the supernatural offers great prizes as well as great risks; but let us for a moment dwell upon the risks. The first is undoubtedly that it removes the shocks and buffetings of experience. In the breakfast-room with Brown and the telegram Henry James was forced to keep moving by the pressure of reality; the door must open; the hour must strike. Directly he sank through the solid ground he gained possession of a world which he could fashion to his liking. In the dream world the door need not open; the clock need not strike; beauty is to be had for the asking. But beauty is the most perverse of spirits; it seems as if she must pass through ugliness or lie down with disorder before she can rise in her own person. The ready-made beauty of the dream world produces only an anaemic and conventionalized version of the world we know. And Henry James was much too fond of the world we know to create one that we do not know. The visionary imagination was by no means his. His genius was dramatic, not lyric. Even his characters wilt in the thin atmosphere he provides for them, and we are presented with a Brother when we would much rather grasp the substantial person of Brown.

We have been piling the risks, rather unfairly, upon one story in particular. The truth is perhaps that we have become fundamentally sceptical. Mrs. Radcliffe amused our ancestors because they were our ancestors; because they lived with very few books, an occasional post, a newspaper superannuated before it reached them, in the depths of the country or in a town which resembled the more modest of our villages, with long hours to spend sitting over the fire drinking wine by the light of half a dozen candles. Nowadays we breakfast upon a richer feast of horror than served them for a twelvemonth. We are tired of violence; we suspect mystery. Surely, we might say to a writer set upon the supernatural, there are facts enough in the world to go round; surely it is safer to stay in the breakfast-room with Brown. Moreover, we are impervious to fear. Your ghosts will only make us laugh, and if you try to express some tender and intimate vision of a world stripped of its hide we shall be forced (and there is nothing more uncomfortable) to look the other way. But writers, if they are worth their salt, never take advice. They always run risks. To admit that the supernatural was used for the last time by Mrs. Radcliffe and that modern nerves are immune from the wonder and terror which ghosts have always inspired would be to throw up the sponge too easily. If the old methods are obsolete, it is the business of a writer to discover new ones. The public can feel again what it has once felt—there can be no doubt about that; only from time to time the point of attack must be changed.

How consciously Henry James set himself to look for the weak place in our armour of insensibility it is not necessary to decide. Let us turn to another story, *The Friends of the Friends*, and judge whether he succeeded. This is the story of a man and woman who have been trying for years to meet but only accomplish their meeting on the night of the woman's death. After her death the meetings are continued, and when this is divined by the woman he is engaged to marry she refuses to go on with the marriage. The relationship is altered. Another person, she says, has come between them. 'You see her—you see her; you see her every night!' It is what we have come to call a typically Henry James situation. It is the same theme that was treated with enormous elaboration in *The Wings of the Dove*. Only there, when Milly has come between Kate and Densher and altered their relationship for ever, she has ceased to exist; here the anonymous lady goes on with her work after death. And yet—does it make very much difference? Henry James has only to take the smallest of steps and he is over the border. His characters with their extreme fineness of perception are already half-way out of the body. There is nothing violent in their release. They seem rather to have achieved at last what they have long been attempting—communication without obstacle. But Henry James, after all, kept his ghosts for his ghost stories. Obstacles are essential to *The Wings of the Dove*. When he removed them by supernatural means as he did in *The Friends of the Friends* he did so in order to produce a particular effect. The story is very short; there is no time to elaborate the relationship; but the point can be pressed home by a shock. The supernatural is brought in to provide that shock. It is the queerest of shocks—tranquil, beautiful, like the closing of chords in harmony; and yet, somehow obscene. The living and the dead by virtue of their superior sensibility have reached across the gulf; that is beautiful. The live man and the dead woman have met alone at night. They have their relationship. The spiritual and the carnal meeting together produce a strange emotion —not exactly fear, nor yet excitement. It is a feeling that we do not immediately recognize. There is a weak spot in our armour somewhere. Perhaps Henry James will penetrate by methods such as these.

Next, however, we turn to *Owen Wingrave*, and the enticing game of pinning your author to the board by detecting once more traces of his fineness, his subtlety, whatever his prevailing characteristics may be, is rudely interrupted. Pinioned, tied down, to all appearance lifeless, up he jumps and walks away. Somehow one has forgotten to account for the genius, for the driving power which is so incalculable and so essential. With Henry James in particular we tend, in wonder at his prodigious dexterity, to forget that he had a crude and simple passion for telling stories. The preface to *Owen Wingrave* throws light upon that fact, and incidentally suggests why it is that *Owen Wingrave* as a ghost story misses its mark. One summer's afternoon, many years ago, he tells us, he sat on a penny chair under a great tree in Kensington Gardens. A slim young man sat down upon another chair near by and began to read a book.

> Did the young man then, on the spot, just *become* Owen Wingrave, establishing by the mere magic of type the situation, creating at a stroke all the implications and filling out all the pictures? . . . my poor point is only that at the beginning of my session in the penny chair the seedless fable hadn't a claim to make or an excuse to give, and that, the very next thing, the penny-worth still partly unconsumed, it was fairly bristling with pretexts. 'Dramatize it, dramatize it!' would seem to have rung with sudden intensity in my ears.

So the theory of a conscious artist taking out his little grain of matter and working it into the finished fabric is another of our critical fables. The truth appears to be that he sat on a chair, saw a young man, and fell asleep. At any rate, once the group, the man, or perhaps only the sky and the trees become significant, the rest is there inevitably. Given Owen Wingrave, then Spencer Coyle, Mrs. Coyle, Kate Julian, the old house, the season, the atmosphere must be in existence. Owen Wingrave implies all that. The artist has simply to see that the relations between these places and people are the right ones. When we say that Henry James had a passion for story-telling we mean that when his significant moment came to him the accessories were ready to flock in.

In this instance they flocked in almost too readily. There they are on the spot with all the stir and importance that belong to living people. Miss Wingrave seated in her Baker Street lodging with 'a fat catalogue of the Army and Navy Stores, which reposed on a vast desolate table-cover of false blue'; Mrs. Coyle, 'a fair fresh slow woman', who admitted and indeed gloried in the fact that she was in love with her husband's pupils, 'Which shows that the subject between them was treated in a liberal spirit'; Spencer Coyle himself, and the boy Lechmere—all bear, of course, upon the question of Owen's temperament and situation, and yet they bear on so many other things besides. We seem to be settling in for a long absorbing narrative; and then, rudely, incongruously, a shriek rings out; poor Owen is found stretched on the threshold of the haunted room; the supernatural has cut the book in two. It is violent; it is sensational; but if Henry James himself were to ask us: 'Now, have I frightened you?' we should be forced to reply: 'Not a bit'. The catastrophe has not the right relations to what has gone before. The vision in Kensington Gardens did not, perhaps, embrace the whole. Out of sheer bounty the author has given us a scene rich in possibilities—a young man whose problem (he detests war and is condemned to be a soldier) has a deep psychological interest; a girl whose subtlety and oddity are purposely defined as if in readiness for future use. Yet what use is made of them? Kate Julian has merely to dare a young man to sleep in a haunted room; a plump Miss from a parsonage would have done as well. What use is made of the supernatural? Poor Owen Wingrave is knocked on the head by the ghost of an ancestor; a stable bucket in a dark passage would have done it better.

The stories in which Henry James uses the supernatural effectively are, then, those where some quality in a character or in a situation can only be given its fullest meaning by being cut free from facts. Its progress in the unseen world must be closely related to what goes on in this. We must be made to feel that the apparition fits the crisis of passion or of conscience which sent it forth so exactly that the ghost story, besides its virtues as a ghost story, has the additional charm of being also symbolical. Thus the ghost of Sir Edmund Orme appears to the lady who jilted him long ago whenever her daughter shows signs of becoming engaged. The apparition is the result of her guilty conscience, but it is more than that. It is the guardian of the rights of lovers. It fits what has gone before; it completes. The use of the super-natural draws out a harmony which would otherwise be inaudible. We hear the first note close at hand, and then, a moment after, the second chimes far away.

Henry James's ghosts have nothing in common with the violent old ghosts—the blood-stained sea captains, the white horses, the headless ladies of dark lanes and windy commons. They have their origin within us. They are present when-ever the significant overflows our powers of expressing it; whenever the ordinary appears ringed by the strange. The baffling things that are left over, the frightening ones that persist—these are the emotions that he takes, embodies, makes consoling and companionable. But how can we be afraid? As the gentleman says when he has seen the ghost of Sir Edmund Orme for the first time: 'I was ready to answer for it to all and sundry that ghosts are much less alarming and more amusing than was commonly supposed'. The beautiful urbane spirits are only not of this world because they are too fine for it. They have taken with them across the border their clothes, their manners, their breeding, their band-boxes, and valets and ladies' maids. They remain always a little worldly. We may feel clumsy in their pres-ence, but we cannot feel afraid. What does it matter, then, if we do pick up the *Turn of the Screw* an hour or so before bedtime? After an exquisite entertainment we shall, if the other stories are to be trusted, end with this fine music in our ears, and sleep the sounder.

Perhaps it is the silence that first impresses us. Everything at Bly is so profoundly quiet. The twitter of birds at dawn, the far-away cries of children, faint footsteps in the distance stir it but leave it unbroken. It accumulates; it weighs us down; it makes us strangely apprehensive of noise. At last the house and garden die out beneath it. 'I can hear again, as I write, the intense hush in which the sounds of evening dropped. The rooks stopped cawing in the golden sky, and the unfriendly hour lost for the unspeakable minute all its voice.' It is unspeakable. We know that the man who stands on the tower staring down at the governess beneath is evil. Some unutterable obscenity has come to the surface. It tries to get in; it tries to get at something. The exquisite little beings who lie innocently asleep must at all costs be protected. But the horror grows. Is it possible that the little girl, as she turns back from the window, has seen the woman outside? Has she been with Miss Jessel? Has Quint visited the boy? It is Quint who hangs about us in the dark; who is there in that corner and again there in that. It is Quint who must be reasoned away, and for all our reasoning returns. Can it be that we are afraid? But it is not a man with red hair and a white face whom we fear. We are afraid of something, perhaps, in ourselves. In short, we turn on the light. If by its beams we examine the story in safety, note how masterly the telling is, how each sentence is stretched, each image filled, how the inner world gains from the robustness of the outer, how beauty and obscenity twined together worm their way to the depths—still we must own that something remains unaccounted for. We must admit that Henry James has conquered. That courtly, worldly, sentimental old gentleman can still make us afraid of the dark.

A Terribly Sensitive Mind[1]

THE most distinguished writers of short stories in England are agreed, says Mr. Murry, that as a writer of short stories Katherine Mansfield was *hors concours*. No one has succeeded her, and no critic has been able to define her quality. But the reader of her journal is well content to let such questions be. It is not the quality of her writing or the degree of her fame that interest us in her diary, but the spectacle of a mind—a terribly sensitive mind—receiving one after another the haphazard impressions of eight years of life. Her diary was a mystical companion. 'Come my unseen, my unknown, let us talk together', she says on beginning a new volume. In it she noted facts—the weather, an engagement; she sketched scenes; she analyzed her character; she described a pigeon or a dream or a conversation. nothing could be more fragmentary; nothing more private. We feel that we are watching a mind which is alone with itself; a mind which has so little thought of an audience that it will make use of a shorthand of its own now and then, or, as the mind in its loneliness tends to do, divide into two and talk to itself. Katherine Mansfield about Katherine Mansfield.

But then as the scraps accumulate we find ourselves giving them, or more probably receiving from Katherine Mansfield herself, a direction. From what point of view is she looking at life as she sits there, terribly sensitive, registering one after another such diverse impressions? She is a writer; a born writer. Everything she feels and hears and sees is not fragmentary and separate; it belongs together as writing. Sometimes the note is directly made for a story. 'Let me remember when I write about that fiddle how it runs up lightly and swings down sorrowful; how it *searches*', she notes.

[1] *New York Herald Tribune*, September 18, 1927.

Or, 'Lumbago. This is a very queer thing. So sudden, so painful, I must remember it when I write about an old man. The start to get up, the pause, the look of fury, and how, lying at night, one seems to get locked.' . . .

Again, the moment itself suddenly puts on significance, and she traces the outline as if to preserve it. 'It's raining, but the air is soft, smoky, warm. Big drops patter on the languid leaves, the tobacco flowers lean over. Now there is a rustle in the ivy. Wingly has appeared from the garden next door; he bounds from the wall. And delicately, lifting his paws, pointing his ears, very afraid the big wave will overtake him, he wades over the lake of green grass.' The Sister of Nazareth 'showing her pale gums and big discoloured teeth' asks for money. The thin dog. So thin that his body is like 'a cage on four wooden pegs', runs down the street. In some sense, she feels, the thin dog is the street. In all this we seem to be in the midst of unfinished stories; here is a beginning; here an end. They only need a loop of words thrown round them to be complete.

But then the diary is so private and so instinctive that it allows another self to break off from the self that writes and to stand a little apart watching it write. The writing self was a queer self; sometimes nothing would induce it to write. 'There is so much to do and I do so little. Life would be almost perfect here if only when I was *pretending* to work I always was working. Look at the stories that wait and wait just at the threshold. . . . *Next day.* Yet take this morning, for instance. I don't want to write anything. It's gray; it's heavy and dull. And short stories seem unreal and not worth doing. I don't want to write; I want to *live*. What does she mean by that? It's not easy to say. But there you are!'

What does she mean by that? No one felt more seriously the importance of writing than she did. In all the pages of her journal, instinctive, rapid as they are, her attitude toward her work is admirable, sane, caustic, and austere. There is no literary gossip; no vanity; no jealousy. Although during her last years she must have been aware of her success she makes no allusion to it. Her own comments upon her work are always penetrating and disparaging. Her stories wanted richness and depth; she was only 'skimming the top—no more'. But writing, the mere expression of things adequately and sensitively, is not enough. It is founded upon something unexpressed; and this something must be solid and entire. Under the desperate pressure of increasing illness she began a curious and difficult search, of which we catch glimpses only and those hard to interpret, after the crystal clearness which is needed if one is to write truthfully. 'Nothing of any worth can come of a disunited being', she wrote. One must have health in one's self. After five years of struggle she gave up the search after physical health not in despair, but because she thought the malady was of the soul and that the cure lay not in any physical treatment, but in some such 'spiritual brotherhood' as that at Fontainebleau, in which the last months of her life were spent. But before she went she wrote the summing up of her position with which the journal ends.

She wanted health, she wrote; but what did she mean by health? 'By health', she wrote, 'I mean the power to lead a full, adult, living, breathing life in close contact with what I love—the earth and the wonders thereof—the sea—the sun. . . . Then I want to *work*. At what? I want so to live that I work with my hands and my feeling and my brain. I want a garden, a small house, grass, animals, books, pictures, music. And out of this, the expression of this, I want to be writing. (Though I may write about cabmen. That's no matter.)' The diary ends with the words 'All is well'. And since she died three months later it is tempting to think that the words stood for some conclusion which illness and the intensity of her own nature drove her to find at an age when most of us are loitering easily among those appearances and impressions, those amusements and sensations, which none had loved better than she.

Women and Fiction[1]

THE title of this article can be read in two ways: it may allude to women and the fiction that they write, or to women and the fiction that is written about them. The ambiguity is intentional, for in dealing with women as writers, as much elasticity as possible is desirable; it is necessary to leave oneself room to deal with other things besides their work, so much has that work been influenced by conditions that have nothing whatever to do with art.

The most superficial inquiry into women's writing instantly raises a host of questions. Why, we ask at once, was there no continuous writing done by women before the eighteenth century? Why did they then write almost as habitually as men, and in the course of that writing produce, one after another, some of the classics of English fiction? And why did their art then, and why to some extent does their art still, take the form of fiction?

A little thought will show us that we are asking questions to which we shall get, as answer, only further fiction. The answer lies at present locked in old diaries, stuffed away in old drawers, half-obliterated in the memories of the aged. It is to be found in the lives of the obscure—in those almost unlit corridors of history where the figures of generations of women are so dimly, so fitfully perceived. For very little is known about women. The history of England is the history of the male line, not of the female. Of our fathers we know always some fact, some distinction. They were soldiers or they were sailors; they filled that office or they made that law. But of our mothers, our grandmothers, our great-grandmothers, what remains? Nothing but a tradition. One was beautiful; one was red-haired; one was kissed by a Queen. We know nothing of them except their names and

[1] *The Forum*, March 1929.

the dates of their marriages and the number of children they bore.

Thus, if we wish to know why at any particular time women did this or that, why they wrote nothing, why on the other hand they wrote masterpieces, it is extremely difficult to tell. Anyone who should seek among those old papers, who should turn history wrong side out and so construct a faithful picture of the daily life of the ordinary woman in Shakespeare's time, in Milton's time, in Johnson's time, would not only write a book of astonishing interest, but would furnish the critic with a weapon which he now lacks. The extraordinary woman depends on the ordinary woman. It is only when we know what were the conditions of the average woman's life—the number of her children, whether she had money of her own, if she had a room to herself, whether she had help in bringing up her family, if she had servants, whether part of the housework was her task—it is only when we can measure the way of life and the experience of life made possible to the ordinary woman that we can account for the success or failure of the extraordinary woman as a writer.

Strange spaces of silence seem to separate one period of activity from another. There was Sappho and a little group of women all writing poetry on a Greek island six hundred years before the birth of Christ. They fall silent. Then about the year 1000 we find a certain court lady, the Lady Murasaki, writing a very long and beautiful novel in Japan. But in England in the sixteenth century, when the dramatists and poets were most active, the women were dumb. Elizabethan literature is exclusively masculine. Then, at the end of the eighteenth century and in the beginning of the nineteenth, we find women again writing—this time in England —with extraordinary frequency and success.

Law and custom were of course largely responsible for these strange intermissions of silence and speech. When a woman was liable, as she was in the fifteenth century, to be beaten and flung about the room if she did not marry the man of her parents' choice, the spiritual atmosphere was not favourable to the production of works of art. When she was married without her own consent to a man who thereupon became her lord and master, 'so far at least as law and custom could make him', as she was in the time of the Stuarts, it is likely she had little time for writing, and less encouragement. The immense effect of environment and suggestion upon the mind, we in our psychoanalytical age are beginning to realize. Again, with memoirs and letters to help us, we are beginning to understand how abnormal is the effort needed to produce a work of art, and what shelter and what support the mind of the artist requires. Of those facts the lives and letters of men like Keats and Carlyle and Flaubert assure us.

Thus it is clear that the extraordinary outburst of fiction in the beginning of the nineteenth century in England was heralded by innumerable slight changes in law and customs and manners. And women of the nineteenth century had some leisure; they had some education. It was no longer the exception for women of the middle and upper classes to choose their own husbands. And it is significant that of the four great women novelists—Jane Austen, Emily Brontë, Charlotte Brontë, and George Eliot—not one had a child, and two were unmarried.

Yet, though it is clear that the ban upon writing had been removed, there was still, it would seem, considerable pressure upon women to write novels. No four women can have been more unlike in genius and character than these four. Jane Austen can have had nothing in common with George Eliot; George Eliot was the direct opposite of Emily Brontë. Yet all were trained for the same profession; all, when they wrote, wrote novels.

Fiction was, as fiction still is, the easiest thing for a woman to write. Nor is it difficult to find the reason. A novel is the least concentrated form of art. A novel can be taken up or put down more easily than a play or a poem. George Eliot left her work to nurse her father. Charlotte Brontë put down her pen to pick the eyes out of the potatoes. And living as she did in the common sitting-room, surrounded by people, a woman was trained to use her mind in observation and upon the analysis of character. She was trained to be a novelist and not to be a poet.

Even in the nineteenth century, a woman lived almost solely in her home and her emotions. And those nineteenth-century novels, remarkable as they were, were profoundly influenced by the fact that the women who wrote them were excluded by their sex from certain kinds of experience. That experience has a great influence upon fiction is indisputable. The best part of Conrad's novels, for instance, would be destroyed if it had been impossible for him to be a sailor. Take away all that Tolstoi knew of war as a soldier, of life and society as a rich young man whose education admitted him to all sorts of experience, and *War and Peace* would be incredibly impoverished.

Yet *Pride and Prejudice, Wuthering Heights, Villette,* and *Middlemarch* were written by women from whom was for-cibly withheld all experience save that which could be met with in a middle-class drawing-room. No first-hand experi-ence of war or seafaring or politics or business was possible for them. Even their emotional life was strictly regulated by law and custom. When George Eliot ventured to live with Mr. Lewes without being his wife, public opinion was scan-dalized. Under its pressure she withdrew into a suburban seclusion which, inevitably, had the worst possible effects upon her work. She wrote that unless people asked of their own accord to come and see her, she never invited them. At the same time, on the other side of Europe, Tolstoi was living a free life as a soldier, with men and women of all classes, for which nobody censured him and from which his novels drew much of their astonishing breadth and vigour.

But the novels of women were not affected only by the necessarily narrow range of the writer's experience. They showed, at least in the nineteenth century, another char-acteristic which may be traced to the writer's sex. In *Middle-march* and in *Jane Eyre* we are conscious not merely of the writer's character, as we are conscious of the character of Charles Dickens, but we are conscious of a woman's presence

—of someone resenting the treatment of her sex and pleading for its rights. This brings into women's writing an element which is entirely absent from a man's, unless, indeed, he happens to be a working-man, a negro, or one who for some other reason is conscious of disability. It introduces a distortion and is frequently the cause of weakness. The desire to plead some personal cause or to make a character the mouthpiece of some personal discontent or grievance always has a distressing effect, as if the spot at which the reader's attention is directed were suddenly twofold instead of single.

The genius of Jane Austen and Emily Brontë is never more convincing than in their power to ignore such claims and solicitations and to hold on their way unperturbed by scorn or censure. But it needed a very serene or a very powerful mind to resist the temptation to anger. The ridicule, the censure, the assurance of inferiority in one form or another which were lavished upon women who practised an art, provoked such reactions naturally enough. One sees the effect in Charlotte Brontë's indignation, in George Eliot's resignation. Again and again one finds it in the work of the lesser women writers—in their choice of a subject, in their unnatural self-assertiveness, in their unnatural docility. Moreover, insincerity leaks in almost unconsciously. They adopt a view in deference to authority. The vision becomes too masculine or it becomes too feminine; it loses its perfect integrity and, with that, its most essential quality as a work of art.

The great change that has crept into women's writing is, it would seem, a change of attitude. The woman writer is no longer bitter. She is no longer angry. She is no longer pleading and protesting as she writes. We are approaching, if we have not yet reached, the time when her writing will have little or no foreign influence to disturb it. She will be able to concentrate upon her vision without distraction from outside. The aloofness that was once within the reach of genius and originality is only now coming within the reach of ordinary women. Therefore the average novel by a woman is far more genuine and far more interesting to-day than it was a hundred or even fifty years ago.

But it is still true that before a woman can write exactly as she wishes to write, she has many difficulties to face. To begin with, there is the technical difficulty—so simple, apparently; in reality, so baffling—that the very form of the sentence does not fit her. It is a sentence made by men; it is too loose, too heavy, too pompous for a woman's use. Yet in a novel, which covers so wide a stretch of ground, an ordinary and usual type of sentence has to be found to carry the reader on easily and naturally from one end of the book to the other. And this a woman must make for herself, altering and adapting the current sentence until she writes one that takes the natural shape of her thought without crushing or distorting it.

But that, after all, is only a means to an end, and the end is still to be reached only when a woman has the courage to surmount opposition and the determination to be true to herself. For a novel, after all, is a statement about a thousand different objects—human, natural, divine; it is an attempt to relate them to each other. In every novel of merit these different elements are held in place by the force of the writer's vision. But they have another order also, which is the order imposed upon them by convention. And as men are the arbiters of that convention, as they have established an order of values in life, so too, since fiction is largely based on life, these values prevail there also to a very great extent.

It is probable, however, that both in life and in art the values of a woman are not the values of a man. Thus, when a woman comes to write a novel, she will find that she is perpetually wishing to alter the established values—to make serious what appears insignificant to a man, and trivial what is to him important. And for that, of course, she will be criticized; for the critic of the opposite sex will be genuinely puzzled and surprised by an attempt to alter the current scale of values, and will see in it not merely a difference of view, but a view that is weak, or trivial, or sentimental, because it differs from his own.

But here, too, women are coming to be more independent of opinion. They are beginning to respect their own sense of values. And for this reason the subject matter of their novels begins to show certain changes. They are less interested, it would seem, in themselves; on the other hand, they are more interested in other women. In the early nineteenth century, women's novels were largely autobiographical. One of the motives that led them to write was the desire to expose their own suffering, to plead their own cause. Now that this desire is no longer so urgent, women are beginning to explore their own sex, to write of women as women have never been written of before; for of course, until very lately, women in literature were the creation of men.

Here again there are difficulties to overcome, for, if one may generalize, not only do women submit less readily to observation than men, but their lives are far less tested and examined by the ordinary processes of life. Often nothing tangible remains of a woman's day. The food that has been cooked is eaten; the children that have been nursed have gone out into the world. Where does the accent fall? What is the salient point for the novelist to seize upon? It is difficult to say. Her life has an anonymous character which is baffling and puzzling in the extreme. For the first time, this dark country is beginning to be explored in fiction; and at the same moment a woman has also to record the changes in women's minds and habits which the opening of the professions has introduced. She has to observe how their lives are ceasing to run underground; she has to discover what new colours and shadows are showing in them now that they are exposed to the outer world.

If, then, one should try to sum up the character of women's fiction at the present moment, one would say that it is courageous; it is sincere; it keeps closely to what women feel. It is not bitter. It does not insist upon its femininity. But at the same time, a woman's book is not written as a man would write it. These qualities are much commoner than they were, and they give even to second- and third-rate work the value of truth and the interest of sincerity.

But in addition to these good qualities, there are two that call for a word more of discussion. The change which has turned the English woman from a nondescript influence, fluctuating and vague, to a voter, a wage-earner, a responsible citizen, has given her both in her life and in her art a turn toward the impersonal. Her relations now are not only emotional; they are intellectual, they are political. The old system which condemned her to squint askance at things through the eyes or through the interests of husband or brother, has given place to the direct and practical interests of one who must act for herself, and not merely influence the acts of others. Hence her attention is being directed away from the personal centre which engaged it exclusively in the past to the impersonal, and her novels naturally become more critical of society, and less analytical of individual lives.

We may expect that the office of gadfly to the state, which has been so far a male prerogative, will now be discharged by women also. Their novels will deal with social evils and remedies. Their men and women will not be observed wholly in relation to each other emotionally, but as they cohere and clash in groups and classes and races. That is one change of some importance. But there is another more interesting to those who prefer the butterfly to the gadfly—that is to say, the artist to the reformer. The greater impersonality of women's lives will encourage the poetic spirit, and it is in poetry that women's fiction is still weakest. It will lead them to be less absorbed in facts and no longer content to record with astonishing acuteness the minute details which fall under their own observation. They will look beyond the personal and political relationships to the wider questions which the poet tries to solve—of our destiny and the meaning of life.

The basis of the poetic attitude is of course largely founded upon material things. It depends upon leisure, and a little money, and the chance which money and leisure give to observe impersonally and dispassionately. With money and leisure at their service, women will naturally occupy themselves more than has hitherto been possible with the craft of letters. They will make a fuller and a more subtle use of the instrument of writing. Their technique will become bolder and richer.

In the past, the virtue of women's writing often lay in its divine spontaneity, like that of the blackbird's song or the thrush's. It was untaught; it was from the heart. But it was also, and much more often, chattering and garrulous—mere talk spilt over paper and left to dry in pools and blots. In future, granted time and books and a little space in the house for herself, literature will become for women, as for men, an art to be studied. Women's gift will be trained and strengthened. The novel will cease to be the dumping-ground for the personal emotions. It will become, more than at present, a work of art like any other, and its resources and its limitations will be explored.

From this it is a short step to the practice of the sophisti-cated arts, hitherto so little practised by women—to the writing of essays and criticism, of history and biography. And that, too, if we are considering the novel, will be of advan-tage; for besides improving the quality of the novel itself, it will draw off the aliens who have been attracted to fiction by its accessibility while their hearts lay elsewhere. Thus will the novel be rid of those excrescences of history and fact which, in our time, have made it so shapeless.

So, if we may prophesy, women in time to come will write fewer novels, but better novels; and not novels only, but poetry and criticism and history. But in this, to be sure, one is looking ahead to that golden, that perhaps fabulous, age when women will have what has so long been denied them—leisure, and money, and a room to themselves.

An Essay in Criticism[1]

HUMAN credulity is indeed wonderful. There may be good reasons for believing in a King or a Judge or a Lord Mayor. When we see them go sweeping by in their robes and their wigs, with their heralds and their outriders, our knees begin to shake and our looks to falter. But what reason there is for believing in critics it is impossible to say. They have neither wigs nor outriders. They differ in no way from other people if one sees them in the flesh. Yet these insignificant fellow creatures have only to shut themselves up in a room, dip a pen in the ink, and call themselves 'we', for the rest of us to believe that they are somehow exalted, inspired, infallible. Wigs grow on their heads. Robes cover their limbs. No greater miracle was ever performed by the power of human credulity. And, like most miracles, this one, too, has had a weakening effect upon the mind of the believer. He begins to think that critics, because they call themselves so, must be right. He begins to suppose that something actually happens to a book when it has been praised or denounced in print. He begins to doubt and conceal his own sensitive, hesitating apprehensions when they conflict with the critics' decrees.

And yet, barring the learned (and learning is chiefly useful in judging the work of the dead), the critic is rather more fallible than the rest of us. He has to give us his opinion of a book that has been published two days, perhaps, with the shell still sticking to its head. He has to get outside that cloud of fertile, but unrealized, sensation which hangs about a reader, to solidify it, to sum it up. The chances are that he does this before the time is ripe; he does it too rapidly and too definitely. He says that it is a great book or a bad book. Yet, as he knows, when he is content to read

[1] *New York Herald Tribune*, October 9, 1927.

only, it is neither. He is driven by force of circumstances and some human vanity to hide those hesitations which beset him as he reads, to smooth out all traces of that crab-like and crooked path by which he has reached what he choses to call 'a conclusion'. So the crude trumpet blasts of critical opinion blow loud and shrill, and we, humble readers that we are, bow our submissive heads.

But let us see whether we can do away with these pretences for a season and pull down the imposing curtain which hides the critical process until it is complete. Let us give the mind a new book, as one drops a lump of fish into a cage of fringed and eager sea anemones, and watch it pausing, pondering, considering its attack. Let us see what prejudices affect it; what influences tell upon it. And if the conclusion becomes in the process a little less conclusive, it may, for that very reason, approach nearer to the truth. The first thing that the mind desires is some foothold of fact upon which it can lodge before it takes flight upon its speculative career. Vague rumours attach themselves to people's names. Of Mr. Hemingway, we know that he is an American living in France, an 'advanced' writer, we suspect, connected with what is called a movement, though which of the many we own that we do not know. It will be well to make a little more certain of these matters by reading first Mr. Hemingway's earlier book, *The Sun Also Rises*, and it soon becomes clear from this that, if Mr. Hemingway is 'advanced', it is not in the way that is to us most interesting. A prejudice of which the reader would do well to take account is here exposed; the critic is a modernist. Yes, the excuse would be because the moderns make us aware of what we feel subconsciously; they are truer to our own experience; they even anticipate it, and this gives us a particular excitement. But nothing new is revealed about any of the characters in *The Sun Also Rises*. They come before us shaped, proportioned, weighed, exactly as the characters of Maupassant are shaped and proportioned. They are seen from the old angle; the old reticences, the old relations between author and character are observed.

But the critic has the grace to reflect that this demand for new aspects and new perspectives may well be overdone. It may become whimsical. It may become foolish. For why should not art be traditional as well as original? Are we not attaching too much importance to an excitement which, though agreeable, may not be valuable in itself, so that we are led to make the fatal mistake of overriding the writer's gift?

At any rate, Mr. Hemingway is not modern in the sense given; and it would appear from his first novel that this rumour of modernity must have sprung from his subject matter and from his treatment of it rather than from any fundamental novelty in his conception of the art of fiction. It is a bare, abrupt, outspoken book. Life as people live it in Paris in 1927 or even in 1928 is described as we of this age do describe life (it is here that we steal a march upon the Victorians) openly, frankly, without prudery, but also without surprise. The immoralities and moralities of Paris are described as we are apt to hear them spoken of in private life. Such candour is modern and it is admirable. Then, for qualities grow together in art as in life, we find attached to this admirable frankness an equal bareness of style. Nobody speaks for more than a line or two. Half a line is mostly sufficient. If a hill or a town is described (and there is always some reason for its description) there it is, exactly and literally built up of little facts, literal enough, but chosen, as the final sharpness of the outline proves, with the utmost care. Therefore, a few words like these: 'The grain was just beginning to ripen and the fields were full of poppies. The pasture land was green and there were fine trees, and sometimes big rivers and chateaux off in the trees'—which have a curious force. Each word pulls its weight in the sentence. And the prevailing atmosphere is fine and sharp, like that of winter days when the boughs are bare against the sky. (But if we had to choose one sentence with which to describe what Mr. Hemingway attempts and sometimes achieves, we should quote a passage from a description of a bullfight: 'Romero never made any contortions, always it was straight and pure and natural in line. The others twisted themselves like corkscrews, their elbows raised and leaned against the flanks of the bull after his horns had passed, to give a faked look of danger. Afterwards, all that was faked turned bad and gave an unpleasant feeling. Romero's bullfighting gave real emotion, because he kept the absolute purity of line in his movements and always quietly and calmly let the horns pass him close each time.') Mr. Hemingway's writing, one might paraphrase, gives us now and then a real emotion, because he keeps absolute purity of line in his movements and lets the horns (which are truth, fact, reality) pass him close each time. But there is something faked, too, which turns bad and gives an unpleasant feeling—that also we must face in course of time.

And here, indeed, we may conveniently pause and sum up what point we have reached in our critical progress. Mr. Hemingway is not an advanced writer in the sense that he is looking at life from a new angle. What he sees is a tolerably familiar sight. Common objects like beer bottles and journalists figure largely in the foreground. But he is a skilled and conscientious writer. He has an aim and makes for it without fear or circumlocution. We have, therefore, to take his measure against somebody of substance, and not merely line him, for form's sake, beside the indistinct bulk of some ephemeral shape largely stuffed with straw. Reluctantly we reach this decision, for this process of measurement is one of the most difficult of a critic's tasks. He has to decide which are the most salient points of the book he has just read; to distinguish accurately to what kind they belong, and then, holding them against whatever model is chosen for comparison, to bring out their deficiency or their adequacy.

Recalling *The Sun Also Rises*, certain scenes rise in memory: the bullfight, the character of the Englishman, Harris; here a little landscape which seems to grow behind the people naturally; here a long, lean phrase which goes curling round a situation like the lash of a whip. Now and again this phrase evokes a character brilliantly, more often a scene. Of character, there is little that remains firmly and solidly elucidated. Something indeed seems wrong with the people. If we place them (the comparison is bad) against Tchekov's people, they are flat as cardboard. If we place them (the comparison is better) against Maupassant's people they are crude as a photograph. If we place them (the comparison may be illegitimate) against real people, the people we liken them to are of an unreal type. They are people one may have seen showing off at some café; talking a rapid, high-pitched slang, because slang is the speech of the herd, seemingly much at their ease, and yet if we look at them a little from the shadow not at their ease at all, and, indeed, terribly afraid of being themselves, or they would say things simply in their natural voices. So it would seem that the thing that is faked is character; Mr. Hemingway leans against the flanks of that particular bull after the horns have passed.

After this preliminary study of Mr. Hemingway's first book, we come to the new book, *Men Without Women*, possessed of certain views or prejudices. His talent plainly may develop along different lines. It may broaden and fill out; it may take a little more time and go into things—human beings in particular—rather more deeply. And even if this meant the sacrifice of some energy and point, the exchange would be to our private liking. On the other hand, his is a talent which may contract and harden still further! it may come to depend more and more upon the emphatic moment; make more and more use of dialogue, and cast narrative and description overboard as an encumbrance.

The fact that *Men Without Women* consists of short stories, makes it probable that Mr. Hemingway has taken the second line. But, before we explore the new book, a word should be said which is generally left unsaid, about the implications of the title. As the publisher puts it . . . 'the softening feminine influence is absent—either through training, discipline, death, or situation'. Whether we are to understand by this that women are incapable of training, discipline, death, or situation, we do not know. But it is undoubtedly true, if we are going to persevere in our attempt to reveal the processes of the critic's mind, that any emphasis laid upon sex is dangerous. Tell a man that this is a woman's book, or a woman that this is a man's, and you have brought into play sympathies and antipathies which have nothing to do with art. The greatest writers lay no stress upon sex one way or the other. The critic is not reminded as he reads them that he belongs to the masculine or the feminine gender. But in our time, thanks to our sexual perturbations, sex consciousness is strong, and shows itself in literature by an exaggeration, a protest of sexual characteristics which in either case is disagreeable. Thus Mr. Lawrence, Mr. Douglas, and Mr. Joyce partly spoil their books for women readers by their display of self-conscious virility; and Mr. Hemingway, but much less violently, follows suit. All we can do, whether we are men or women, is to admit the influence, look the fact in the face, and so hope to stare it out of countenance.

To proceed then—*Men Without Women* consists of short stories in the French rather than in the Russian manner. The great French masters, Mérimée and Maupassant, made their stories as self-conscious and compact as possible. There is never a thread left hanging; indeed, so contracted are they that when the last sentence of the last page flares up, as it so often does, we see by its light the whole circumference and significance of the story revealed. The Tchekov method is, of course, the very opposite of this. Everything is cloudy and vague, loosely trailing rather than tightly furled. The stories move slowly out of sight like clouds in the summer air, leaving a wake of meaning in our minds which gradually fades away. Of the two methods, who shall say which is the better? At any rate, Mr. Hemingway, enlisting under the French masters, carries out their teaching up to a point with considerable success.

There are in *Men Without Women* many stories which, if life were longer, one would wish to read again. Most of them indeed are so competent, so efficient, and so bare of superfluity that one wonders why they do not make a deeper dent in the mind than they do. Take the pathetic story of the Major whose wife died—'In Another Country'; or the sardonic story of a conversation in a railway carriage—'A Canary for One'; or stories like 'The Undefeated' and 'Fifty Grand' which are full of the sordidness and heroism of bull-fighting and boxing—all of these are good trenchant stories, quick, terse, and strong. If one had not summoned the ghosts of Tchekov, Mérimée, and Maupassant, no doubt one would be enthusiastic. As it is, one looks about for something, fails to find something, and so is brought again to the old familiar business of ringing impressions on the counter, and asking what is wrong?

For some reason the book of short stories does not seem to us to go as deep or to promise as much as the novel. Perhaps it is the excessive use of dialogue, for Mr. Hemingway's use of it is surely excessive. A writer will always be chary of dialogue because dialogue puts the most violent pressure upon the reader's attention. He has to hear, to see, to supply the right tone, and to fill in the background from what the characters say without any help from the author. Therefore, when fictitious people are allowed to speak it must be because they have something so important to say that it stimulates the reader to do rather more than his share of the work of creation. But, although Mr. Hemingway keeps us under the fire of dialogue constantly, his people, half the time, are saying what the author could say much more economically for them. At last we are inclined to cry out with the little girl in 'Hills Like White Elephants': 'Would you please please please please please please stop talking?'

And probably it is this superfluity of dialogue which leads to that other fault which is always lying in wait for the writer of short stories: the lack of proportion. A paragraph in excess will make these little craft lopsided and will bring about that blurred effect which, when one is out for clarity and point, so baffles the reader. And both these faults, the tendency to flood the page with unnecessary dialogue and the lack of sharp, unmistakable points by which we can take hold of the story, come from the more fundamental fact that, though Mr. Hemingway is brilliantly and enormously skilful, he lets his dexterity, like the bullfighter's cloak, get between him and the fact. For in truth story-writing has much in common with bullfighting. One may twist one's self like a corkscrew and go through every sort of contortion so that the public thinks one is running every risk and displaying superb gallantry. But the true writer stands close up to the bull and lets the horns—call them life, truth, reality, whatever you like—pass him close each time.

Mr. Hemingway, then, is courageous; he is candid; he is highly skilled; he plants words precisely where he wishes; he has moments of bare and nervous beauty; he is modern in manner but not in vision; he is self-consciously virile; his talent has contracted rather than expanded; compared with his novel his stories are a little dry and sterile. So we sum him up. So we reveal some of the prejudices, the instincts and the fallacies out of which what it pleases us to call criticism is made.

Phases of Fiction [1]

THE following pages attempt to record the impressions made upon the mind by reading a certain number of novels in succession. In deciding which book to begin with and which book to go on with, the mind was not pressed to make a choice. It was allowed to read what it liked. It was not, that is to say, asked to read historically, nor was it asked to read critically. It was asked to read only for interest and pleasure, and, at the same time, to comment as it read upon the nature of the interest and the pleasure that it found. It went its way, therefore, independent of time and reputation. It read Trollope before it read Jane Austen and skipped, by chance or negligence, some of the most celebrated books in English fiction. Thus, there is little reference or none to Fielding, Richardson, or Thackeray.

Yet, if nobody save the professed historian and critic reads to understand a period or to revise a reputation, nobody reads simply by chance or without a definite scale of values. There is, to speak metaphorically, some design that has been traced upon our minds which reading brings to light. Desires, appetites, however we may come by them, fill it in, scoring now in this direction, now in that. Hence, an ordinary reader can often trace his course through literature with great exactness and can even think himself, from time to time, in possession of a whole world as inhabitable as the real world. Such a world, it may be urged against it, is always in process of creation. Such a world, it may be added, likewise against it, is a personal world, a world limited and unhabitable perhaps by other people, a world created in obedience to tastes that may be peculiar to one temperament and distasteful to another—indeed, any such

[1] *The Bookman*, April, May, & June, 1929.

record of reading, it will be concluded, is bound to be limited, personal, erratic.

In its defence, however, it may be claimed that if the critic and the historian speak a more universal language, a more learned language, they are also likely to miss the centre and to lose their way for the simple reason that they know so many things about a writer that a writer does not know about himself. Writers are heard to complain that influences —education, heredity, theory—are given weight of which they themselves are unconscious in the act of creation. Is the author in question the son of an architect or a bricklayer? Was he educated at home or at the university? Does he come before or after Thomas Hardy? Yet not one of these things is in his mind, perhaps, as he writes and the reader's ignorance, narrowing and limiting as it is, has at least the advantage that it leaves unhampered what the reader has in common with the writer, though much more feebly: the desire to create.

Here, then, very briefly and with inevitable simplifications, an attempt is made to show the mind at work upon a shelf full of novels and to watch it as it chooses and rejects, making itself a dwelling-place in accordance with its own appetites. Of these appetites, perhaps, the simplest is the desire to believe wholly and entirely in something which is fictitious. That appetite leads on all the others in turn. There is no saying, for they change so much at different ages, that one appetite is better than another. The common reader is, moreover, suspicious of fixed labels and settled hierarchies. Still, since there must be an original impulse, let us give the lead to this one and start upon the shelf full of novels in order to gratify our wish to believe.

The Truth-Tellers

In English fiction there are a number of writers who gratify our sense of belief—Defoe, Swift, Trollope, Borrow, W. E. Norris, for example; among the French, one thinks instantly of Maupassant. Each of them assures us that things are precisely as they say they are. What they describe happens actually before our eyes. We get from their novels the same sort of refreshment and delight that we get from seeing something actually happen in the street below. A dustman, for example, by an awkward movement of his arm knocks over a bottle apparently containing Condy's Fluid which cracks upon the pavement. The dustman gets down; he picks up the jagged fragments of the broken bottle; he turns to a man who is passing in the street. We cannot take our eyes off him until we have feasted our powers of belief to the full. It is as if a channel were cut, into which suddenly and with great relief an emotion hitherto restrained rushes and pours. We forget whatever else we may be doing. This positive experience overpowers all the mixed and ambiguous feelings of which we may be possessed at the moment. The dustman has knocked over a bottle; the red stain is spreading on the pavement. It happens precisely so.

The novels of the great truth-tellers, of whom Defoe is easily the English chief, procure for us a refreshment of this kind. He tells us the story of Moll Flanders, of Robinson Crusoe, of Roxana, and we feel our powers of belief rush into the channel, thus cut, instantly, fertilizing and refreshing our entire being. To believe seems the greatest of all pleasures. It is impossible to glut our greed for truth, so rapacious is it. There is not a shadowy or insubstantial word in the whole book to startle our nervous sense of security. Three or four strong, direct strokes of the pen carve out Roxana's character. Her dinner is set indisputably on the table. It consists of veal and turnips. The day is fine or cloudy; the month is April or September. Persistently, naturally, with a curious, almost unconscious iteration, emphasis is laid upon the very facts that most reassure us of stability in real life, upon money, furniture, food, until we seem wedged among solid objects in a solid universe.

One element of our delight comes from the sense that this world, with all its circumstantiality, bright and round and hard as it is, is yet complete, so that in whatever direction we reach out for assurance we receive it. If we press on beyond the confines of each page, as it is our instinct to do, completing what the writer has left unsaid, we shall find that we can trace our way; that there are indications which let us realize them; there is an under side, a dark side to this world. Defoe presided over his universe with the omnipotence of a God, so that his world is perfectly in scale. Nothing is so large that it makes another thing too small; nothing so small that it makes another thing too large.

The name of God is often found on the lips of his people, but they invoke a deity only a little less substantial than they are themselves, a being seated solidly not so very far above them in the tree tops. A divinity more mystical, could Defoe have made us believe in him, would so have discredited the landscape and cast doubt upon the substance of the men and women that our belief in them would have perished at the heart. Or, suppose that he let himself dwell upon the green shades of the forest depths or upon the sliding glass of the summer stream. Again, however much we were delighted by the description, we should have been uneasy because this other reality would have wronged the massive and monumental reality of Crusoe and Moll Flanders. As it is, saturated with the truth of his own universe, no such discrepancy is allowed to intrude. God, man, nature are all real, and they are all real with the same kind of reality—an astonishing feat, since it implies complete and perpetual submission on the writer's part to his conviction, an obdurate deafness to all the voices which seduce and tempt him to gratify other moods. We have only to reflect how seldom a book is carried through on the same impulse of belief, so that its perspective is harmonious throughout, to realize how great a writer Defoe was. One could number on one's fingers half a dozen novels which set out to be masterpieces and yet have failed because the belief flags; the realities are mixed; the perspective shifts and, instead of a final clarity, we get a baffling, if only a momentary, confusion.

Having, now, feasted our powers of belief to the full and so enjoyed the relief and rest of this positive world existing so

palpably and completely outside of us, there begins to come
over us that slackening of attention which means that the
nerve in use is sated for the time being. We have absorbed
as much of this literal truth as we can and we begin to crave
for something to vary it that will yet be in harmony with it.
We do not want, except in a flash or a hint, such truth
as Roxana offers us when she tells us how her master, the
Prince, would sit by their child and 'loved to look at it when
it was asleep'. For that truth is hidden truth; it makes us
dive beneath the surface to realize it and so holds up the
action. It is, then, action that we want. One desire having
run its course, another leaps forward to take up the burden
and no sooner have we formulated our desire than Defoe has
given it to us. 'On with the story'—that cry is forever on his
lips. No sooner has he got his facts assembled than the
burden is floated. Perpetually springing up, fresh and effort-
less, action and event, quickly succeeding each other thus
set in motion this dense accumulation of facts and keep the
breeze blowing in our faces. It becomes obvious, then, that
if his people are sparely equipped and bereft of certain
affections, such as love of husband and child, which we
expect of people at leisure, it is that they may move quicker.
They must travel light since it is for adventure that they are
made. They will need quick wits, strong muscles, and rocky
common sense on the road they are to travel rather than
sentiment, reflection, or the power of self-analysis.

Belief, then, is completely gratified by Defoe. Here, the
reader can rest himself and enter into possession of a large
part of his domain. He tests it; he tries it; he feels nothing
give under him or fade before him. Still, belief seeks fresh
sustenance as a sleeper seeks a fresh side of the pillow. He
may turn, and this is likely, to someone closer to him in
time than Defoe in order to gratify his desire for belief (for
distance of time in a novel sets up picturesqueness, hence
unfamiliarity). If he should take down, for example, some
book of a prolific and once esteemed novelist, like W. E.
Norris, he will find that the juxtaposition of the two books
brings each out more clearly.

W. E. Norris was an industrious writer who is well worth singling out for inquiry if only because he represents that vast body of forgotten novelists by whose labours fiction is kept alive in the absence of the great masters. At first, we seem to be given all that we need: girls and boys, cricket, shooting, dancing, boating, lovemaking, marriage; a park here; a London drawing-room there; here, an English gentleman; there, a cad; dinners, tea-parties, canters in the Row; and, behind it all, green and gray, domestic and venerable, the fields and manor houses of England. Then, as one scene succeeds another, half-way through the book, we seem to have a great deal more belief on our hands than we know what to do with. We have exhausted the vividness of slang; the modernity, the adroit turn of mood. We loiter on the threshold of the scene, asking to be allowed to press a little further; we take some phrase, and look at it as if it ought to yield us more. Then, turning our eyes from the main figures, we try to sketch out something in the background, to pursue these feelings and relations away from the present moment; not, needless to say, with a view to discovering some over-arching conception, something which we may call 'a reading of life'. No, our desire is otherwise: some shadow of depth appropriate to the bulk of the figures; some Providence such as Defoe provides or morality such as he suggests, so that we can go beyond the age itself without falling into inanity.

Then, we discover it is the mark of a second-rate writer that he cannot pause here or suggest there. All his powers are strained in keeping the scene before us, its brightness and its credibility. The surface is all; there is nothing beyond.

Our capacity for belief, however, is not in the least exhausted. It is only a question of finding something that will revive it for us. Not Shakespeare and not Shelley and not Hardy; perhaps, Trollope, Swift, Maupassant. Above all, Maupassant is the most promising at the moment, for Maupassant enjoys the great advantage that he writes in French. Not from any merit of his own, he gives us that little fillip which we get from reading a language whose edges have not been smoothed for us by daily use. The very sentences shape themselves in a way that is definitely charming. The words tingle and sparkle. As for English, alas, it is *our* language—shop-worn, not so desirable, perhaps. Moreover, each of these compact little stories has its pinch of gunpowder, artfully placed so as to explode when we tread on its tail. The last words are always highly charged. Off they go, *bang*, in our faces and there is lit up for us in one uncompromising glare someone with his hand lifted, someone sneering, someone turning his back, someone catching an omnibus, as if this insignificant action, whatever it may be, summed up the whole situation forever.

The reality that Maupassant brings before us is always one of the body, of the senses—the ripe flesh of a servant girl, for example, or the succulence of food. 'Elle restait inerte, ne sentant plus son corps, et l'esprit dispersé, comme si quelqu'un l'eût d'échiqueté avec un de ces instruments dont se servent les cardeurs pour effiloquer la laine des matelas.' Or her tears dried themselves upon her cheeks 'comme des gouttes d'eau sur du fer rouge'. It is all concrete; it is all visualized. It is a world, then, in which one can believe with one's eyes and one's nose and one's senses; nevertheless, it is a world which secretes perpetually a little drop of bitterness. Is this all? And, if this is all, is it enough? Must we, then, believe this? So we ask. Now that we are given truth unadorned, a disagreeable sensation seems attached to it, which we must analyse before we go further.

Suppose that one of the conditions of things as they are is that they are unpleasant, have we strength enough to support that unpleasantness for the sake of the delight of believing in it? Are we not shocked somehow by *Gulliver's Travels* and *Boule de suif* and *La Maison Tellier*? Shall we not always be trying to get round the obstacle of ugliness by saying that Maupassant and his like are narrow, cynical, and unimaginative when, in fact, it is their truthfulness that we resent—the fact that leeches suck the naked legs of servant girls, that there are brothels, that human nature is fundamentally cold, selfish, corrupt? This discomfort at the

disagreeableness of truth is one of the first things that shakes
very lightly our desire to believe. Our Anglo-Saxon blood,
perhaps, has given us an instinct that truth is, if not exactly
beautiful, at least pleasant or virtuous to behold. But let us
look once more at truth and, this time, through the eyes
of Anthony Trollope, 'a big, blustering, spectacled, loud
voiced hunting man . . . whose language in male society
was, I believe, so lurid that I was not admitted to breakfast
with him . . . who rode about the country establishing penny
posts, and wrote, as the story goes, so many thousand words
before breakfast every day of his life'.[1]

Certainly, the Barchester novels tell the truth, and the
English truth, at first sight, is almost as plain of feature as
the French truth, though with a difference. Mr. Slope is a
hypocrite, with a 'pawing, greasy way with him'. Mrs.
Proudie is a domineering bully. The Archdeacon is well-
meaning but coarse-grained and thick-cut. Thanks to the
vigour of the author, the world of which these are the most
prominent inhabitants goes through its daily rigmarole of
feeding and begetting children and worshipping with a
thoroughness, a gusto, which leave us no loophole of escape.
We believe in Barchester as we believe in the reality of our
own weekly bills. Nor, indeed, do we wish to escape from
the consequences of our belief, for the truth of the Slopes
and the Proudies, the truth of the evening party where Mrs.
Proudie has her dress torn off her back under the light of
eleven gas jets, is entirely acceptable.

At the top of his bent Trollope is a big, if not first-rate
novelist, and the top of his bent came when he drove his pen
hard and fast after the humours of provincial life and scored,
without cruelty but with hale and hearty common sense,
the portraits of those well-fed, black-coated, unimaginative men and women of the fifties. In his manner with
them, and his manner is marked, there is an admirable
shrewdness, like that of a family doctor or solicitor, too well
acquainted with human foibles to judge them other than
tolerantly and not above the human weakness of liking one

[1] *Vignettes of Memory*, by Lady Violet Greville, 1927.

person a great deal better than another for no good reason. Indeed, though he does his best to be severe and is at his best when most so, he could not hold himself aloof, but let us know that he loved the pretty girl and hated the oily humbug so vehemently that it is only by a great pull on his reins that he keeps himself straight. It is a family party over which he presides and the reader who becomes, as time goes on, one of Trollope's most intimate cronies has a seat at his right hand. Their relation becomes confidential.

All this, of course, complicates what was simple enough in Defoe and Maupassant. There, we were plainly and straightforwardly asked to believe. Here, we are asked to believe, but to believe through the medium of Trollope's temperament and, thus, a second relationship is set up with Trollope himself which, if it diverts us, distracts us also. The truth is no longer quite so true. The clear cold truth, which seems to lie before us unveiled in *Gulliver's Travels* and *Moll Flanders* and *La Maison Tellier*, is here garnished with a charming embroidery. But it is not from this attractive embellishment of Trollope's personality that the disease comes which in the end proves fatal to the huge, substantial, well buttressed, and authenticated truth of the Barchester novels. Truth itself, however unpleasant, is interesting always. But, unfortunately, the conditions of storytelling are harsh; they demand that scene shall follow scene; that party shall be supported by another party, one parsonage by another parsonage; that all shall be of the same calibre; that the same values shall prevail. If we are told here that the palace was lit by gas, we must be told there that the manor house was faithful to the oil lamp. But what will happen if, in process of solidifying the entire body of his story, the novelist finds himself out of facts or flagging in his invention? Must he then go on? Yes, for the story has to be finished: the intrigue discovered, the guilty punished, the lovers married in the end. The record, therefore, becomes at times merely a chronicle. Truth peters out into a thin-blooded catalogue. Better would it be, we feel, to leave a blank or even to outrage our sense of probability than to stuff the crevices with this makeshift substance: the wrong side of truth is a worn, dull fabric, unsteeped in the waters of imagination and scorched. But the novel has issued her orders; I consist, she says, of two and thirty chapters; and who am I, we seem to hear the sagacious and humble Trollope ask, with his usual good sense, that I should go disobeying the novel? And he manfully provides us with makeshifts.

If, then, we reckon up what we have got from the truth-tellers, we find that it is a world where our attention is always being drawn to things which can be seen, touched, and tasted, so that we get an acute sense of the reality of our physical existence. Having thus established our belief, the truth-tellers at once contrive that its solidity shall be broken before it becomes oppressive by action. Events happen; coincidence complicates the plain story. But their actions are all in keeping one with another and they are extremely careful not to discredit them or alter the emphasis in any way by making their characters other than such people as naturally express themselves to the full in active and adventurous careers. Then, again, they hold the three great powers which dominate fiction—God, Nature, and Man—in stable relation so that we look at a world in proper perspective; where, moreover, things hold good not only here at the moment in front of us but, there, behind that tree or among those unknown people far away in the shadow behind those hills. At the same time, truth-telling implies disagreeableness. It is part of truth—the sting and edge of it. We cannot deny that Swift, Defoe, and Maupassant all convince us that they reach a more profound depth in their ugliness than Trollope in his pleasantness. For this reason, truth-telling easily swerves a little to one side and becomes satiric. It walks beside the fact and apes it, like a shadow which is only a little more humped and angular than the object which casts it. Yet, in its perfect state, when we can believe absolutely, our satisfaction is complete. Then, we can say, though other states may exist which are better or more exalted, there is none that makes this unnecessary,

none that supersedes it. But truth-telling carries in its breast
a weakness which is apparent in the works of the lesser
writers or in the masters themselves when they are exhausted. Truth-telling is liable to degenerate into perfunctory fact-recording, the repetition of the statement that it
was on Wednesday that the Vicar held his mother's meeting
which was often attended by Mrs. Brown and Miss Dobson
in their pony carriage, a statement which, as the reader is
quick to perceive, has nothing of truth in it but the respectable outside.

At length, then, taking into account the perfunctory fact-
recording, the lack of metaphor, the plainness of the language, and the fact that we believe most when the truth is
most painful to us, it is not strange that we should become
aware of another desire welling up spontaneously and
making its way into those cracks which the great monuments
of the truth-tellers wear inevitably upon their solid bases.
A desire for distance, for music, for shadow, for space, takes
hold of us. The dustman has picked up his broken bottle;
he has crossed the road; he begins to lose solidity and detail
over there in the evening dusk.

The Romantics

'It was a November morning, and the cliffs which overlooked the ocean were hung with thick and heavy mist,
when the portals of the ancient and half ruinous tower, in
which Lord Ravenswood had spent the last and troubled
years of his life, opened, that his mortal remains might pass
forward to an abode yet more dreary and lonely.'

No change could be more complete. The dustman has
become a Lord; the present has become the past; homely
Anglo-Saxon speech has become Latin and many syllabled;
instead of pots and pans, gas jets and snug broughams, we
have a half-ruinous tower and cliffs, the ocean and November, heavy in mist. This past and this ruin, this lord and this
autumn, this ocean and this cliff are as delightful to us as

the change from a close room and voices to the night and the open air. The curious softness and remoteness of the *Bride of Lammermoor*, the atmosphere of rusty moorland and splashing waves, the dark and the distance actually seem to be adding themselves to that other more truthful scene which we still hold in mind, and to be giving it completeness. After that storm this peace, after that glare this coolness. The truth-tellers had very little love, it seems, of nature. They used nature almost entirely as an obstacle to overcome or as a background to complete, not æsthetically for contemplation or for any part it might play in the affairs of their characters. The town, after all, was their natural haunt. But let us compare them in more essential qualities: in their treatment of people. There comes towards us a girl tripping lightly and leaning on her father's arm:

. . . 'Lucy Ashton's exquisitely beautiful, yet somewhat girlish features, were formed to express peace of mind, serenity, and indifference to the tinsel of worldly pleasure. Her locks, which were of shadowy gold, divided on a brow of exquisite whiteness, like a gleam of broken and pallid sunshine upon a hill of snow. The expression of the countenance was in the last degree gentle, soft, timid and feminine, and seemed rather to shrink from the most casual look of a stranger than to court his admiration.'

Nobody could less resemble Moll Flanders or Mrs. Proudie. Lucy Ashton is incapable of action or of self-control. The bull runs at her and she sinks to the ground; the thunder peals and she faints. She falters out the strangest little language of ceremony and politeness, 'O if you be a man, if you be a gentleman assist me to find my father'. One might say that she has no character except the traditional; to her father she is filial; to her lover, modest; to the poor, benevolent. Compared with Moll Flanders, she is a doll with sawdust in her veins and wax in her cheeks. Yet we have read ourselves into the book and grow familiar with its proportions. We come, at length, to see that anything more individual or eccentric or marked would lay emphasis where we want none. This tapering wraith hovers over the landscape and is part of it. She and Edgar Ravenswood are needed to support this romantic world with their bare forms, to clasp it round with that theme of unhappy love which is needed to hold the rest together. But the world that they clasp has its own laws. It leaves out and eliminates no less drastically than the other. On the one hand, we have feelings of the utmost exaltation—love, hate, jealousy, remorse; on the other hand, raciness and simplicity in the extreme. The rhetoric of the Ashtons and Ravenswoods is completed by the humours of peasants and cackle of village women. The true romantic can swing us from earth to sky; and the great master of romantic fiction, who is undoubtedly Sir Walter Scott, uses his liberty to the full. At the same time, we retort upon this melancholy which he has called forth, as in the *Bride of Lammermoor*. We laugh at ourselves for having been so moved by machinery so absurd. However, before we impute this defect to romance itself, we must consider whether it is not Scott's fault. This lazy-minded man was quite capable when the cold fit was on him of filling a chapter or two currently, conventionally, from a fountain of empty, journalistic phrases which, for all that they have a charm of their own, let the slackened attention sag still further.

Carelessness has never been laid to the charge of Robert Louis Stevenson. He was careful, careful to a fault—a man who combined most strangely boy's psychology with the extreme sophistication of an artist. Yet, he obeyed no less implicitly than Walter Scott the laws of romance. He lays his scene in the past; he is always putting his characters to the sword's point with some desperate adventure; he caps his tragedy with homespun humour. Nor can there be any doubt that his conscience and his seriousness as a writer have stood him in good stead. Take any page of *The Master of Ballantrae* and it still stands wear and tear; but the fabric of the *Bride of Lammermoor* is full of holes and patches; it is scamped, botched, hastily flung together. Here, in Stevenson, romance is treated seriously and given all the advantages of the most refined literary art, with the result that we are never left to consider what an absurd situation this is or to reflect that we have no emotion left with which to meet the demand made upon us. We get, on the contrary, a firm, credible story, which never betrays us for a second, but is corroborated, substantiated, made good in every detail. With what precision and cunning a scene will be made visible to us as if the pen were a knife which sliced away the covering and left the core bare!

'It was as he said: there was no breath stirring; a windless stricture of frost had bound the air; and as we went forth in the shine of the candles, the blackness was like a roof over our heads.' Or, again: 'All the 27th that rigorous weather endured; a stifling cold; folk passing about like smoking chimneys; the wide hearth in the hall piled high with fuel; some of the spring birds that had already blundered north into our neighbourhood besieging the windows of the house or trotting on the frozen turf like things distracted.'

'A windless stricture of frost . . . folk passing about like smoking chimneys'—one may search the Waverley Novels in vain for such close writing as this. Separately, these descriptions are lovely and brilliant. The fault lies elsewhere, in the whole of which they are a part. For in those critical minutes which decide a book's fate, when it is finished and the book swims up complete in the mind and lets us look at it, something seems lacking. Perhaps it is that the detail sticks out too prominently. The mind is caught up by this fine passage of description, by that curious exactitude of phrase; but the rhythm and sweep of emotion which the story has started in us are denied satisfaction. We are plucked back when we should be swinging free. Our attention is caught by some knot of ribbon or refinement of tracery when in fact we desire only a bare body against the sky.

Scott repels our taste in a thousand ways. But the crisis, that is the point where the accent falls and shapes the book under it, is right. Slouching, careless as he is, he will at the critical moment pull himself together and strike the one stroke needed, the stroke which gives the book its vividness in memory. Lucy sits gibbering 'couched like a hare upon its form'. 'So, you have ta'en up your bonnie bridegroom?' she says, dropping her fine lady's mincing speech for the vernacular. Ravenswood sinks beneath the quicksands. 'One only vestige of his fate appeared. A large sable feather had been detached from his hat, and the rippling waves of the rising tide wafted it to Caleb's feet. The old man took it up, dried it, and placed it in his bosom.' At both these points the writer's hand is on the book and it falls from him shaped. But in *The Master of Ballantrae*, though each detail is right and wrought so as separately to move our highest admiration, there is no such final consummation. What should have gone to help it seems, in retrospect, to stand apart from it. We remember the detail, but not the whole. Lord Durisdeer and the Master die together but we scarcely notice it. Our attention has been frittered away elsewhere.

It would seem that the romantic spirit is an exacting one; if it sees a man crossing the road in the lamplight and then lost in the gloom of the evening, it at once dictates what course the writer must pursue. We do not wish, it will say, to know much about him. We desire that he shall express our capacity for being noble and adventurous; that he shall dwell among wild places and suffer the extremes of fortune; that he be endowed with youth and distinction and allied with moors, winds, and wild birds. He is, moreover, to be a lover, not in a minute, introspective way, but largely and in outline. His feelings must be part of the landscape; the shallow browns and blues of distant woods and harvest fields are to enter into them; a tower, perhaps, and a castle where the snapdragon flowers. Above all, the romantic spirit demands here a crisis and there a crisis in which the wave that has swollen in the breast shall break. Such feelings Scott gratifies more completely than Stevenson, though with enough qualification to make us pursue the question of romance and its scope and its limitations a little further. Perhaps here it might be interesting to read *The Mysteries of Udolpho*.

The Mysteries of Udolpho have been so much laughed at as

the type of Gothic absurdity that it is difficult to come at the book with a fresh eye. We come, expecting to ridicule. Then, when we find beauty, as we do, we go to the other extreme and rhapsodize. But the beauty and the absurdity of romance are both present and the book is a good test of the romantic attitude, since Mrs. Radcliffe pushes the liberties of romance to the extreme. Where Scott will go back a hundred years to get the effect of distance, Mrs. Radcliffe will go back three hundred. With one stroke, she frees herself from a host of disagreeables and enjoys her freedom lavishly.

As a novelist, it is her desire to describe scenery and it is there that her great gift lies. Like every true writer, she shoulders her way past every obstacle to her goal. She brings us into a huge, empty, airy world. A few ladies and gentlemen, who are purely eighteenth century in mind, manner, and speech, wander about in vast champaigns, listen to nightingales singing amorously in midnight woods; see the sun set over the lagoon of Venice; and watch the distant Alps turn pink and blue from the turrets of an Italian castle. These people, when they are well born, are of the same blood as Scott's gentry; attenuated and formal silhouettes who have the same curious power of being in themselves negligible and insipid but of merging harmoniously in the design.

Again, we feel the force which the romantic acquires by obliterating facts. With the sinking of the lights, the solidity of the foreground disappears, other shapes become apparent and other senses are roused. We become aware of the danger and darkness of our existence; comfortable reality has proved itself a phantom too. Outside our little shelter we hear the wind raging and the waves breaking. In this mood our senses are strained and apprehensive. Noises are audible which we should not hear normally. Curtains rustle. Something in the semi-darkness seems to move. Is it alive? And what is it? And what is it seeking here? Mrs. Radcliffe succeeds in making us feel all this, largely because she is able to make us aware of the landscape and, thus, induces a detached mood favourable to romance; but in her, more plainly than in Scott or Stevenson, the absurdity is evident, the wheels of the machine are visible and the grinding is heard. She lets us see more clearly than they do what demands the romantic writer makes upon us.

Both Scott and Stevenson, with the true instinct of the imagination, introduced rustic comedy and broad Scots dialect. It is in that direction, as they rightly divined, that the mind will unbend when it relaxes. Mrs. Radcliffe, on the other hand, having climbed to the top of her pinnacle, finds it impossible to come down. She tries to solace us with comic passages, put naturally into the mouths of Annette and Ludovico who are servants. But the break is too steep for her limited and ladylike mind and she pieces out her high moments and her beautiful atmosphere with a pale reflection of romance which is more tedious than any ribaldry. Mysteries abound. Murdered bodies multiply; but she is incapable of creating the emotion to feel them by, with the result that they lie there, unbelieved in; hence, ridiculous. The veil is drawn; there is the concealed figure; there is the decayed face; there are the writhing worms— and we laugh.

Directly the power which lives in a book sinks, the whole fabric of the book, its sentences, the length and shape of them, its inflections, its mannerisms, all that it wore proudly and naturally under the impulse of a true emotion become stale, forced, unappetizing. Mrs. Radcliffe slips limply into the faded Scott manner and reels off page after page in a style illustrated by this example:

> Emily, who had always endeavoured to regulate her conduct by the nicest laws, and whose mind was finely sensible, not only of what is just in morals, but of whatever is beautiful in the feminine character, was shocked by these words.

And so it slips along and so we sink and drown in the pale tide. Nevertheless, Udolpho passes this test: it gives us an emotion which is both distinct and unique, however high or low we rate the emotion itself.

If we see now where the danger of romance lies: how difficult the mood is to sustain; how it needs the relief of comedy; how the very distance from common human experience and strangeness of its elements become ridiculous—if we see these things, we see also that these emotions are in themselves priceless jewels. The romantic novel realizes for us an emotion which is deep and genuine. Scott, Stevenson, Mrs. Radcliffe, all in their different ways, unveil another country of the land of fiction; and it is not the least proof of their power that they breed in us a keen desire for something different.

The Character-Mongers and Comedians

The novels which make us live imaginatively, with the whole of the body as well as the mind, produce in us the physical sensations of heat and cold, noise and silence, one reason perhaps why we desire change and why our reactions to them vary so much at different times. Only, of course, the change must not be violent. It is rather that we need a new scene; a return to human faces; a sense of walls and towns about us, with their lights and their characters after the silence of the wind-blown heath.

After reading the romances of Scott and Stevenson and Mrs. Radcliffe, our eyes seem stretched, their sight a little blurred, as if they had been gazing into the distance and it would be a relief to turn for contrast to a strongly marked human face, to characters of extravagant force and character in keeping with our romantic mood. Such figures are most easily to be found in Dickens, of course, and particularly in *Bleak House* where, as Dickens said, 'I have purposely dwelt upon the romantic side of familiar things'. They are found there with peculiar aptness—for if the characters satisfy us by their eccentricity and vigour, London and the landscape of the Dedlocks' place at Chesney Wold are in the mood of the moor, only more luridly lit up and more sharply dark and bright because in Dickens the character-making power is so prodigious that the very houses and streets and fields are strongly featured in sympathy with the people. The character-making power is so prodigious, indeed, that it has little need to make use of observation, and a great part of the delight of Dickens lies in the sense we have of wantoning with human beings twice or ten times their natural size of smallness who retain only enough human likeness to make us refer their feelings very broadly, not to our own, but to those of odd figures seen casually through the half-opened doors of public houses, lounging on quays, slinking mysteriously down little alleys which lie about Holborn and the Law Courts. We enter at once into the spirit of exaggeration.

Who, in the course of a long life, has met Mr. Chadband or Mr. Turveydrop or Miss Flite? Who has met anybody who, whatever the day of the occasion, can be trusted to say the same phrase, to repeat the same action? This perpetual repetition has, of course, an enormous power to drive these characters home, to stabilize them. Mr. Vholes, with his three dear girls at home and his father to support in the Vale of Taunton, Mrs. Jellyby and the natives of Borrioboola-Gha, Mr. Turveydrop and his deportment, all serve as stationary points in the flow and confusion of the narrative; they have a decorative effect as if they were gargoyles carved, motionless, at the corner of a composition. Wherever we may have wandered, we shall come back and find them there. They uphold the extraordinary intricacy of the plot in whose confusion we are often sunk up to our lips. For it is impossible to imagine that the Jellybys and the Turveydrops are ever affected by human emotions or that their habitual routine is disturbed by the astonishing events which blow through the pages of the book, from so many quarters at the same time. Thus they have a force, a sublimity, which the slighter and more idiosyncratic characters miss.

After all, is not life itself, with its coincidences and its convolutions, astonishingly queer? 'What connexion,' Dickens himself exclaims, 'can there have been between many people in the innumerable histories of this world, who, from opposite sides of great gulfs, have, nevertheless, been very

curiously brought together!' One after another his characters come into being, called into existence by an eye
which has only to glance into a room to take in every object,
human or inanimate, that is there; by an eye which sees
once and for all; which snatches at a woman's steel hair-
curlers, a pair of red-rimmed eyes, a white scar and makes
them somehow reveal the essence of a character; an eye
gluttonous, restless, insatiable, creating more than it can
use. Thus, the prevailing impression is one of movement, of
the endless ebb and flow of life round one or two stationary
points.

Often we cease to worry about the plot and wander off
down some strange avenue of suggestion stirred in this vast
and mobile world by a casual movement, a word, a glance.
'Still, very steadfastly and quietly walking towards it, a
peaceful figure, too, in the landscape, went Mademoiselle
Hortense, shoeless, through the wet grass.' She goes and
she leaves a strange wake of emotion behind her. Or, again,
a door is flung open in the misty purlieus of London; there
is Mr. Tulkinghorn's friend, who appears once and once
only—'a man of the same mould and a lawyer too, who
lived the same kind of life until he was seventy-five years
old, and then, suddenly conceiving (as it is supposed) an
impression that it was too monotonous, gave his gold watch
to his hairdresser one summer evening, and walked leisurely
home to the Temple, and hanged himself'.

This sense that the meaning goes on after the words are
spoken, that doors open and let us look through them, is full
of romance. But romance in Dickens is impressed on us
through characters, through extreme types of human beings,
not through castles or banners, not through the violence of
action, adventure, or nature. Human faces, scowling, grinning, malignant, benevolent, are projected at us from every
corner. Everything is unmitigated and extreme.

But at last, among all these characters who are so static
and so extreme, we come upon one—Inspector Bucket, the
detective—which is not, as the others are, of a piece, but
made up of contrasts and discrepancies. The romantic power

of the single-piece character is lost. For the character is no longer fixed and part of the design; it is in itself of interest. Its movements and changes compel us to watch it. We try to understand this many-sided man who has brushed his hair, which is thin, with a wet brush; who has his bombastic, official side, yet with it combines, as we see when the mine sprung, ability, conscience, even compassion—for all these qualities are displayed by turns in the astonishingly vivid account of the drive through the night and the storm, in pursuit of Esther's mother. If much more were added, so that Inspector Bucket drew more of our attention to him and diverted it from the story, we should begin with his new scale of values in our eyes to find the glaring opposites in use elsewhere too violent to be tolerable. But Dickens committed no such sin against his readers. He uses this clear-cut, many-faced figure to sharpen his final scenes and, then, letting Inspector Bucket of the detective force disappear, gathers the loose folds of the story into one prodigious armful and makes an end. But he has sharpened our curiosity and made us dissatisfied with the limitations and even with the exuberance of his genius. The scene becomes too elastic, too voluminous, too cloud-like in its contours. The very abundance of it tires us, as well as the impossibility of holding it all together. We are always straying down bypaths and into alleys where we lose our way and cannot remember where we were going.

Though the heart of Dickens burned with indignation for public wrongs, he lacked sensitiveness privately, so that his attempts at intimacy failed. His great figures are on too large a scale to fit nicely into each other. They do not interlock. They need company to show them off and action to bring out their humours. They are often out of touch with each other. In Tolstoy, in the scenes between Princess Marya and her father, the old Prince, the pressure of character upon character is never relaxed. The tension is perpetual, every nerve in the character is alive. It may be for this reason that Tolstoy is the greatest of novelists. In Dickens the characters are impressive in themselves but not in their personal relations. Often, indeed, when they talk to each other they are vapid in the extreme or sentimental beyond belief. One thinks of them as independent, existing forever, unchanged, like monoliths looking up into the sky. So it is that we begin to want something smaller, more intense, more intricate. Dickens has, himself, given us a taste of the pleasure we derive from looking curiously and intently into another character. He has made us instinctively reduce the size of the scene in proportion to the figure of a normal man, and now we seek this intensification, this reduction, carried out more perfectly and more completely, we shall find, in the novels of Jane Austen.

At once, when we open *Pride and Prejudice*, we are aware that the sentence has taken on a different character. Dickens, of course, at full stride is as free-paced and far-stretched as possible. But in comparison with this nervous style, how large-limbed and how loose. The sentence here runs like a knife, in and out, cutting a shape clear. It is done in a drawing-room. It is done by the use of dialogue. Half a dozen people come together after dinner and begin, as they so well might, to discuss letter-writing. Mr. Darcy writes slowly and 'studies too much for words of four syllables'. Mr. Bingley, on the other hand (for it is necessary that we should get to know them both and they can be quickest shown if they are opposed) 'leaves out half his words and blots the rest'. But such is only the first rough shaping that gives the outline of the face. We go on to define and distinguish. Bingley, says Darcy, is really boasting, when he calls himself a careless letter-writer because he thinks the defect interesting. It was a boast when he told Mrs. Bennet that if he left Nethfield he would be gone in five minutes. And this little passage of analysis on Darcy's part, besides proving his astuteness and his cool observant temper, rouses Bingley to show us a vivacious picture of Darcy at home. 'I don't know a more awful object than Darcy, on particular occasions, and in particular places; at his own house especially, and of a Sunday evening, when he has nothing to do.'

So, by means of perfectly natural question and answer,

everyone is defined and, as they talk, they become not only more clearly seen, but each stroke of the dialogue brings them together or moves them apart, so that the group is no longer casual but interlocked. The talk is not mere talk; it has an emotional intensity which gives it more than brilliance. Light, landscape—everything that lies outside the drawing-room is arranged to illumine it. Distances are made exact; arrangements accurate. It is one mile from Meryton; it is Sunday and not Monday. We want all suspicions and questions laid at rest. It is necessary that the characters should lie before us in as clear and quiet a light as possible since every flicker and tremor is to be observed. Nothing happens, as things so often happen in Dickens, for its own oddity or curiosity but with relation to something else. No avenues of suggestion are opened up, no doors are suddenly flung wide; the ropes which tighten the structure, since they are all rooted in the heart, are so held firmly and tightly. For, in order to develop personal relations to the utmost, it is important to keep out of the range of the abstract, the impersonal; and to suggest that there is anything that lies outside men and women would be to cast the shadow of doubt upon the comedy of their relationships and its sufficiency. So with edged phrases where often one word, set against the current of the phrase, serves to fledge it (thus: 'and whenever any of the cottagers were disposed to be quarrelsome, discontented, or *too poor*') we go down to the depths, for deep they are, for all their clarity.

But personal relations have limits, as Jane Austen seems to realize by stressing their comedy. Everything, she seems to say, has, if we could discover it, a reasonable summing up; and it is extremely amusing and interesting to see the efforts of people to upset the reasonable order, defeated as they invariably are. But if, complaining of the lack of poetry or the lack of tragedy, we are about to frame the familiar statement that this is a world which is too small to satisfy us, a prosaic world, a world of inches and blades of grass, we are brought to a pause by another impression which requires a moment further of analysis. Among all the elements which play upon us in reading fiction there has always been, though in different degrees, some voice, accent, or temperament clearly heard, though behind the scenes of the book. 'Trollope, the novelist, a big, blustering, spectacled, loud-voiced, hunting man'; Scott, the ruined, country gentleman, whose very pigs trotted after him, so gracious was the sound of his voice—both come to us with the gesture of hosts, welcoming us, and we fall under the spell of their charm or the interest of their characters.

We cannot say this of Jane Austen, and her absence has the effect of making us detached from her work and of giving it, for all its sparkle and animation, a certain aloofness and completeness. Her genius compelled her to absent herself. So truthful, so clear, so sane a vision would not tolerate distraction, even if it came from her own claims, nor allow the actual experience of a transitory woman to colour what should be unstained by personality. For this reason, then, though we may be less swayed by her, we are less dissatisfied. It may be the very idiosyncrasy of a writer that tires us of him. Jane Austen, who has so little that is peculiar, does not tire us, nor does she breed in us a desire for those writers whose method and style differ altogether from hers. Thus, instead of being urged as the last page is finished to start in search of something that contrasts and completes, we pause when we have read *Pride and Prejudice*.

The pause is the result of a satisfaction which turns our minds back upon what we have just read, rather than forward to something fresh. Satisfaction is, by its nature, removed from analysis, for the quality which satisfies us is the sum of many different parts, so that if we begin praising *Pride and Prejudice* for the qualities that compose it—its wit, its truth, its profound comic power—we shall still not praise it for the quality which is the sum of all these. At this point, then, the mind, brought to bay, escapes the dilemma and has recourse to images. We compare *Pride and Prejudice* to something else because, since satisfaction can be defined no further, all the mind can do is to make a likeness of the thing, and, by giving it another shape, cherish the illusion that it is explaining it, whereas it is, in fact, only looking at it afresh. To say that *Pride and Prejudice* is like a shell, a gem, a crystal, whatever image we may choose, is to see the same thing under a different guise. Yet, perhaps, if we compare *Pride and Prejudice* to something concrete, it is because we are trying to express the sense we have in other novels imperfectly, here with distinctness, of a quality which is not in the story but above it, not in the things themselves but in their arrangement.

Pride and Prejudice, one says, has form; *Bleak House* has not. The eye (so active always in fiction) gives its own interpretation of impressions that the mind has been receiving in different terms. The mind has been conscious in *Pride and Prejudice* that things are said, for all their naturalness, with a purpose; one emotion has been contrasted with another; one scene has been short, the next long; so that all the time, instead of reading at random, without control, snatching at this and that, stressing one thing or another, as the mood takes us, we have been aware of check and stimulus, of spectral architecture built up behind the animation and variety of the scene. It is a quality so precise it is not to be found either in what is said or in what is done; that is, it escapes analysis. It is a quality, too, that is much at the mercy of fiction. Its control is invariably weak there, much weaker than in poetry or in drama because fiction runs so close to life the two are always coming into collison. That this architectural quality can be possessed by a novelist, Jane Austen proves. And she proves, too, that far from chilling the interest or withdrawing the attention from the characters, it seems on the contrary to focus it and add an extra pleasure to the book, a significance. It makes it seem that here is something good in itself, quite apart from our personal feelings.

Not to seek contrast but to start afresh—this is the impulse which urges us on after finishing *Pride and Prejudice*. We must make a fresh start altogether. Personal relations, we recall, have limits. In order to keep their edges sharp, the mysterious, the unknown, the accidental, the strange subside;

their intervention would be confusing and distressing. The writer adopts an ironic attitude to her creatures, because she has denied them so many adventures and experiences. A suitable marriage is, after all, the upshot of all this coming together and drawing apart. A world which so often ends in a suitable marriage is not a world to wring one's hands over. On the contrary, it is a world about which we can be sarcastic; into which we can peer endlessly, as we fit the jagged pieces one into another. Thus, it is possible to ask not that her world shall be improved or altered (that our satisfaction forbids) but that another shall be struck off, whose constitution shall be different and shall allow of the other relations. People's relations shall be with God or nature. They shall think. They shall sit, like Dorothea Casaubon in *Middlemarch*, drawing plans for other people's houses; they shall suffer like Gissing's characters in solitude; they shall be alone. *Pride and Prejudice*, because it has such integrity of its own, never for an instant encroaches on other provinces, and, thus, leaves them more clearly defined.

Nothing could be more complete than the difference between *Pride and Prejudice* and *Silas Marner*. Between us and the scene which was so near, so distinct, is now cast a shadow. Something intervenes. The character of Silas Marner is removed from us. It is held in relation to other men and his life compared with human life. This comparison is perpetually made and illustrated by somebody not implicit in the book but inside it, somebody who at once reveals herself as 'I', so that there can be no doubt from the first that we are not going to get the relations of people together, but the spectacle of life so far as 'I' can show it to us. 'I' will do my best to illumine these particular examples of men and women with all the knowledge, all the reflections that 'I' can offer you.

'I', we at once perceive, has access to many more experiences and reflections than can have come the way of the rustics themselves. She discovers what a simple weaver's emotions on leaving his native village are, by comparing them with those of other people. 'People whose lives have been made various by learning, sometimes find it hard to keep a fast hold on their habitual views of life, on their faith in the Invisible. . . .' It is the observer speaking and we are at once in communication with a grave mind—a mind which it is part of our business to understand. This, of course, darkens and thickens the atmosphere, for we see through so many temperaments; so many side-lights from knowledge, from reflection, play upon what we see; often, even as we are watching the weaver, our minds circle round him and we observe him with an amusement, compassion, or interest which it is impossible that he should feel himself.

Raveloe is not simply a town like Meryton now in existence with certain shops and assembly room; it has a past and therefore the present becomes fleeting, and we enjoy, among other things, the feeling that this is a world in process of change and decay, whose charm is due partly to the fact that it is past. Perhaps we compare it in our own minds with the England of to-day and the Napoleonic wars with those of our own time. All this, if it serves to enlarge the horizon, also makes the village and the people in it who are placed against so wide a view smaller and their impact on each other less sharp. The novelist who believes that personal relations are enough, intensifies them and sharpens them and devotes his power to their investigation. But if the end of life is not to meet, to part, to love, to laugh, if we are at the mercy of other forces, some of them unknown, all of them beyond our power, the urgency of these meetings and partings is blurred and lessened. The edges of the coming together are blunted and the comedy tends to widen itself into a larger sphere and so to modulate into something melancholy, tolerant, and perhaps resigned. George Eliot has removed herself too far from her characters to dissect them keenly or finely, but she has gained the use of her own mind upon these same characters. Jane Austen went in and out of her people's minds like the blood in their veins.

George Eliot has kept the engine of her clumsy and powerful mind at her own disposal. She can use it, when she has created enough matter to use it upon, freely. She can stop at any moment to reason out the motives of the mind that has created it. When Silas Marner discovers that his gold has been stolen, he has recourse to 'that sort of refuge which always comes with the prostration of thought under an overpowering passion; it was that expectation of impossibilities, that belief in contradictory images, which is still distinct from madness, because it is capable of being dissipated by the external fact'. Such analysis is unthinkable in Dickens or in Jane Austen. But it adds something to the character which the character lacked before. It makes us feel not only that the working of the mind is interesting but that we shall get a much truer and subtler understanding of what is actually said and done if we so observe it. We shall perceive that often an action has only a slight relation to a feeling and, thus, that the truth-tellers, who are content to record accurately what is said and done are often ludicrously deceived and out in their estimate. In other directions there are changes. The use of dialogue is limited; for people can say very little directly. Much more can be said for them or about them by the writer himself. Then, the writer's mind, his knowledge, his skill, not merely the colour of his temperament, become means for bringing out the disposition of the character and also for relating it to other times and places. There is thus revealed underneath a state of mind which often runs counter to the action and the speech.

It is in this direction that George Eliot turns her characters and her scenes. Shadows checker them. All sorts of influences of history, or time, or reflection play upon them. If we consult our own difficult and mixed emotions as we read, it becomes clear that we are fast moving out of the range of pure character-mongering, of comedy, into a far more dubious region.

The Psychologists

Indeed, we have a strange sense of having left every world when we take up *What Maisie Knew*; of being without some support which, even if it impeded us in Dickens and George Eliot, upheld us and controlled us. The visual sense which has hitherto been so active, perpetually sketching fields and farmhouses and faces, seems now to fail or to use its powers to illumine the mind within rather than the world without. Henry James has to find an equivalent for the processes of the mind, to make concrete a mental state. He says, she was 'a ready vessel for bitterness, a deep little porcelain cup in which biting acids could be mixed'. He is forever using this intellectual imagery. The usual supports, the props and struts of the conventions, expressed or observed by the writer, are removed. Everything seems aloof from interference, thrown open to discussion and light, though resting on no visible support. For the minds of which this world is composed seem oddly freed from the pressure of the old encumbrances and raised above the stress of circumstances.

Crises cannot be precipitated by any of the old devices which Dickens and George Eliot used. Murders, rapes, seductions, sudden deaths have no power over this high, aloof world. Here the people are the sport only of delicate influences: of thoughts that people think, but hardly state, about each other; of judgments which people whose time is unoccupied have leisure to devise and apply. In consequence, these characters seem held in a vacuum at a great move from the substantial, lumbering worlds of Dickens and George Eliot or from the precise crisscross of convention which metes out the world of Jane Austen. They live in a cocoon, spun from the finest shades of meaning, which a society, completely unoccupied by the business of getting its living, has time to spin round and about itself. Hence, we are at once conscious of using faculties hitherto dormant, ingenuity and skill, a mental nimbleness and dexterity such as serve to solve a puzzle ingeniously; our pleasure becomes split up, refined, its substance infinitely divided instead of being served to us in one lump.

Maisie, the little girl who is the bone of contention between two parents, each of them claiming her for six months, each of them finally marrying a second husband or wife, lies sunk beneath the depths of suggestion, hint, and conjecture, so that she can only affect us very indirectly, each feeling of hers being deflected and reaching us after glancing off the mind of some other person. Therefore she rouses in us no simple and direct emotion. We always have time to watch it coming and to calculate its pathway, now to the right, now to the left. Cool, amused, intrigued, at every second trying to refine our senses still further and to marshal all that we have of sophisticated intelligence into one section of our-selves, we hang suspended over this aloof little world and watch with intellectual curiosity for the event.

In spite of the fact that our pleasure is less direct, less the result of feeling strongly in sympathy with some pleasure or sorrow, it has a fineness, a sweetness, which the more direct writers fail to give us. This comes in part from the fact that a thousand emotional veins and streaks are perceptible in this twilight or dawn which are lost in the full light of midday.

Besides this fineness and sweetness we get another pleasure which comes when the mind is freed from the perpetual demand of the novelist that we shall feel with his characters. By cutting off the responses which are called out in actual life, the novelist frees us to take delight, as we do when ill or travelling, in things in themselves. We can see the strange-ness of them only when habit has ceased to immerse us in them, and we stand outside watching what has no power over us one way or the other. Then we see the mind at work; we are amused by its power to make patterns; by its power to bring out relations in things and disparities which are covered over when we are acting by habit or driven on by the ordinary impulses. It is a pleasure somewhat akin, per-haps, to the pleasure of mathematics or the pleasure of music. Only, of course, since the novelist is using men and women as his subjects, he is perpetually exciting feelings which are opposed to the impersonality of numbers and sound; he seems, in fact, to ignore and to repress their natural feelings, to be coercing them into a plan which we call with vague resentment 'artificial' though it is probable that we are not so foolish as to resent artifice in art. Either through a feeling of timidity or prudery or through a lack of imaginative audacity, Henry James diminishes the interest and importance of his subject in order to bring about a symmetry which is dear to him. This his readers resent. We feel him there, as the suave showman, skilfully manipulating his characters; nipping, repressing; dexterously evading and ignoring, where a writer of greater depth or natural spirits would have taken the risk which his material imposes, let his sails blow full and so, perhaps, achieved symmetry and pattern, in themselves so delightful, all the same.

But it is the measure of Henry James's greatness that he has given us so definite a world, so distinct and peculiar a beauty that we cannot rest satisfied but want to experiment further with these extraordinary perceptions, to understand more and more, but to be free from the perpetual tutelage of the author's presence, his arrangements, his anxieties. To gratify this desire, naturally, we turn to the work of Proust, where we find at once an expansion of sympathy so great that it almost defeats its own object. If we are going to become conscious of everything, how shall we realize anything? Yet if Henry James's world, after the worlds of Dickens and George Eliot, seemed without material boundaries, if everything was pervious to thought and susceptible of twenty shades of meaning, here illumination and analysis are carried far beyond those bounds. For one thing, Henry James himself, the American, ill at ease for all his magnificent urbanity in a strange civilization, was an obstacle never perfectly assimilated even by the juices of his own art. Proust, the product of the civilization which he describes, is so porous, so pliable, so perfectly receptive that we realize him only as an envelope, thin but elastic, which stretches wider and wider and serves not to enforce a view but to enclose a world. His whole universe is steeped in the light of intelligence. The commonest object, such as the telephone, loses its simplicity, its solidity, and becomes a part of life and transparent. The commonest actions, such as going up in an elevator or eating cake, instead of being discharged automatically, rake up in their progress a whole series of thoughts, sensations, ideas, memories which were apparently sleeping on the walls of the mind.

What are we to do with it all? we cannot help asking, as these trophies are piled up round us. The mind cannot be content with holding sensation after sensation passively to itself; something must be done with them; their abundance must be shaped. Yet at first it would seem as if this vitalizing power has become so fertile that it cumbers the way and trips us up, even when we have need to go quickest, by putting some curious object enticingly in our way. We have to stop and look even against our will.

Thus, when his mother calls him to come to his grandmother's deathbed, the author says, '"I was not asleep," I answered as I awoke'. Then, even in this crisis, he pauses to explain carefully and subtly why at the moment of waking we so often think for a second that we have not been to sleep. The pause, which is all the more marked because the reflection is not made by 'I' himself but is supplied impersonally by the narrator and therefore, from a different angle, lays a great strain upon the mind, stretched by the urgency of the situation to focus itself upon the dying woman in the next room.

Much of the difficulty of reading Proust comes from this content obliquity. In Proust, the accumulation of objects which surround any central point is so vast and they are often so remote, so difficult of approach and of apprehension that this drawing-together process is gradual, tortuous, and the final relation difficult in the extreme. There is so much more to think about them than one had supposed. One's relations are not only with another person but with the weather, food, clothes, smells, with art and religion and science and history and a thousand other influences.

If one begins to analyse consciousness, it will be found that it is stirred by thousands of small, irrelevant ideas stuffed with odds and ends of knowledge. When, therefore, we come to say something so usual as 'I kissed her', we may well have to explain also how a girl jumped over a man in a deck-chair on the beach before we come tortuously and gradually to the difficult process of describing what a kiss means. In any crisis, such as the death of the grandmother or that moment when the Duchess learns as she steps into her carriage that her old friend Swann is fatally ill, the number of emotions that compose each of these scenes is immensely larger, and they are themselves much more incongruous and difficult of relation than any other scene laid before us by a novelist.

Moreover, if we ask for help in finding our way, it does not come through any of the usual channels. We are never told, as the English novelists so frequently tell us, that one way is right and the other wrong. Every way is thrown open without reserve and without prejudice. Everything that can be felt can be said. The mind of Proust lies open with the sympathy of a poet and the detachment of a scientist to everything that it has the power to feel. Direction or emphasis, to be told that that is right, to be nudged and bidden to attend to that, would fall like a shadow on this profound luminosity and cut off some section of it from our view. The common stuff of the book is made of this deep reservoir of perception. It is from these depths that his characters rise, like waves forming, then break and sink again into the moving sea of thought and comment and analysis which gave them birth.

In retrospect, thus, though as dominant as any characters in fiction, the characters of Proust seem made of a different substance. Thoughts, dreams, knowledge are part of them. They have grown to their full stature, and their actions have met with no rebuff. If we look for direction to help us put them in their places in the universe, we find it negatively in an absence of direction—perhaps sympathy is of more value than interference, understanding than judgment. As a consequence of the union of the thinker and the poet, often, on the heel of some fanatically precise observation, we come upon a flight of imagery—beautiful, coloured, visual, as if the mind, having carried its powers as far as possible in analysis, suddenly rose in the air and from a station high up

gave us a different view of the same object in terms of metaphor. This dual vision makes the great characters in Proust
and the whole world from which they spring more like a
globe, of which one side is always hidden, than a scene laid
flat before us, the whole of which we can take in at one
glance.

To make this more precise, it might be well to choose
another writer, of foreign birth also, who has the same power
of illuminating the consciousness from its roots to the surface.
Directly we step from the world of Proust to the world of
Dostoevsky, we are startled by differences which for a time
absorb all our attention. How positive the Russian is, in
comparison with the Frenchman. He strikes out a character
or a scene by the use of glaring oppositions which are left
unbridged. Extreme terms like 'love' and 'hate' are used
so lavishly that we must race our imaginations to cover the
ground between them. One feels that the mesh of civilization here is made of a coarse netting and the holes are wide
apart. Men and women have escaped, compared with the
imprisonment that they suffer in Paris. They are free to
throw themselves from side to side, to gesticulate, to hiss, to
rant, to fall into paroxysms of rage and excitement. They
are free, with the freedom that violent emotion gives, from
hesitation, from scruple, from analysis. At first we are
amazed by the emptiness and the crudity of this world compared with the other. But when we have arranged our
perspective a little, it is clear that we are still in the same
world—that it is the mind which entices us and the adventures of the mind that concern us. Other worlds, such as
Scott's or Defoe's, are incredible. Of this we are assured
when we begin to encounter those curious contradictions of
which Dostoevsky is so prolific. There is a simplicity in
violence which we find nowhere in Proust, but violence also
lays bare regions deep down in the mind where contradiction prevails. That contrast which marked Stavrogin's
appearance, so that he was at once 'a paragon of beauty,
yet at the same time there seemed something repellent
about him', is but the crude outer sign of the vice and

virtue we meet, at full tilt, in the same breast. The simplification is only on the surface; when the bold and ruthless
process, which seems to punch out characters, then to group
them together and then to set them all in violent motion, so
energetically, so impatiently, is complete, we are shown
how, beneath this crude surface, all is chaos and complication. We feel at first that we are in a savage society where
the emotions are much simpler and stronger and more
impressive than any we encounter in *A la Recherche du Temps
perdu*.

Since there are so few conventions, so few barriers
(Stavrogin, for instance, passes easily from the depths to
the heights of society) the complexity would appear to lie
deeper, and these strange contradictions and anomalies
which make a man at once divine and bestial would seem
to be deep in the heart and not superimposed. Hence, the
strange emotional effect of *The Possessed*. It appears to be
written by a fanatic ready to sacrifice skill and artifice in
order to reveal the soul's difficulties and confusions. The
novels of Dostoevsky are pervaded with mysticism; he
speaks not as a writer but as a sage, sitting by the roadside
in a blanket, with infinite knowledge and infinite patience.

> 'Yes,' she answered, 'the mother of God is the great
> mother—the damp earth, and therein lies great joy for
> men. And every earthly woe and every earthly fear is a
> joy for us; and when you water the earth with your tears
> a foot deep, you will rejoice at everything at once, and
> your sorrow will be no more, such is the prophecy.' That
> word sank into my heart at the time. Since then when I
> bow down to the ground at my prayers, I've taken to
> kissing the earth.   I kiss it and weep.

Such is a characteristic passage. But in a novel the voice of
the teacher, however exalted, is not enough. We have too
many interests to consider, too many problems to face. Consider a scene like that extraordinary party to which Varvara
Petrovna has brought Marya, the lame idiot, whom Stavrogin has married 'from a passion for martyrdom, from a
craving for remorse, through moral sensuality'. We cannot

read to the end without feeling as if a thumb were pressing on a button in us, when we have no emotion left to answer the call. It is a day of surprises, a day of startling revelations, a day of strange coincidences. For several of the people there (and they come flocking to the room from all quarters) the scene has the greater emotional importance. Everything is done to suggest the intensity of their emotions. They turn pale; they shake with terror; they go into hysterics. They are thus brought before us in flashes of extreme brilliance—the mad woman with the paper rose in her hat; the young man whose words patter out 'like smooth big grains. . . . One somehow began to imaging that he must have a tongue of special shape, somehow exceptionally long and thin, and extremely red, with a very sharp everlastingly active little tip.'

Yet though they stamp and scream, we hear the sound as if it went on next door. Perhaps the truth is that hate, surprise, anger, horror, are all too strong to be felt continuously. This emptiness and noise lead us to wonder whether the novel of psychology, which projects its drama in the mind, should not, as the truth-tellers showed us, vary and diversify its emotions, lest we shall become numb with exhaustion. To brush aside civilization and plunge into the depths of the soul is not really to enrich. We have, if we turn to Proust, more emotion in a scene which is not supposed to be remarkable, like that in the restaurant in the fog. There we live along a thread of observation which is always going in and out of this mind and that mind; which gathers information from different social levels, which makes us now feel with a prince, now with a restaurant keeper, and brings us into touch with different physical experiences such as light after darkness, safety after danger, so that the imagination is being stimulated on all sides to close slowly, gradually, without being goaded by screams or violence, completely round the object. Proust is determined to bring before the reader every piece of evidence upon which any state of mind is founded; so convinced is Dostoevsky of some point of truth that he sees before him, he will skip and leap to his conclusion with a spontaneity that is in itself stimulating.

By this distortion the psychologist reveals himself. The intellect, which analyses and discriminates, is always and almost at once overpowered by the rush to feeling; whether it is sympathy or anger. Hence, there is something illogical and contradictory often in the characters, perhaps because they are exposed to so much more than the usual current of emotional force. Why does he act like this? we ask again and again, and answer rather doubtfully, that so perhaps madmen act. In Proust, on the other hand, the approach is equally indirect, but it is through what people think and what is thought about them, through the knowledge and thoughts of the author himself, that we come to understand them very slowly and laboriously, but with the whole of our minds.

The books, however, with all these dissimilarities, are alike in this; both are permeated with unhappiness. And this would seem to be inevitable when the mind is not given a direct grasp of whatever it may be. Dickens is in many ways like Dostoevsky; he is prodigiously fertile and he has immense powers of caricature. But Micawber, David Copperfield, and Mrs. Gamp are placed directly before us, as if the author saw them from the same angle, and had nothing to do, and no conclusion to draw, except direct amusement or interest. The mind of the author is nothing but a glass between us, or, at most, serves to put a frame round them. All the author's emotional power has gone into them. The surplus of thought and feeling which remained after the characters had been created in George Eliot, to cloud and darken her page, has been used up in the characters of Dickens. Nothing of importance remains over.

But in Proust and Dostoevsky, in Henry James, too, and in all those who set themselves to follow feelings and thoughts, there is always an overflow of emotion from the author as if characters of such subtlety and complexity could be created only when the rest of the book is a deep reservoir of thought and emotion. Thus, though the author himself is not present, characters like Stephen Trofimovitch and Charlus can exist only in a world made of the same stuff as they are, though left unformulated. The effect of this brooding and analysing mind is always to produce an atmosphere of doubt, of questioning, of pain, perhaps of despair. At least, such would seem to be the result of reading *A la Recherche du Temps perdu* and *The Possessed*.

The Satirists and Fantastics

The confused feelings which the psychologists have roused in us, the extraordinary intricacy which they have revealed to us, the network of fine and scarcely intelligible yet profoundly interesting emotions in which they have involved us, set up a craving for relief, at first so primitive that it is almost a physical sensation. The mind feels like a sponge saturated full with sympathy and understanding; it needs to dry itself, to contract upon something hard. Satire and the sense that the satirist gives us that he has the world well within his grasp, so that it is at the mercy of his pen, precisely fulfil our needs.

A further instinct will lead us to pass over such famous satirists as Voltaire and Anatole France in favour of someone writing in our own tongue, writing English. For without any disrespect to the translator we have grown intolerably weary in reading Dostoevsky, as if we were reading with the wrong spectacles or as if a mist had formed between us and the page. We come to feel that every idea is slipping about in a suit badly cut and many sizes too large for it. For a translation makes us understand more clearly than the lectures of any professor the difference between raw words and written words; the nature and importance of what we call style. Even an inferior writer, using his own tongue upon his own ideas, works a change at once which is agreeable and remarkable. Under his pen the sentence shrinks and wraps itself firmly round the meaning, if it be but a little one. The loose, the baggy, shrivels up. And while a writer of passable English will do this, a writer like Peacock does infinitely more.

When we open *Crotchet Castle* and read that first very long sentence which begins, 'In one of those beautiful valleys, through which the Thames (not yet polluted by the tide, the scouring of cities or even the minor defilement of the sandy streams of Surrey)', it would be difficult to describe the relief it gives us, except metaphorically. First there is the shape which recalls something visually delightful, like a flowing wave or the lash of a whip vigorously flung; then as phrase joins phrase and one parenthesis after another pours in its tributary, we have a sense of the whole swimming stream gliding beneath old walls with the shadows of ancient buildings and the glow of green lawns reflected in it. And what is even more delightful after the immensities and obscurities in which we have been living, we are in a world so manageable in scale that we can take its measure, tease it and ridicule it. It is like stepping out into the garden on a perfect September morning when every shadow is sharp and every colour bright after a night of storm and thunder. Nature has submitted to the direction of man. Man himself is dominated by his intelligence. Instead of being many-sided, complicated, elusive, people possess one idiosyncrasy apiece, which crystallizes them into sharp separate characters, colliding briskly when they meet. They seem ridiculously and grotesquely simplified out of all knowledge. Dr. Folliott, Mr. Firedamp, Mr. Skionar, Mr. Chainmail, and the rest seem after the tremendous thickness and bulk of the Guermantes and the Stavrogins nothing but agreeable caricatures which a clever old scholar has cut out of a sheet of black paper with a pair of scissors. But on looking closer we find that though it would be absurd to credit Peacock with any desire or perhaps capacity to explore the depths of the soul, his reticence is not empty but suggestive. The character of Dr. Folliott is drawn in three strokes of the pen. What lies between is left out. But each stroke indicates the mass behind it, so that the reader can make it out for himself; while it has, because of this apparent simplicity, all the sharpness of a caricature. The world so happily constituted that there is always trout for breakfast, wine in the cellar, and some amusing contretemps, such as the cook setting herself alight and being put out by the footman, to make us laugh—a world where there is nothing more pressing to do than to 'glide over the face of the waters, discussing everything and settling nothing', is not the world of pure fantasy; it is close enough to be a parody of our world and to make our own follies and the solemnities of our institutions look a little silly.

The satirist does not, like the psychologist, labour under the oppression of omniscience. He has leisure to play with his mind freely, ironically. His sympathies are not deeply engaged. His sense of humour is not submerged.

But the prime distinction lies in the changed attitude towards reality. In the psychologists the huge burden of facts is based upon a firm foundation of dinner, luncheon, bed and breakfast. It is with surprise, yet with relief and a start of pleasure, that we accept Peacock's version of the world, which ignores so much, simplifies so much, gives the old globe a spin and shows another face of it on the other side. It is unnecessary to be quite so painstaking, it seems. And, after all, is not this quite as real, as true as the other? And perhaps all this pother about 'reality' is overdone. The great gain is perhaps that our relation with things is more distant. We reap the benefit of a more poetic point of view. A line like the charming 'At Godstow, they gathered hazel on the grave of Rosamond' could be written only by a writer who was at a certain distance from his people, so that there need be no explanations. For certainly with Trollope's people explanations would have been necessary; we should have wanted to know what they had been doing, gathering hazel, and where they had gone for dinner afterwards and how the carriage had met them. 'They', however, being Chainmail, Skionar, and the rest, are at liberty to gather hazel on the grave of Rosamond if they like; as they are free to sing a song if it so pleases them or to debate the march of mind.

The romantic took the same liberty but for another purpose. In the satirist we get not a sense of wildness and the soul's adventures, but that the mind is free and therefore sees through and dispenses with much that is taken seriously by writers of another calibre.

There are, of course, limitations, reminders, even in the midst of our pleasure, of boundaries that we must not pass. We cannot imagine in the first place that the writer of such exquisite sentences can cover many reams of paper; they cost too much to make. Then again a writer who gives us so keen a sense of his own personality by the shape of his phrase is limited. We are always being brought into touch, not with Peacock himself, as with Trollope himself (for there is no giving away of his own secrets; he does not conjure up the very shape of himself and the sound of his laughter as Trollope does), but all the time our thought is taking the colour of his thought, we are insensibly thinking in his measure. If we write, we try to write in his manner, and this brings us into far greater intimacy with him than with writers like Trollope again or Scott, who wrap their thought up quite adequately in a duffle gray blanket which wears well and suits everything. This may in the end, of course, lead to some restriction. Style may carry with it, especially in prose, so much personality that it keeps us within the range of that personality. Peacock pervades his book.

In order that we may consider this more fully let us turn from Peacock to Sterne, a much greater writer, yet sufficiently in the family of Peacock to let us carry on the same train of thought uninterruptedly.

At once we are aware that we are in the presence of a much subtler mind, a mind of far greater reach and intensity. Peacock's sentences, firmly shaped and beautifully polished as they are, cannot stretch as these can. Here our sense of elasticity is increased so much that we scarcely know where we are. We lose our sense of direction. We go backwards instead of forwards. A simple statement starts a digression; we circle; we soar; we turn round; and at last back we come again to Uncle Toby who has been sitting meanwhile in his black plush breeches with his pipe in his hand. Proust, it may be said, was as tortuous, but his indirectness was due to his immense powers of analysis and to the fact that directly he had made a simple statement he perceived and must make us perceive all that it implied. Sterne is not an analyst of other people's sensations. Those remain simple, eccentric, erratic. It is his own mind that fascinates him, its oddities and its whims, its fancies and its sensibilities; and it is his own mind that colours the book and gives it walls and shape. Yet it is obvious that his claim is just when he says that however widely he may digress, to my Aunt Dinah and the coachman and then 'some millions of miles into the very heart of the planetary system', when he is by way of telling about Uncle Toby's character, still 'the drawing of my Uncle Toby's character went on gently all the time—not the great contours of it—that was impossible—but some familiar strokes and faint designations of it . . . so that you are much better acquainted with my Uncle Toby now than you were before'. It is true, for we are always alighting as we skim and circle to deposit some little grain of observation upon the figure of Uncle Toby sitting there with his pipe in his hand. There is thus built up intermittently, irregularly, an extraordinary portrait of a character—a character shown most often in a passive state, sitting still, through the quick glancing eyes of an erratic observer, who never lets his character speak more than a few words or take more than a few steps in his proper person, but is forever circling round and playing with the lapels of his coat and peering up into his face and teasing him affectionately, whimsically, as if he were the attendant sprite in charge of some unconscious mortal. Two such opposites were made to see each other off and draw each other out. One relishes the simplicity, the modesty, of Uncle Toby all the more for comparing them with the witty, indecent, disagreeable, yet highly sympathetic, character of the author.

All through *Tristram Shandy* we are aware of this blend and contrast. Laurence Sterne is the most important character in the book. It is true that at the critical moment the author obliterates himself and gives his characters that little extra push which frees them from his tutelage so that they are something more than the whims and fancies of a brilliant brain. But since character is largely made up of surroundings and circumstances, these people whose surroundings are so queer, who are often silent themselves but always so whimsically talked about, are a race apart among the people of fiction. There is nothing like them elsewhere, for in no other book are the characters so closely dependent on the author. In no other book are the writer and reader so involved together. So, finally, we get a book in which all the usual conventions are consumed and yet no ruin or catastrophe comes to pass; the whole subsists complete by itself, like a house which is miraculously habitable without the help of walls, staircases, or partitions. We live in the humours, contortions, and oddities of the spirit, not in the slow unrolling of the long length of life. And the reflection comes, as we sun ourselves on one of these high pinnacles, can we not escape even further, so that we are not conscious of any author at all? Can we not find poetry in some novel or other? For Sterne by the beauty of his style has let us pass beyond the range of personality into a world which is not altogether the world of fiction. It is above.

The Poets

Certain phrases have brought about this change in us. They have raised us out of the atmosphere of fiction; they have made us pause to wonder.   For instance:

> I will not argue the matter; Time wastes too fast: every letter I trace tells me with what rapidity Life follows my pen; the days and hours of it more precious,—my dear Jenny—than the rubies about thy neck, are flying over our heads like light clouds of a windy day, never to return more; everything presses on,—whilst thou art twisting that lock;—see! it grows grey; and every time I kiss thy hand to bid adieu, and every absence which follows it, are preludes to that eternal separation which we are shortly to make.

Phrases like this bring, by the curious rhythm of their phrasing, by a touch on the visual sense, an alteration in the movement of the mind which makes it pause and widen its gaze and slightly change its attention. We are looking out at life in general.

But though Sterne with his extraordinary elasticity could use this effect, too, without incongruity, that is only possible because his genius is rich enough to let him sacrifice some of the qualities that are native to the character of the novel without our feeling it. It is obvious that there is no massing together of the experiences of many lives and many minds as in *War and Peace*; and, too, that there is something of the essayist, something of the soliloquist in the quips and quirks of this brilliant mind. He is sometimes sentimental, as if after so great a display of singularity he must assert his interest in the normal lives and affections of his people. Tears are necessary; tears are pumped up. Be that as it may, exquisite and individual as his poetry is, there is another poetry which is more natural to the novel, because it uses the material which the novelist provides. It is the poetry of situation rather than of language, the poetry which we perceive when Catherine in *Wuthering Heights* pulls the feathers from the pillow; when Natasha in *War and Peace* looks out of the window at the stars. And it is significant that we recall this poetry, not as we recall it in verse, by the words, but by the scene. The prose remains casual and quiet enough so that to quote it is to do little or nothing to explain its effect. Often we have to go far back and read a chapter or more before we can come by the impression of beauty or intensity that possessed us.

Yet it is not to be denied that two of the novelists who are most frequently poetical—Meredith and Hardy—are as novelists imperfect. Both *The Ordeal of Richard Feverel* and *Far from the Madding Crowd* are books of great inequality. In both we feel a lack of control, an incoherence such as we never feel in *War and Peace* or in *A la Recherche du Temps perdu* or in *Pride and Prejudice*. Both Hardy and Meredith are too fully charged, it would seem, with a sense of poetry and have too limited or too imperfect a sympathy with human beings to express it adequately through that channel. Hence, as we so often find in Hardy, the impersonal element—Fate, the Gods, whatever name we choose to call it—dominates the people. They appear wooden, melodramatic, unreal. They cannot express the poetry with which the writer himself is charged through their own lips, for their psychology is inadequate, and thus the expression is left to the writer, who assumes a character apart from his people and cannot return to them with perfect ease when the time comes.

Again, in Meredith the writer's sense of the poetry of youth, of love, of nature is heard like a song to which the characters listen passively without moving a muscle; and then, when the song is done, on they move again with a jerk. This would seem to prove that a profound poetic sense is a dangerous gift for the novelist; for in Hardy and Meredith poetry seems to mean something impersonal, generalized, hostile to the idiosyncrasy of character, so that the two suffer if brought into touch. It may be that the perfect novelist expresses a different sort of poetry, or has the power of expressing it in a manner which is not harmful to the other qualities of the novel. If we recall the passages that have seemed to us, in retrospect at any rate, to be poetical in fiction we remember them as part of the novel. When Natasha in *War and Peace* looks out of the window at the stars, Tolstoy produces a feeling of deep and intense poetry without any disruption or that disquieting sense of song being sung to people who listen. He does this because his poetic sense finds expression in the poetry of the situation or because his characters express it in their own words, which are often of the simplest. We have been living in them and knowing them, so that, when Natasha leans on the window sill and thinks of her life to come, our feelings of the poetry of the moment do not lie in what she says so much as in our sense of her who is saying it.

Wuthering Heights again is steeped in poetry. But here there is a difference, for one can hardly say that the profound poetry of the scene where Catherine pulls the feathers from the pillow has anything to do with our knowledge of her or adds to our understanding or our feeling about her future. Rather it deepens and controls the wild, stormy atmosphere of the whole book. By a master stroke of vision, rarer in prose than in poetry, people and scenery and atmosphere are all in keeping. And, what is still rarer and more impressive, through that atmosphere we seem to catch sight of larger men and women, of other symbols and significances. Yet the characters of Heathcliff and Catherine are perfectly natural; they contain all the poetry that Emily Brontë herself feels without effort. We never feel that this is a poetic moment, apart from the rest, or that here Emily Brontë is speaking to us through her characters. Her emotion has not overflowed and risen up independently, in some comment or attitude of her own. She is using her characters to express her conception, so that her people are active agents in the book's life, adding to its impetus and not impeding it. The same thing happens, more explicitly but with less concentration, in *Moby Dick*. In both books we get a vision of presence outside the human beings, of a meaning that they stand for, without ceasing to be themselves. But it is notable that both Emily Brontë and Herman Melville ignore the greater part of those spoils of the modern spirit which Proust grasps so tenaciously and transforms so triumphantly. Both the earlier writers simplify their characters till only the great contour, the clefts and ridges of the face, are visible. Both seem to have been content with the novel as their form and with prose as their instrument provided that they could remove the scene far from towns, simplify the actors and allow nature at her wildest to take part in the scene. Thus we can say that there is poetry in novels both where the poetry is expressed not so much by the particular character in a particular situation, like Natasha in the window, but rather by the whole mood and temper of the book, like the mood and temper of *Wuthering Heights* or *Moby Dick* to which the characters of Catherine or Heathcliff or Captain Ahab give expression.

In *A la Recherche du Temps perdu*, however, there is as much poetry as in any of these books; but it is poetry of a different kind. The analysis of emotion is carried further by Proust than by any other novelist; and the poetry comes, not in the situation, which is too fretted and voluminous for such an effect, but in those frequent passages of elaborate metaphor, which spring out of the rock of thought like fountains of sweet water and serve as translations from one language into another. It is as though there were two faces to every situation; one full in the light so that it can be described as accurately and examined as minutely as possible; the other half in shadow so that it can be described only in a moment of faith and vision by the use of metaphor. The longer the novelist pores over his analysis, the more he becomes conscious of something that forever escapes. And it is this double vision that makes the work of Proust to us in our generation so spherical, so comprehensive. Thus, while Emily Brontë and Herman Melville turn the novel away from shore out to sea, Proust on the other hand rivets his eyes on men.

And here we may pause, not, certainly, that there are no more books to read or no more changes of mood to satisfy, but for a reason which springs from the youth and vigour of the art itself. We can imagine so many different sorts of novels, we are conscious of so many relations and suscepti- bilities the novelist had not expressed that we break off in the middle with Emily Brontë or with Tolstoy without any pretence that the phases of fiction are complete or that our desires as a reader have received full satisfaction. On the contrary, reading excites them; they well up and make us inarticulately aware of a dozen different novels that wait just below the horizon unwritten. Hence the futility at present of any theory of 'the future of fiction'. The next ten years will certainly upset it; the next century will blow it to the winds. We have only to remember the comparative youth of the novel, that it is, roughly speaking, about the age of English poetry in the time of Shakespeare, to realize the folly of any summary, or theory of the future of the art. Moreover, prose itself is still in its infancy, and capable, no doubt, of infinite change and development.

But our rapid journey from book to book has left us with some notes made by the way and these we may sort out, not so much to seek a conclusion as to express the brooding, the meditative mood which follows the activity of reading. So then, in the first place, even though the time at our disposal has been short, we have travelled, in reading these few books, a great distance emotionally. We have plodded soberly along the high road talking plain sense and meeting many interesting adventures; turning romantic, we have lived in castles and been hunted on moors and fought gallantly and died; then tired of this, we have come into touch with humanity again, at first romantically prodigiously, enjoying the society of giants and dwarfs, the huge and the deformed, and then again tiring of this extravagance, have reduced them, by means of Jane Austen's microscope, to perfectly proportioned and normal men and women and the chaotic world to English parsonage, shrubberies, and lawns.

But a shadow next falls upon that bright prospect, distorting the lovely harmony of its proportions. The shadow of our own minds has fallen upon it and gradually we have drawn within, and gone exploring with Henry James endless filaments of feeling and relationship in which men and women are enmeshed, and so we have been led on with Dostoevsky to descend miles and miles into the deep and yeasty surges of the soul.

At last Proust brings the light of an immensely civilized and saturated intelligence to bear upon this chaos and reveals the infinite range and complexity of human sensibility. But in following him we lose the sense of outline, and to recover it seek out the satirists and the fantastics, who stand aloof and hold the world at a distance and eliminate and reduce so that we have the satisfaction of seeing round things after being immersed in them. And the satirists and the fantastics, like Peacock and Sterne, because of their detachment, write often as poets write, for the sake of the beauty of the sentence and not for the sake of its use, and so stimulate us to wish for poetry in the novel. Poetry, it would seem, requires a different ordering of the scene; human beings are needed, but needed in their relation to love, or death, or nature rather than to each other. For this reason their psychology is simplified, as it is both in Meredith and Hardy, and instead of feeling the intricacy of life, we feel its passion, its tragedy. In *Wuthering Heights* and in *Moby Dick* this simplification, far from being empty, has greatness, and we feel that something beyond, which is not human yet does not destroy their humanity or the actions. So, briefly, we may sum up our impressions. Brief and fragmentary as they are, we have gained some sense of the vastness of fiction and the width of its range.

As we look back it seems that the novelist can do anything. There is room in a novel for story-telling, for comedy, for tragedy, for criticism and information and philosophy and poetry. Something of its appeal lies in the width of its scope and the satisfaction it offers to so many different moods, desires, and instincts on the part of the reader. But however the novelist may vary his scene and alter the relations of one thing to another—and as we look back we see the whole world in perpetual transformation—one element remains constant in all novels, and that is the human element; they are about people, they excite in us the feelings that people excite in us in real life. The novel is the only form of art which seeks to make us believe that it is giving a full and truthful record of the life of a real person. And in order to give that full record of life, not the climax and the crisis but the growth and development of feelings, which is the novelist's aim, he copies the order of the day, observes the sequence of ordinary things even if such fidelity entails chapters of description and hours of research. Thus we glide into the novel with far less effort and less break with our surroundings than into any other form of imaginative literature. We seem to be continuing to live, only in another house or country perhaps. Our most habitual and natural sympathies are roused with the first words; we feel them expand and contract, in liking or disliking, hope or fear on every page. We watch the character and behaviour of Becky Sharp or

Richard Feverel and instinctively come to an opinion about them as about real people, tacitly accepting this or that impression, judging each motive, and forming the opinion that they are charming but insincere, good or dull, secretive but interesting, as we make up our minds about the characters of the people we meet.

This engaging lack of artifice and the strength of the emotion that he is able to excite are great advantages to the novelist, but they are also great dangers. For it is inevitable that the reader who is invited to live in novels as in life should go on feeling as he feels in life. Novel and life are laid side by side. We want happiness for the character we like, punishment for those we dislike. We have secret sympathies for those who seem to resemble us. It is difficult to admit that the book may have merit if it outrages our sympathies, or describes a life which seems unreal to us. Again we are acutely aware of the novelist's character and speculate upon his life and adventures. These personal standards extend in every direction, for every sort of prejudice, every sort of vanity, can be snubbed or soothed by the novelist. Indeed the enormous growth of the psychological novel in our time has been prompted largely by the mistaken belief, which the reader has imposed upon the novelist, that truth is always good; even when it is the truth of the psycho-analyst and not the truth of imagination.

Such vanities and emotions on the part of the reader are perpetually forcing the novelist to gratify them. And the result, though it may give the novel a short life of extreme vigour, is, as we know even while we are enjoying the tears and laughs and excitement of that life, fatal to its endurance. For the accuracy of representation, the looseness and simplicity of its method, its denial of artifice and convention, its immense power to imitate the surface reality—all the qualities that make a novel the most popular form of literature—also make it, even as we read it, turn stale and perish on our hands. Already some of the 'great novels' of the past, like *Robert Elsmere* or *Uncle Tom's Cabin*, are perished except in patches because they were originally bolstered up with so much that had virtue and vividness only for those who lived at the moment that the books were written. Directly manners change, or the contemporary idiom alters, page after page, chapter after chapter, become obsolete and lifeless.

But the novelist is aware of this too and, while he uses the power of exciting human sympathy which belongs to him, he also attempts to control it. Indeed the first sign that we are reading a writer of merit is that we feel this control at work on us. The barrier between us and the book is raised higher. We do not slip so instinctively and so easily into a world that we know already. We feel that we are being compelled to accept an order and to arrange the elements of the novel—man, nature, God—in certain relations at the novelist's bidding. In looking back at the few novels that we have glanced at here we can see how astonishingly we lend ourselves to first one vision and then to another which is its opposite. We obliterate a whole universe at the command of Defoe; we see every blade of grass and snail shell at the command of Proust. From the first page we feel our minds trained upon a point which becomes more and more perceptible as the book proceeds and the writer brings his conception out of darkness. At last the whole is exposed to view. And then, when the book is finished, we seem to see (it is strange how visual the impression is) something girding it about like the firm road of Defoe's storytelling; or we see it shaped and symmetrical with dome and column complete, like *Pride and Prejudice* and *Emma*. A power which is not the power of accuracy or of humour or of pathos is also used by the great novelists to shape their work. As the pages are turned, something is built up which is not the story itself. And this power, if it accentuates and concentrates and gives the fluidity of the novel endurance and strength, so that no novel can survive even a few years without it, is also a danger. For the most characteristic qualities of the novel— that it registers the slow growth and development of feeling, that it follows many lives and traces their unions and fortunes over a long stretch of time—are the very qualities that are most incompatible with design and order. It is the gift of style, arrangement, construction, to put us at a distance from the special life and to obliterate its features; while it is the gift of the novel to bring us into close touch with life. The two powers fight if they are brought into combination. The most complete novelist must be the novelist who can balance the two powers so that the one enhances the other.

This would seem to prove that the novel is by its nature doomed to compromise, wedded to mediocrity. Its province, one may conclude, is to deal with the commoner but weaker emotions; to express the bulk and not the essence of life. But any such verdict must be based upon the supposition that 'the novel' has a certain character which is now fixed and cannot be altered, that 'life' has a certain limit which can be defined. And it is precisely this conclusion that the novels we have been reading tend to upset.

The process of discovery goes on perpetually. Always more of life is being reclaimed and recognized. Therefore, to fix the character of the novel, which is the youngest and most vigorous of the arts, at this moment would be like fixing the character of poetry in the eighteenth century and saying that because Gray's *Elegy* was 'poetry' *Don Juan* was impossible. An art practised by hosts of people, sheltering diverse minds, is also bound to be simmering, volatile, unstable. And for some reason not here to be examined, fiction is the most hospitable of hosts; fiction to-day draws to itself writers who would even yesterday have been poets, dramatists, pamphleteers, historians. Thus 'the novel', as we still call it with such parsimony of language, is clearly splitting apart into books which have nothing in common but this one inadequate title. Already the novelists are so far apart that they scarcely communicate, and to one novelist the work of another is quite genuinely unintelligible or quite genuinely negligible.

The most significant proof of this fertility, however, is provided by our sense of feeling something that has not yet been said; of some desire still unsatisfied. A very general, a very elementary, view of this desire would seem to show that it points in two directions. Life—it is a commonplace—is growing more complex. Our self-consciousness is becoming far more alert and better trained. We are aware of relations and subtleties which have not yet been explored. Of this school Proust is the pioneer, and undoubtedly there are still to be born writers who will carry the analysis of Henry James still further, who will reveal and relate finer threads of feeling, stranger and more obscure imaginations.

But also we desire synthesis. The novel, it is agreed, can follow life; it can amass details. But can it also select? Can it symbolize? Can it give us an epitome as well as an inventory? It was some such function as this that poetry discharged in the past. But, whether for the moment or for some longer time, poetry with her rhythms, her poetic diction, her strong flavour of tradition, is too far from us to-day to do for us what she did for our parents. Prose perhaps is the instrument best fitted to the complexity and difficulty of modern life. And prose—we have to repeat it—is still so youthful that we scarcely know what powers it may not hold concealed within it. Thus it is possible that the novel in time to come may differ as widely from the novel of Tolstoy and Jane Austen as the poetry of Browning and Byron differs from the poetry of Lydgate and Spenser. In time to come—but time to come lies far beyond our province.

PART II

THE ART OF BIOGRAPHY

The New Biography[1]

'THE aim of biography', said Sir Sydney Lee, who had perhaps read and written more lives than any man of his time, 'is the truthful transmission of personality', and no single sentence could more neatly split up into two parts the whole problem of biography as it presents itself to us to-day. On the one hand there is truth; on the other there is personality. And if we think of truth as something of granite-like solidity and of personality as something of rainbow-like intangibility and reflect that the aim of biography is to weld these two into one seamless whole, we shall admit that the problem is a stiff one and that we need not wonder if biographers have for the most part failed to solve it.

For the truth of which Sir Sidney speaks, the truth which biography demands, is truth in its hardest, most obdurate form; it is truth as truth is to be found in the British Museum; it is truth out of which all vapour of falsehood has been pressed by the weight of research. Only when truth had been thus established did Sir Sidney Lee use it in the building of his monument; and no one can be so foolish as to deny that the piles be raised of such hard facts, whether one is called Shakespeare or King Edward the Seventh, are worthy of all our respect. For there is a virtue in truth; it has an almost mystic power. Like radium, it seems able to give off forever and ever grains of energy, atoms of light. It stimulates the mind, which is endowed with a curious susceptibility in this direction as no fiction, however artful or highly coloured, can stimulate it. Truth being thus efficacious and supreme, we can only explain the fact that Sir Sidney's life of Shakespeare is dull, and that his life of Edward the Seventh is unreadable, by supposing that though both are stuffed with truth, he failed to choose those truths which transmit

[1] *New York Herald Tribune*, October 30, 1927.

149

personality. For in order that the light of personality may shine through, facts must be manipulated; some must be brightened; others shaded; yet, in the process, they must never lose their integrity. And it is obvious that it is easier to obey these precepts by considering that the true life of your subject shows itself in action which is evident rather than in that inner life of thought and emotion which meanders darkly and obscurely through the hidden channels of the soul. Hence, in the old days, the biographer chose the easier path. A life, even when it was lived by a divine, was a series of exploits. The biographer, whether he was Izaak Walton or Mrs. Hutchinson or that unknown writer who is often so surprisingly eloquent on tombstones and memorial tablets, told a tale of battle and victory. With their stately phrasing and their deliberate artistic purpose, such records transmit personality with a formal sincerity which is perfectly satis-factory of its kind. And so, perhaps, biography might have pursued its way, draping the robes decorously over the recumbent figures of the dead, had there not arisen toward the end of the eighteenth century one of those curious men of genius who seem able to break up the stiffness into which the company has fallen by speaking in his natural voice. So Boswell spoke. So we hear booming out from Boswell's page the voice of Samuel Johnson. 'No, sir; stark insensibility', we hear him say. Once we have heard those words we are aware that there is an incalculable presence among us which will go on ringing and reverberating in widening circles however times may change and ourselves. All the draperies and decencies of biography fall to the ground. We can no longer maintain that life consists in actions only or in works. It consists in personality. Something has been liberated beside which all else seems cold and colourless. We are freed from a servitude which is now seen to be intolerable. No longer need we pass solemnly and stiffly from camp to council chamber. We may sit, even with the great and good, over the table and talk.

Through the influence of Boswell, presumably, biography all through the nineteenth century concerned itself as much with the lives of the sedentary as with the lives of the active. It sought painstakingly and devotedly to express not only the outer life of work and activity but the inner life of emotion and thought. The uneventful lives of poets and painters were written out as lengthily as the lives of soldiers and statesmen. But the Victorian biography was a parti-coloured, hybrid, monstrous birth. For though truth of fact was observed as scrupulously as Boswell observed it, the personality which Boswell's genius set free was hampered and distorted. The convention which Boswell had destroyed settled again, only in a different form, upon biographers who lacked his art. Where the Mrs. Hutchinsons and the Izaak Waltons had wished to prove that their heroes were prodigies of courage and learning the Victorian biographer was dominated by the idea of goodness. Noble, upright, chaste, severe; it is thus that the Victorian worthies are presented to us. The figure is almost always above life size in top-hat and frock-coat, and the manner of presentation becomes increasingly clumsy and laborious. For lives which no longer express themselves in action take shape in innumerable words. The conscientious biographer may not tell a fine tale with a flourish, but must toil through endless labyrinths and embarrass himself with countless documents. In the end he produces an amorphous mass, a life of Tennyson, or of Gladstone, in which we go seeking disconsolately for voice or laughter, for curse or anger, for any trace that this fossil was once a living man. Often, indeed, we bring back some invaluable trophy, for Victorian biographies are laden with truth; but always we rummage among them with a sense of the prodigious waste, of the artistic wrongheadedness of such a method.

With the twentieth century, however, a change came over biography, as it came over fiction and poetry. The first and most visible sign of it was in the difference in size. In the first twenty years of the new century biographies must have lost half their weight. Mr. Strachey compressed four stout Victorians into one slim volume; M. Maurois boiled the usual two volumes of a Shelley life into one little book the size of a novel. But the diminution of size was only the outward token of an inward change. The point of view had completely altered. If we open one of the new school of biographies its bareness, its emptiness makes us at once aware that the author's relation to his subject is different. He is no longer the serious and sympathetic companion, toiling even slavishly in the footsteps of his hero. Whether friend or enemy, admiring or critical, he is an equal. In any case, he preserves his freedom and his right to independent judgment. Moreover, he does not think himself constrained to follow every step of the way. Raised upon a little eminence which his independence has made for him, he sees his subject spread about him. He chooses; he synthesizes; in short, he has ceased to be the chronicler; he has become an artist.

Few books illustrate the new attitude to biography better than *Some People*, by Harold Nicolson. In his biographies of Tennyson and of Byron Mr. Nicolson followed the path which had been already trodden by Mr. Strachey and others. Here he has taken a step on his own initiative. For here he has devised a method of writing about people and about himself as though they were at once real and imaginary. He has succeeded remarkably, if not entirely, in making the best of both worlds. *Some People* is not fiction because it has the substance, the reality of truth. It is not biography because it has the freedom, the artistry of fiction. And if we try to discover how he has won the liberty which enables him to present us with these extremely amusing pages we must in the first place credit him with having had the courage to rid himself of a mountain of illusion. An English diplomat is offered all the bribes which usually induce people to swallow humbug in large doses with composure. If Mr. Nicolson wrote about Lord Curzon it should have been solemnly. If he mentioned the Foreign Office it should have been respectfully. His tone toward the world of Bognors and Whitehall should have been friendly but devout. But thanks to a number of influences and people, among whom one might mention Max Beerbohm and Voltaire, the attitude of the bribed and docile official has been blown to atoms. Mr. Nicolson laughs. He laughs at Lord Curzon; he laughs at the Foreign Office; he laughs at himself. And since his laughter is the laughter of the intelligence it has the effect of making us take the people he laughs at seriously. The figure of Lord Curzon concealed behind the figure of a drunken valet is touched off with merriment and irreverence; yet of all the studies of Lord Curzon which have been written since his death none makes us think more kindly of that preposterous but, it appears, extremely human man.

So it would seem as if one of the great advantages of the new school to which Mr. Nicolson belongs is the lack of pose, humbug, solemnity. They approach their bigwigs fearlessly. They have no fixed scheme of the universe, no standard of courage or morality to which they insist that he shall conform. The man himself is the supreme object of their curiosity. Further, and it is this chiefly which has so reduced the bulk of biography, they maintain that the man himself, the pith and essence of his character, shows itself to the observant eye in the tone of a voice, the turn of a head, some little phrase or anecdote picked up in passing. Thus in two subtle phrases, in one passage of brilliant description, whole chapters of the Victorian volume are synthesized and summed up. *Some People* is full of examples of this new phase of the biographer's art. Mr. Nicolson wants to describe a governess and he tells us that she had a drop at the end of her nose and made him salute the quarterdeck. He wants to describe Lord Curzon, and he makes him lose his trousers and recite 'Tears, Idle Tears'. He does not cumber himself with a single fact about them. He waits till they have said or done something characteristic, and then he pounces on it with glee. But, though he waits with an intention of pouncing which might well make his victims uneasy if they guessed it, he lays suspicion by appearing himself in his own proper person in no flattering light. He has a scrubby dinner-jacket, he tells us; a pink bumptious face, curly hair, and a curly nose. He is as much the subject of his own irony and observation as they are. He lies in wait for his own absurdities as artfully as for theirs. Indeed, by the end of the book we realize that the figure which has been most completely and most subtly displayed is that of the author. Each of the supposed subjects holds up in his or her small bright diminishing mirror a different reflection of Harold Nicolson. And though the figure thus revealed is not noble or impressive or shown in a very heroic attitude, it is for these very reasons extremely like a real human being. It is thus, he would seem to say, in the mirrors of our friends, that we chiefly live.

To have contrived this effect is a triumph not of skill only, but of those positive qualities which we likely to treat as if they were negative—freedom from pose, from sentimentality, from illusion. And the victory is definite enough to leave us asking what territory it has won for the art of biography. Mr. Nicolson has proved that one can use many of the devices of fiction in dealing with real life. He has shown that a little fiction mixed with fact can be made to transmit personality very effectively. But some objections or qualifications suggest themselves. Undoubtedly the figures in *Some People* are all rather below life size. The irony with which they are treated, though it has its tenderness, stunts their growth. It dreads nothing more than that one of these little beings should grow up and becomes serious or perhaps tragic. And, again, they never occupy the stage for more than a few brief moments. They do not want to be looked at very closely. They have not a great deal to show us. Mr. Nicolson makes us feel, in short, that he is playing with very dangerous elements. An incautious movement and the book will be blown sky high. He is trying to mix the truth of real life and the truth of fiction. He can only do it by using no more than a pinch of either. For though both truths are genuine, they are antagonistic; let them meet and they destroy each other. Even here, where the imagination is not deeply engaged, when we find people whom we know to be real like Lord Oxford or Lady Colefax, mingling with Miss Plimsoll and Marstock, whose reality we doubt, the one casts suspicion upon the other. Let it be fact, one feels, or let it be fiction; the imagination will not serve under two masters simultaneously.

And here we again approach the difficulty which, for all

his ingenuity, the biographer still has to face. Truth of fact and truth of fiction are incompatible; yet he is now more than ever urged to combine them. For it would seem that the life which is increasingly real to us is the fictitious life; it dwells in the personality rather than in the act. Each of us is more Hamlet, Prince of Denmark, than he is John Smith of the Corn Exchange. Thus, the biographer's imagination is always being stimulated to use the novelist's art of arrangement, suggestion, dramatic effect to expound the private life. Yet if he carries the use of fiction too far, so that he disregards the truth, or can only introduce it with incongruity, he loses both worlds; he has neither the freedom of fiction nor the substance of fact. Boswell's astonishing power over us is based largely upon his obstinate veracity, so that we have implicit belief in what he tells us. When Johnson says 'No, sir; stark insensibility', the voice has a ring in it because we have been told, soberly and prosaically, a few pages earlier, that Johnson 'was entered a Commoner of Pembroke, on the 31st of October, 1728, being then in his nineteenth year'. We are in the world of brick and pavement; of birth, marriage, and death; of Acts of Parliament; of Pitt and Burke and Sir Joshua Reynolds. Whether this is a more real world than the world of Bohemia and Hamlet and Macbeth we doubt; but the mixture of the two is abhorrent.

Be that as it may we can assure ourselves by a very simple experiment that the days of Victorian biography are over. Consider one's own life; pass under review a few years that one has actually lived. Conceive how Lord Morley would have expounded them; how Sir Sidney Lee would have documented them; how strangely all that has been most real in them would have slipped through their fingers. Nor can we name the biographer whose art is subtle and bold enough to present that queer amalgamation of dream and reality, that perpetual marriage of granite and rainbow. His method still remains to be discovered. But Mr. Nicolson with his mixture of biography and autobiography, of fact and fiction, of Lord Curzon's trousers and Miss Plimsoll's nose, waves his hand airily in a possible direction.

A Talk about Memoirs[1]

JUDITH: I wonder—shall I give my bird a real beak or
an orange one? Whatever they may say, silks have been
ruined by the war. But what are you looking behind the
curtain for? *Ann:* There is no gentleman present? *Judith:*
None, unless you count the oil portrait of Uncle John. *Ann:*
Oh, then, we can talk about the Greeks! There is not a single
memoir in the whole of Greek literature. There! You can't
contradict me; and so we go on to wonder how the ladies of
the race spent the morning when it was wet and the hours
between tea and dinner when it was dark. *Judith:* The mornings never are wet in Athens. Then they don't drink tea.
They drink a red sweet stuff out of glasses, and eat lumps of
Turkish delight with it. *Ann:* Ah, that explains! A dry, hot
climate, no twilight, wine, and blue sky. In England the
atmosphere is naturally aqueous, and as if there weren't
enough outside, we drench ourselves with tea and coffee at
least four times a day. It's atmosphere that makes English
literature unlike any other—clouds, sunsets, fogs, exhala-
tions, miasmas. And I believe that the element of water is
supplied chiefly by the memoir writers. Look what great
swollen books they are! (She lifts five volumes in her hands,
one after another.) Dropsical. Still, there are times—I suppose it's the lack of wine in my blood—when the mere
thought of a classic is repulsive. *Judith:* I agree with you.
The classics—oh dear, what was I going to say?—something
very wise, I know. But I can't embroider a parrot and talk
about Milton in the same breath. *Ann:* Whereas you could
embroider a parrot and talk about Lady Georgiana Peel?
Judith: Precisely. Do tell me about Lady Georgiana Peel
and the rest. Those are the books I love. *Ann:* I do more than
love them; I reverence them as the parents and begetters of

[1] *New Statesman*, March 6, 1920.

our race. And if I knew Mr. Lytton Strachey, I'd tell him what I think of him for behaving disrespectfully of the great English art of biography. My dear Judith, I had a vision last night of a widow with a taper setting fire to a basketful of memoirs—half a million words—two volumes—stout— blue—with a crest—genealogical trees—family portraits— all complete. 'Art be damned!' I cried, and woke in a frenzy. *Judith:* Well, I fancy she heard you. But let's begin on Lady Georgiana Peel. *Ann:* Lady Georgiana Peel [1] was born in the year 1836, and was the daughter of Lord John Russell. The Russells are said to be descended from Thor, the God of Thunder; their more direct ancestor being one Henri de Rozel, who, in the eleventh century— *Judith:* We'll take their word for it. *Ann:* Very well. But don't forget it. The Russells are cold in temperament, contradictious by nature. Ahem! Lord and Lady John were resting under an oak tree in Richmond Park when Lord John remarked how pleasant it would be to live in that white house behind the palings for the rest of their lives. No sooner said than the owner falls ill and dies. The Queen, with that unfailing insight, etc., sends for Lord John, etc., and offers him the lodge for life, etc., etc., etc. I mean they lived happily ever after, though as time went by, a factory chimney somewhat spoilt the view. *Judith:* And Lady Georgiana? *Ann:* Well, there's not much about Lady Georgiana. She saw the Queen having her hair brushed, and she went to stay at Woburn. And what d'you think they did there? They threw mutton chops out of the window 'for whoever cared to pick them up'. And each guest had a piece of paper by his plate 'in which to wrap up an eatable for the people waiting outside'. *Judith:* Mutton chops! people waiting outside! *Ann:* Ah, now the charm begins to work. A snowy Christmas —imagine a fair-haired little girl at the window—early in the forties the scene is—frost on the ground—a mutton chop descending. Don't you see all the arms going up and the poor wretches trampling the flower-beds in their struggles? But,

[1] *Recollections of Lady Georgiana Peel.* Compiled by her daughter Ethel Peel.

'I think', she says, 'the custom died out.' And then she married, and her husband's riding was the pride of the county; and when he won a race he gave something to the village church. But I don't know that there's much more to be said. *Judith:* Please go on. The charm is working; I'm not asleep; I'm in the drawing-room at Woburn in the forties. *Ann:* Lady Georgiana being, as I told you, descended from the God of Thunder, is not one to take liberties with life. The scene is a little empty. There's Charles Dickens wearing a pink shirt front embroidered with white; the Russell mausoleum in the background; sailors with icicles hanging from their whiskers; the Grosvenor boys shooting snipe in Belgrave Square; Lord John handing the Queen down to dinner—and so forth. Let's consult Mr. Bridges.[1] He may help us to fill it in. 'Our mothers were modelled as closely as might be on the example of the Great Queen. . . . If they were not always either beautiful or wise they gained love and respect everywhere without being either. . . . But, whatever happens, women will still be women and men men.' Shall I go on skipping? *Judith:* I seem to gather that the wall-papers were dark and the sideboards substantial. *Ann:* Yes, but we've too much furniture already. Life is what we want. (She turns over the pages of several volumes without saying anything.) *Judith:* Oh, Ann; it's fearfully dull at Woburn in the forties. Moreover, my parrot is turning into a sacred fowl. I shall be presenting him to the village church next. Is no one coming to call? *Ann:* Wait a moment. I fancy I see Miss Dempster[2] approaching. *Judith:* Quick; let me look at her picture. A devout, confidential lady—Bedchamber woman to Queen Victoria, I should guess. I can fancy her murmuring: 'Poor, poor Princess'; or, 'Dearest Lady Charlotte has had a sad loss in the death of her favourite gillie', as she extracts from the Royal Head a sleek tortoiseshell pin and lays it reverently in the golden tray. By the way, can you imagine Queen Victoria's hair? I can't. *Ann:* Lady Georgiana says it was 'long and fair'. Be that as it may, Miss

[1] *Victorian Recollections*, by John A. Bridges.
[2] *The Manners of My Time*, by C. L. H. Dempster.

Dempster had nothing to do with her hair-pins—save that, I think it likely her daydreams took that direction. She was a penniless lass with a long pedigree; Scotch, of course, moving in the best society—'one of the Shropshire Corbets who (through the Leycesters) is a cousin of Dean Stanley'— that's her way of describing people; and for my part I find it very descriptive. But wait—here's a scene that promises well. Imagine the terrace of the Blythswoods' villa at Cannes. An eclipse of the moon is taking place; the Emperor Dom Pedro of Portugal has his eye fixed to the telescope; it is chilly, and a copper-coloured haze suffuses the sky. Meanwhile, Miss Dempster and the Prince of Hohenzollern walk up and down talking. What d'ye think they talk about? . . . 'we agreed that it had never occurred to us before that *somewhere* our Earth's shadow must be ever falling. . . . Speaking of the dark and shadowed days of human life I quoted Mrs. Browning's lines: "Think, the passing of a trail, To the nature most undone, Like the shadow on the dial, *Proves* the presence of the *sun.*"' You don't want to hear about the death of the Duke of Albany and his appearance in his coffin or the Emperor of Germany and his cancer? *Judith:* For Heaven's sake, no! *Ann:* Well, then, we must shut up Miss Dempster. But isn't it queer how Lady Georgiana and the rest have made us feel like naughty, dirty, mischievous children? I don't altogether enjoy the feeling, and yet there is something august in their unyielding authority. They have fronts of brass; not a doubt or a desire disturbs them outwardly; and so they proceed over a world which for us is alternately a desert or a flowering wilderness stuck about with burning bushes and mocking macaws, as if it were Piccadilly or the Cromwell Road at three o'clock in the afternoon. I detect passions and pieties and convictions all dumb and deep sunk which serve them for a kind of spiritual petrol. What, my dear Judith, have we got in its place? *Judith:* If, like me, you'd been sitting in the drawing-room at Woburn for the past fifty years, you would be feeling a little stiff. Did they never amuse themselves? Was death their only amusement, and rank their sole romance? *Ann:*

There were horses. I see your eyes turned with longing to Dorothea Conyers [1] and John Porter.[2] Now you can get up and come to the stables. Now, I assure you, things are going to hum a little. In both these books we get what I own was somewhat disguised in the others—a passion for life. I confess that I like John Porter's view of life better than Dorothea Conyers', though, from the lips of a novelist, there is charm in her reflection: 'Unfortunately, I shall never be a popular short-story writer: I do something just wrong'; one feels inclined to tell her to shorten her stirrups or have her fetlocks fired and see whether *that* wouldn't do the trick. But this cherry-cheeked elderly gentleman, this quintessence of all good coachmen and trusty servants, this lean old trainer with his shrewd little eyes, and the horseshoe tiepin and the look of integrity and service honestly performed, of devotion given and returned—I can't help feeling that he is the pick of the bunch. I like his assumption that the whole world exists for racing, or, as he is careful to put it, for 'the amelioration of the thoroughbred'. I like the warmth with which he praises his horses for holding their own on the course and begetting fine children at the stud. 'I thought the world of him,' he says of Isonomy, 'and his achievements as a sire strengthened my regard and admiration.' 'That the horse I almost worshipped was afflicted with wind infirmity', he says in another place, nearly killed him; and when Ormonde, for he it was, proved incurable and went to Australia, John Porter plucked a few hairs from tail and mane to keep, doubtless in some inner pocket, 'as a memento of a great and noble creature'. What character he detects in them, and how humanely he respects it! Madam Eglantyne must be humoured in her fancy to be delivered of her children under a tree in the park. Sir Joseph Hawley—not a race-horse, but the owner of race-horses—what a character— what a fine fellow he was!—'a really great man . . . a noble friend to me and my family . . . stern, straight and fearless';

[1] *Sporting Reminiscences*, by Dorothea Conyers.
[2] *John Porter of Kingsclere*. An anthology written in collaboration with Edward Monkhouse.

so John Porter writes of him, and when the Baronet for the last time left his cigar to waste on the mantelpiece, John Porter pocketed the ashes and has them now 'put carefully away' in memory of his master. Then I like to read how Ormonde was born at half-past six on a Sunday evening, as the stable boys were going to Church, with a mane three inches long, and how always at the critical moment Fred Archer made a little movement in the saddle and 'lengthening his stride, Ormonde shot ahead, to win in a canter'; and how he was not only a giant among giants, but, like all magnanimous heroes, had the disposition of a lamb, and would eat cakes and carnations out of a Queen's hand. How splendid we should think it if it were written in Greek! Indeed, how Greek it all is! *Judith:* Are you sure there is nothing about the village church? *Ann:* Well, yes. John Porter did in token of gratitude add 'some suitable embellishments to the village church'; but, then (as there are no gentlemen present) so did the Greeks, and we think no worse of them for doing so. *Judith:* Perhaps. Anyhow, John Porter is the pick of the bunch. He enjoyed life; that's what the Victorians—but, go on—tell me how Orme was poisoned.

Sir Walter Raleigh [1]

TO most of us, says Miss Hadow in her introduction to a book of selections from the prose of Sir Walter Raleigh, 'the Elizabethan Age stands for one of two things: it is the age of jewelled magnificence, of pomp and profusion and colour, of stately ceremonial and Court pageant, of poetry and drama; or it is the age of enterprise and exploration'. But though we have every reason for being grateful to Miss Hadow for her part in the production of this astonishing little book, we cannot go with her in this initial distinction. If Shakespeare, as literature is the only thing that survives in its completeness, may be held to represent the Elizabethan age, are not enterprise and exploration a part of Shakespeare? If there are some who read him without any thought save for the poetry, to most of us, we believe, the world of Shakespeare is the world of Hakluyt and of Raleigh; on that map Guiana and the River of the Plate are not very far distant or easily distinguishable from the Forest of Arden and Elsinore. The navigator and the explorer made their voyage by ship instead of by the mind, but over Hakluyt's pages broods the very same lustre of the imagination. Those vast rivers and fertile valleys, those forests of odorous trees and mines of gold and ruby, fill up the background of the plays as, in our fancy, the blue of the distant plains of America seems to lie behind the golden cross of St. Paul's and the bristling chimneys of Elizabethan London.

No man was a truer representative of this Elizabethan world than Sir Walter Raleigh. From the intrigues and splendours of the Court he sailed to an unknown land inhabited by savages; from discourse with Marlowe and Spenser he went to sea-battle with the Spaniard. Merely to

1 *Times Literary Supplement*, March 15, 1917.

read over the list of his pursuits gives one a sense of the space and opportunity of the Elizabethan age; courtier and admiral, soldier and explorer, member of Parliament and poet, musician and historian—he was all those things, and still kept such a curiosity alive in him that he must practise chemistry in his cabin when he had leisure at sea, or beg an old henhouse from the Governor of the Tower in which to pursue his search for 'the Great Elixir'. It is little wonder that Rumour should still be telling her stories about his cloak, his pipe with the silver bowl, his potatoes, his mahogany, his orange trees, after all these years; for though Rumour may lie, there is always good judgment in her falsehood.

When we come to read what remains of his writing—and in this little book the indispensable part of it is preserved— we get what Rumour cannot give us: the likeness of an extremely vigorous and individual mind, scarcely dominated by the 'vast and devouring space' of the centuries. It is well, perhaps, to begin by reading the last fight of the *Revenge*, the letters about Cadiz and Guiana, and that to his wife written in expectation of death, before reading the extracts from the *Historie of the World*, and to end with the preface to that work, as one leaves a church with the sound of the organ in one's ears. His adventures by sea and land, his quest of Eldorado and the great gold mine of his dreams, his sentence of death and long imprisonment—glimpses of that 'day of a tempestuous life' are to be found in these pages. They give us some idea of its storm and its sunshine. Naturally the style of them is very different from that of the preface. They are full of hurry and turmoil, or impetuosity and self-assertiveness. He is always eager to justify his own daring, and to proclaim the supremacy of the English among other peoples. Even 'our common English soldier, leavied in haste, from following the Cart, or sitting on the shop-stall', surpasses in valour the best of Roman soldiers. Of the landing in Fayal in the year 1597 he writes, 'For I thought it to belong unto the honor of our Prince & Nation, that a few Ilanders should not think any advantage great enough, against a fleet set forth by Q. Elizabeth'; although he had to admit that 'I had more regard of reputation, in that businesse, than of safetie'.

But if we had to justify our love of these old voyagers we should not lay stress upon the boastful and magnificent strain in them; we should point, rather, to the strain of poetry—the meditative mood fostered by long days at sea, sleep and dreams under strange stars, and lonely effort in the face of death. We would recall the words of Sir Humfrey Gilbert, when the storm broke upon his ship, 'sitting abaft with a book in his hand . . . and crying (so oft as we did approach within hearing) "We are as near to Heaven by sea as by land"'. And so Sir Walter Raleigh, whose character was subject to much criticism during his lifetime, who had been alternately exalted and debased by fortune, who had lived with the passion of a great lover, turns finally to thoughts of the littleness of all human things and to a magnanimous contemplation of the lot of mankind. His thoughts seem inspired by a knowledge of life both at its best and its worst; in the solitude of the Tower his memory is haunted by the sound of the sea. From the sea he takes his most frequent and splendid imagery. It comes naturally to him to speak of the 'Navigation of this life', of 'the Port of death, to which all winds drive us'. Our false friends, he says, 'forsake us in the first tempest of misfortune and steere away before the Sea and Winde.' So in old age we find that our joy and our woe have 'sayled out of sight'. Often he must have looked into the sky from the deck of his ship and thought how 'The Heavens are high, farr off, and unsearcheable'; and his experience as a ruler of uncivilized races must have made him consider what fame 'the boundless ambition in mortal men' is wont to leave behind it:

'They themselves would then rather have wished, to have stolen out of the world without noise, than to be put in minde, that they have purchased the report of their actions in the world, by rapine, oppression, and crueltie, by giving in spoile the innocent and labouring soul to the idle and insolent, and by having emptied the cities of the world of their ancient Inhabitants, and filled them againe with so many and so variable sorts of sorrowes.'

But although the sounds of life and the waves of the sea are constantly in his ears, so that at any moment he is ready to throw away his pen and take command of an expedition, he seems in his deepest moods to reject the show and splendour of the world, to see the vanity of gold mines and of all expeditions save those of the soul.

'For the rest, as all fables were commonly grounded upon some true stories of other things done; so might these tales of the Griffins receive this moral. That if those men which fight against so many dangerous passages for gold, or other riches of this world, had their perfect senses . . . they would content themselves with a quiet and moderate estate.'

The thought of the passing of time and the uncertainty of human lot was a favourite one with the Elizabethans, whose lives were more at the mercy of fortune than ours are. In Raleigh's prose the same theme is constantly treated, but with an absence of the characteristic Elizabethan conceits, which brings it nearer to the taste of our own time; a divine unconsciousness seems to pervade it. Take this passage upon the passing of youth:

'So as who-so-ever hee bee, to whome Fortune hath beene a servant, and the Time a friend: let him but take the accompt of his memory (for wee have no other keeper of our pleasures past) and truelie examine what it hath reserved, either of beauty and youth, or foregone delights; what it hath saved, that it might last, of his dearest affections, or of whatever else the amorous Springtime gave his thoughts of contentment, then unvaluable; and hee shall finde that all the art which his elder yeares have, can draw no other vapour out of these dissolutions, than heavie, secret, and sad sighs. . . . Onely those few blacke Swans I must except; who having had the grace to value worldly vanities at no more than their owne price; doe, by retayning the comfortable memorie of a well acted life, behold death without dread, and the grave without feare; and embrace both, as necessary guides to endlesse glorie.'

This is no sudden effort of eloquence; it is prefaced and continued by words of almost equal beauty. In its melody and strength, its natural symmetry of form, it is a perfect speech, fit for letters of gold and the echoes of cathedral aisles, or for the tenderness of noble human intercourse. It reaches us almost with the very accent of Raleigh's voice. There is a magnificence with which such a being relinquishes his hopes in life and dismisses the cares of 'this ridiculous world' which is the counterpart of his great zest in living. We hear it in the deeply burdened sigh with which he takes his farewell of his wife. 'For the rest, when you have travailled and wearied all your thoughts, over all sorts of worldly cogitations, you shall but sitt downe by sorrowe in the end.' But it is most evident in his thought upon death. The thought of death tolls all through Elizabethan literature lugubriously enough in our ears, for whom, perhaps, existence has been made less palpable by dint of much thinking and death more of a shade than a substance. But to the Elizabethans a great part of the proper conduct of life consisted in meeting the idea of death, which to them was not an idea but a person, with fortitude. And to Raleigh in particular, death was a very definite enemy—death, 'which doth pursue us and hold us in chace from our infancy'. A true man, he says, despises death. And yet even as he says this there come to life before his eyes the 'mishapen and ouglye shapes' with which death tortures the imagination. And at last, when he has taken the idea of death to him and triumphed over it, there rises from his lips that magnificent strain of reconciliation and acknowledgment which sounds for ever in the ears of those who have heard it once: 'O eloquent, just and mightie Death! whom none could advise, thou hast perswaded: what none hath dared, thou hast done.'

Sterne[1]

IT is the custom to draw a distinction between a man and his works and to add that, although the world has a claim to read every line of his writing, it must not ask questions about the author. The distinction has arisen, we may believe, because the art of biography has fallen very low, and people of good taste infer that a 'life' will merely gratify a base curiosity, or will set up a respectable figure of sawdust. It is therefore a wise precaution to limit one's study of a writer to the study of his works; but, like other precautions, it implies some loss. We sacrifice an aesthetic pleasure, possibly of first-rate value—a life of Johnson, for example— and we raise boundaries where there should be none. A writer is a writer from his cradle; in his dealings with the world, in his affections, in his attitude to the thousand small things that happen between dawn and sunset, he shows the same point of view as that which he elaborates afterwards with a pen in his hand. It is more fragmentary and incoherent, but it is also more intense. To this, which one may call the aesthetic interest of his character, there are added the various interests of circumstance—where and how he was born and bred and educated—which all men share, but which are of greater interest as they affect a more original talent. The weakness of modern biographers seems to lie not in their failure to realize that both elements are present in the life of a writer, but in their determination to separate them. It is easier for them to draw distinctions than to see things whole. There is a common formula, in which, having delivered judgment upon his work, they state that 'a few facts about his life' may not be inappropriate, or, writing from the opposite standpoint, proclaim that their concern is 'with the man and not with his works'. A distinction is made

[1] *Times Literary Supplement*, August 12, 1909.

in this way which we do not find in the original, and from this reason mainly arises the common complaint against a biography, that it is 'not like'. We have lives that are all ceremony and work; and lives that are all chatter and scandal. A certain stigma is attached to the biography which deals mainly with a man's personal history, and the writer who sees him most clearly in that light is driven to represent him under the cover of fiction. The fascination of novel writing lies in its freedom; the dull parts can be skipped, and the excitements intensified; but above all the character can be placed artistically, set, that is, in fitting surroundings and composed so as to give whatever impression you choose. The traditional form is far less definite in the case of novels than in the case of biographies, because (one may guess) the sensibilities of conventional people have much less say in the matter. One of the objects of biography is to make men appear as they ought to be, for they are husbands and brothers; but no one takes a character in fiction quite seriously. It is there, indeed, that the main disadvantage of novel writing lies, for the aesthetic effect of truth is only to be equalled by the imagination of genius. There are a dozen incidents in a second-rate novel which might have happened in a dozen different ways, and the least consciousness of indecision blurs the effect; but the bare statement of facts has an indisputable power, if we have reason to think them true. The knowledge that they are true, it may be, leads us to connect them with other ideas; but if we know that they never happened at all, and doubt that they could have happened in this way, they suggest nothing distinct, because they are not distinct themselves. Again, a real life is wonderfully prolific; it passes through such strange places and draws along with it a train of adventure that no novelist can better them, if only he can deal with them as with his own inventions.

Certainly, no novelist could wish for finer material than the life of Sterne affords him. His story was 'like a romance' and his genius was of the rarest. There is a trace of the usual apology in Professor Cross's preface,[1] to the effect that he is

[1] *The Life and Times of Laurence Sterne*, by Wilbur L. Cross.

not going to pass judgment on the writings, but merely to
give the facts of the life. In his opinion such facts would be
dull enough, if it did not 'turn out', as he remarks, that the
writings are in part autobiographical, so that one may consider his life without irrelevance. But Professor Cross has
surely underrated the value of his material, or the use he
has made of it, for the book makes excellent reading from
start to finish, and persuades us that we know Sterne better
than we did before.

There are certain scenes upon which, were one writing a
novel, one would like to dwell. The story of his youth is one;
he was dragged about England and Ireland in the train of
the regiment which his father served. His mother was a
vulgar woman, daughter of a sutler, and his father was a
'little smart man' who got the wound that killed him in a
quarrel over a goose. The family trailed about, always in
straits for money, from one garrison town to another. Sometimes they were taken in by a rich cousin, for the Sternes
were of old descent; sometimes in crossing the Channel they
were 'nearly cast away by a leak springing up on board
ship'. Little brothers and sisters were born on their wander-
ings, and died, 'being of a fine delicate frame not made to
last long'. Sterne, after the death of his father, was taken in
charge by his cousin, Richard Sterne of Elvington, and sent
to Cambridge. He sat with John Hall-Stevenson under a
great walnut tree in the court of Jesus College, reading
Rabelais, Rochester, and Aphra Behn, Homer, Virgil, and
Theocritus, evil books and good books, so that they called
the tree the tree of knowledge. Sterne, further, railed at
'rhetoric, logic, and metaphysics . . . amused that intellect
should employ itself in that way'.

But it is at Sutton, eight miles from York, that we should
like to pause and draw the portrait of the vicar. 'So slovenly
was his dress and strange his gait, that the little boys used to
flock round him and walk by his side.' He would stop on his
way to church, if his pointer started a covey of partridges,
and leave his flock without a sermon while he shot. Once,
when his wife was out of her mind for a while and thought

herself Queen of Bohemia, Sterne drove her through the
stubble fields with bladders fastened to the wheels of her
chaise to make a noise 'and then I told her this is the way
they course in Bohemia'. He farmed his own land, played
the violin, took lessons in painting and drawing, and drove
into York for the races. In addition he was a violent partisan
in the ecclesiastical disputes and drew Dr. Slop from the life.
Then, when he was tired of parochial life he could drive over
to the great stone house with the moat of stagnant water
round it where John Hall-Stevenson lived, in retreat from
the world, humouring his fancies. If the weathercock which
he saw from his bed pointed to the north-east, for example,
Mr. Hall-Stevenson would lie all day in bed. If he could be
induced to rise, he spent his time in writing indecent rhymes
and in reading with his friend among the old and obscene
books in the library. Then, in October, the brotherhood of
the Demoniacs met at the Hall, in imitation of the monks of
Medmenham Abbey; but it was a rustic copy, for they were
'noisy Yorkshire squires and gentlemen', who hunted by
day, drank deep into the night, and told rude stories over
their burgundy. Their spirit and their oddity (for they were
the freaks of the countryside) rejoiced Sterne hugely, just as
he loved the immense freedom of the old writers. When he
was back in his parsonage again he had books all round him
to take the place of talk. York was full of books, for the sales
of the county took place there. Sterne's love of books reminds
us sometimes of Charles Lamb. He loved the vast forgotten
folios, where a lifetime of learning and fancy has been poured
into the notes; he loved Burton and Bouchet and Bruscam-
bille; Montaigne, Rabelais, and Cervantes he loved of
course; but one may believe that he delighted most in his
wild researches into medicine, midwifery, and military
engineering. He was only brought to a stop by the difficulty
of understanding in what way a cannon ball travels, for the
'laws of the parabola' were not to his mind.

He was forty-five before it occurred to him that these
vivid experiences among the parsons, the country peasants,
and the wits of Crazy Castle had given him a view of the

world which it would be possible to put into shape. The first books of *Tristram Shandy* were written at fever heat, 'quaint demons grinning and clawing at his head', ideas striking him as he walked, and sending him back home at a run to secure them. It is in this way that the first books still impress us; a wonderful conception, long imprisoned in the brain and delicately formed, seems to leap out, surprising and intoxicating the writer himself. He had found a key to the world. He thought he could go on like this, at the rate of two volumes a year, for ever, for a miracle had happened which turned all his experiences to words; to write about them was to be master of all that was in him and all that was to come. A slight knowledge of his life is enough to identify many of the characters with real people and to trace the humours of Uncle Toby and Mr. Shandy to the oddities of Crazy Castle and to the studies of the writer himself. But these are merely marks on the surface, and the source from which they sprang lies very deep. Wilfully strange and whimsical of course Sterne was, but the spirit which inspires his humours and connects them is the spirit of the humourist; the world is an absurd place, and to prove it he invents absurdities which he shows to be as sensible as the views by which the world is governed. The stranger's nose, it will be remembered, 'just served as a frigate to launch them into a gulf of school divinity, and then they all sailed before the wind'. Whichever way the story winds it is accompanied by a jibing at 'great wigs, grave faces, and other implements of deceit', and thus the innumerable darts and spurts of fancy, in spite of their variety, have a certain likeness.

Shandy Hall, the home of cranks and eccentricities, nevertheless contrives to make the whole of the outer world appear heavy, and dull and brutal, and teased by innumerable imps. But it is probable that this effect is given quite as much by indirect means as by direct satire and parody. The form of the book, which seems to allow the writer to put down at once the first thought that comes into his head, suggests freedom; and then the thoughts themselves are so informal, so small, private, and far-fetched, that the reader is amazed and delighted to think how easy it must be to write. Even his indecency impresses one as an odd kind of honesty. In comparison other novels seem intolerably portly and platitudinous and remote from life. At the same time, what kind of life is it that Sterne can show us? It is easy to see that it has nothing in common with what, in the shorthand of speech, one calls 'real life'. Sterne skips immense tracts of living in order to concentrate upon the little whim or the oddity which most delighted him. His people are always at high pressure, with their brains in a state of abnormal activity. Their wills and their affections can make small way against their intellects. Uncle Toby, it will be remembered, picks up a Bible directly he has made his offer of marriage, and becomes so much engrossed by the siege of Jericho that he leaves his proposal 'to work with her after its own way'. When the news of his son's death reaches Mr. Shandy, his mind at once fills with the fine sayings of the philosophers, and in spouting them his private sorrow is completely forgotten. Nevertheless, although such reversals of ordinary experience startle us, they do not seem to us unnatural— they do not turn to chill conceits—because Sterne, the first of 'motive-mongers', has observed the humours of man with an exquisite subtlety. His sphere is in the most exalted regions, where the thought and not the act is the thing criticized; where the thought, moreover, is almost completely severed from ordinary associations and the support of facts. Uncle Toby, with his simple questionings and avowals—'You puzzle me to death'—plays a most important part by bringing his brother's flights to earth and giving them that contrast with normal human thought in which the essence of humour lies.

Yet there are moments, especially in the later books of *Tristram Shandy*, where the hobby-horse is ridden to death, and Mr. Shandy's invariable eccentricity tries our patience. The truth is that we cannot live happily in such fine air for long, and that we begin to become conscious of limitations; moreover, this astonishing vivacity has something a little chill about it. The same qualities that were so exhilarating

at first—the malice, the wit, and the irresponsibility—are
less pleasing when they seem less spontaneous, like the grin
on a weary face; or, it may be, when one has had enough of
them. A writer who feels his responsibility to his characters
tries to give vent to portentous groans at intervals; he does
his best to insist that he is a showman merely, that his judgments are fallible, and that a great mystery lies round us all.
But Sterne's sense of humour will suffer no mystery to settle
on his page; he is never sublime like Meredith, but on the
other hand he is never ridiculous like Thackeray. When he
wished to get some relief from his fantastic brilliancy, he
sought it in the portrayal of exquisite instants and pangs of
emotion. The famous account of Uncle Toby and the fly—
'"Go," says he, lifting up the sash, and opening his hand as
he spoke, to let it escape; "go, poor devil; get thee gone,
why should I hurt thee? The world surely is wide enough to
hold both thee and me"'—is followed by a description of
the effect which such words had upon Sterne himself. They
'instantly set my whole frame into one vibration of most
pleasurable sensation'. It is this strange contradiction, as
it seems, between feeling pain and joy acutely, and at the
same time, observing and admiring his own power to do so,
that has thrown so much discredit upon the famous 'sentimentality', and has so much perplexed his admirers. The
amazing truth of these observations is the best proof that he
felt them; but when it becomes obvious that he has now
time to think of himself our attention strays also, and we
ask irrelevant questions—whether, for instance, Sterne was
a good man. Sometimes—the incident of the donkey in
Tristram Shandy is a good example—his method is brilliantly
successful, for he touches upon the emotion, and passes on
to show us how it travels through his mind, and what associations cling to it; different ideas meet and disperse, naturally as it seems; and the whole scene is lit for the moment
with air and colour. In *The Sentimental Journey*, however,
Sterne seems anxious to suppress his natural curiosity, and
to have a double intention in his sentiment—to convey a
feeling to the reader, but with the object of winning admira-

tion for his own simple virtues. It is when his unmixed sentiment falls very flat that we begin to ask ourselves whether
we like the writer, and to call him hypocrite. 'The *pauvre
honteux* [to whom Sterne had given alms] could say nothing;
he pull'd out a little handkerchief, and wiped his face as he
turned away—and I thought he thanked me more than
them all.' The last words, with their affectation of simplicity,
are like eyes turned unctiously to Heaven.

There is abundant evidence in the story of his life to show
how strange and complicated was the state of mind that
produced such works of art. Sterne was a man of many
passions, driven 'according as the fly stings'; but the most
serious was said to have been inspired by Mrs. Draper, the
Eliza of the letters. Nevertheless, sentiments that had done
duty for his wife in 1740 were copied out, with a change of
name, and made to serve again for Eliza, in the year 1767;
and again if he had turned a phrase happily in writing to
Eliza, Lydia, his daughter, was given the benefit of it. Shall
we infer from this that Sterne cared nothing for wife or
mistress or daughter, or shall we believe that he was, before
everything else, and with all the failing of his kind, a great
artist? If he had been among the greatest, no doubt these
little economies would not have been necessary; but with
his exquisite and penetrating but not very exuberant genius
it was essential to make shifts and to eke out as best he might.
Accordingly, we have, as Professor Cross demonstrates, the
strange spectacle of a man who uses his emotions twice over,
for different purposes. The *Journal to Eliza* in which the most
secret passions of his heart are laid bare is but the note-book
for passages in *The Sentimental Journey* which all the world
may read. Sterne himself, no doubt, scarcely knew at what
point his own pain was dissolved in the joy of an artist. We
at this distance of time, might speculate indefinitely.

Indeed, however we may test it, there is no life which is
harder to judge; its eccentricities are often genuine, and its
impulses are often premeditated. In the same way the final
impression is twofold in its nature, for we must combine a
life of extraordinary flightiness and oddity with the infinite

painstaking and self-consciousness of an artist. This thin, excitable man, who was devoured by consumption, who said of himself that he generally acted on the first impulse, and was a bundle of sensations scarcely checked by reason, not only kept a record of all that he felt, but could sit close at his table, arranging and rearranging, adding and altering, until every scene was clear, every tone was felt, and each word was fit and in its place. 'How do the slight touches of the chisel,' he exclaimed in *Tristram Shandy*, 'the pencil, the pen, the fiddle stick, et cetera, give the true swell, which gives the true pleasure! O, my fellow countrymen!—be nice; be cautious of your language—and never, O! never let it be forgotten upon what small particles your eloquence and your fame depend.' His fame depends partly upon that inimitable style, but rests most safely upon the extraordinary zest with which he lived, and upon the joy with which his mind worked ceaselessly upon the world.

Eliza and Sterne[1]

OF the many difficulties which afflict the biographer, the moral difficulty must surely be the greatest. By what standard, that is to say, is he to judge the morals of the dead? By that of their day, or that of his own? Or should he, before putting pen to paper, arrive at some absolute standard of right and wrong by which he can try Socrates and Shelley and Byron and Queen Victoria and Mr. Lloyd George? The problem, though it lies at the root of biography and affects it in every fibre, is for the most part solved or shelved by taking it for granted that the truth was revealed about the year 1850 to the fortunate natives of the British Isles, who need only in future take into account circumstances of date, country, and sex in order to come to a satisfactory conclusion upon all cases of moral eccentricity submitted to their judgment. If we write the life of Elizabeth Draper, for instance, we must lay great stress upon the question of the morality or immorality of her relations with Sterne. We must ransack the evidence and profess relief or censure as the balance sways for her or against. We must attach more importance to her conduct in this respect than in any other. Mr. Wright and Mr. Sclater go through the ceremony with rigid consistency. Her 'moral culpability' is debated at every point, and we are invited to assist at a trial which, as it proceeds, comes to have less and less reality either for us or for anybody else. But in saying that we admit no levity. We are only saying what every reader of biography knows but few writers care to confess—that times are changed; that in 1850 Eliza would not have been invited to Court, but that in 1922 we should all be delighted to sit next her at dinner.

Yet morality, though it may be the crucial difficulty, is by

¹ *Times Literary Supplement*, December 14, 1922.

no means the only difficulty that the biographer has to face. There are the white ants of Anjengo—'a peculiarly voracious breed', who, not satisfied with devouring the 'bulk of the old archives' of a town which is at once the birthplace of Eliza and the seat of the pepper industry, have eaten away a much more precious material—the life of Eliza herself. Again and again her conscientious biographers have to admit that the facts are lost. 'History . . . is often most tantalizingly silent upon points of real interest.' The chief actor leaves the stage, often at the crisis of her fate, and in her absence our attention is directed to the antiseptic quality of wood ashes in the treatment of smallpox; to the different natures of the Hooka, the Calloon, and the Kerim Can; to the method, still in vogue, of hunting deer with cheetahs; and to the fact that one of Eliza's uncles was killed by a sack of caraway seeds falling on his head as he walked up St. Mary-at-Hill in the year 1778. These familiar diversions, which do not perhaps advance the cause of biography, are excusable when the subject is, as Eliza Draper was, an obscure woman, dead almost a century and a half, whose thirty-five years would have been utterly forgotten were it not that for three months in one of them she was loved by Laurence Sterne.

She was loved, but the depredations of time and the white ants leave us in little doubt that the love was on his side, not on hers. If she was anybody's Eliza (which is by no means certain) she was Thomas Limbrey Sclater's Eliza. To him she wrote affectionately all her life; to him she sent one of Sterne's love-letters; and it was of him she thought when the ship was carrying her back to India and away from Sterne for ever. She should have had more sense of the becoming. She should have realized the predicament in which she places posterity. But Eliza was a woman of impulse rather than of reflection. 'Committing matrimony', as her sister called it, with Daniel Draper of Bombay at the age of fourteen she ruined her chances for ever. He was thirty-four, had several illegitimate children, was afflicted with the writer's cramp, and possessed all those virtues which lead officials to the highest promotion and make their wives jump into the arms of Commodore Clarke.

'. . . By nature cool, Phlegmatic, and not adorned by Education with any of those pleasing Acquirements which help to fill up the Vacuums of time agreeably, if not usefully, added to which, Methodically formed, in the Extreme, by long habit, and not easily roused into active measures by any Motive Unconnected with his sense of duty.'

Such a man (Eliza wrote of her husband in words which, since her emotions were strong and her grammar weak, we take the liberty of paraphrasing) is quite unfitted to be the husband of a lady entitled to 'the Appellation of Belle Indian'; who loved society much but solitude more; who read Montaigne and the *Spectator*; who was fourth if not third upon the Governor's invitation list; who wrote letters which some thought worthy of publication; who had been told finally by a friend that nature designed her for the wife of 'a very feeling Poet and Philosopher, rather than to a Gentleman of Independance and General Talents, and the reason he was pleased to assign to it was, the natural and supposed qualities of my heart, together with an expressive Countenance and a manner capable of doing justice to the tender Passions'.

This 'acknowledged Judge of Physiognomy' was, we may guess, no less a person than the great Mr. Sterne. Eliza met him at the house of Mrs. James in Gerrard Street in the year 1767. Draper's increasing cramp had the somewhat incongruous effect of bringing them together. Having tried the English spas without success, Draper returned to Bombay and Eliza was left in London to continue the conversation with Sterne. From the Journal to Eliza we can judge fairly accurately what they talked about. Eliza was the most charming of women, Sterne the most passionate of men. Life was cruel, Mrs. Sterne intolerable, early marriages deplorable, Bombay distant, and husbands exacting. The only happiness to mingle thoughts and tears, to share ecstasies and exchange portraits, and pray for some miracle, such as the simultaneous deaths of Elizabeth Sterne and

Daniel Draper, which might unite them eternally in the future. But though this was undoubtedly what they said, it is no such easy matter to be certain what they meant. Sterne was fifty-four, and Eliza twenty-two. Sterne was at the height of his fame, and Eliza at the height not of her beauty, which was little, but of her charm, which was great. But Sterne was engaged in writing *The Sentimental Journey*, and Eliza must sometimes have felt that though it was most wonderful and flattering to have a celebrated author sitting by her bedside when she fell ill, and reading her letters aloud to the ladies and gentlemen of the highest rank, and displaying her picture, and buying ten handsome brass screws for her cabin, and running her errands round London, still he was fifty-four, had a dreadful cough, and sometimes, she noticed, looked out of the window in a very curious way. No doubt he was thinking about his writing. He assured her that he found her of the very greatest help. And he told her that he had brought her name and picture into his work, 'where', he said, 'they will remain when you and I are at rest'; and he went on to write an elegy upon her, and no doubt worked himself up into one of those accesses of emotion which any woman would have given her eyes to inspire, yet lying ill in bed Eliza found them a little fatiguing, and could not help thinking that Thomas Limbrey Sclater, who was not in the least likely to become immortal, was a great deal more to her taste than Laurence Sterne. Thus, if we must censure Eliza, it is not for being in love with Sterne, but for not being in love with him. She let him write her the letters of a lover and propose to her the rights of a husband. But when she reached India she had almost forgotten him, and his death recalled only 'the mild generous good Yorick' whose picture hung, not above her heart, but over her writing-table.

Arrived in India with eleven years of life before her, the provoking creature proceeded to live them as if she did not care a straw for those 'Annotators and Explainers' who would, Sterne said, busy themselves in after ages with their names. She gave herself up to trivial interests and nameless captains; to sitting till three in the morning upon a 'cool

Terrasse'; to hunting antelopes with leopards; to driving down the streets of Tellicherry with an escort of armed Sepoys; to playing with her children and pouring out her soul in long, long letters to Mr. Sclater and Mrs. James; to that petty process of living, in short, which is of such inexplicable interest to others engaged in the same pursuit. It is all very obscure and highly conjectural. She was very happy at Tellicherry in the year 1769 and very unhappy in the year 1770. She was always being happy and then unhappy and blaming herself and hoping that her daughter would be a better woman than her mother. Yet Eliza did not think altogether badly of herself. It was her complexion that was to blame, and the 'happy flexibility' of her temper. Vain, charming, gifted, sympathetic, her relations with her husband grew steadily more and more desperate. At last, when it was quite certain that Draper loved Leeds, her maid, and neither on Tuesday nor on Wednesday did he say that word 'sympathetick of regret' which 'would have saved me the perilous adventure', Eliza either jumped from her window into a boat or was otherwise conveyed to the flagship of Sir John Clarke and thence to her uncle's house at Masulipatam. This time, without a doubt, her biographers regretfully conclude, 'Eliza was "lost"'. But Eliza was not in the least of that opinion herself. She turned up imperturbably in Queen Anne Street, Cavendish Square, 'which shows that she had considerable social resources'; but there, alas, proceeded to fall in love with the Abbé Raynal. Was she incorrigible or was he, perhaps like others of his countrymen, apt to exaggerate? The terms in which he addressed Anjengo would lead one to suspect the latter. But death, with infinite discretion, spares us the inquiry. Eliza died at the age of thirty-five, and some unknown friend raised a monument to her memory in Bristol Cathedral with the figures of Genius and Benevolence on either side and a bird in the act of feeding its young. So after all somebody liked Eliza, and it is as certain as anything can be that a woman with such a tombstone was moving in the highest circles of Bristol society at the time of her death.

Horace Walpole[1]

ONE hundred and ten letters by Horace Walpole are here printed by Dr. Toynbee for the first time.[2] These, together with twenty-three now printed in full, new matter from hitherto unpublished material, and Dr. Toynbee's notes, make up two volumes of rare delight. If the two volumes were ten we should still urge Dr. Toynbee to fresh researches; we should still welcome the discovery of a large chest put away in some old country house and stuffed to the brim with Walpole's letters. Although there is nothing in the new letters of surpassing brilliance, nothing that draws a new line on the familiar face, there is once more, and for too short a time, the peculiar and unmistakable pleasure of Walpole's society. He does not need to be brilliant; he does not need to be indiscreet; let him draw up to the table, take the pen in his gouty fingers, and write—anything, everything, so long as he continues to write. These last letters, swept up from many different sources with intervals between them and lacking continuity, are yet neither trivial nor disconnected. We fall into step at once. We take our delightful promenade through the greater part of the eighteenth century. We see in passing many old friends. It is as entertaining as ever. The first solemn chimes of the nineteenth century, which mean that Horace Walpole must retire, are as vexatious to us as the clock that strikes and sends a child complaining up to bed.

Perhaps it is fanciful to detect the charm of the mature Walpole in 'My first letter to my mother', with which the book opens: 'Dear Mama, I hop you are wall and I am very wall and I hop papa is wall . . . and I am very glad to hear

[1] *Times Literary Supplement*, July 31, 1919.
[2] Supplement to the Letters of Horace Walpole, fourth Earl of Orford. Chronologically arranged and edited with notes and indices by Paget Toynbee. Two volumes.

by Tom that all my cruataurs ar all wall'. Yet this is an engaging letter, as the dark-eyed little boy in the miniature is a charming little boy; and there can be no doubt that Walpole far sooner than most children knew his own mind and could overcome the difficulties of spelling. There was never a transition stage of awkward immaturity when he said more than he meant, or less than he meant, or what he did not mean. At the age of twenty-three he appears in Rome a complete man of the world, and so much his own master that he can already quiz the great ladies who are seeing the sights, execute commissions for fans and snuff-boxes, exchange compliments with learned men, keep his own mind admirably free from enthusiasm, and end a letter:

> Good-night, child, I am in a violent hurry. Oh, Porto Bello, the delightful news! Corradini is certainly to be Pope, and soon. Next post I shall probably be able to tell you he certainly is not.

The author of that sentence is already completely equipped for his part. He has broken the back of the stubborn English tongue; for ever more it is going to run his errands, carry his light burdens, do his behests; he has at his disposal an indefatigable slave. More than that, he has already taken up his position, sees the spectacle from his own angle, and for close on eighty years there will he stand, witty, malicious, observant, detached, the liveliest of gossips, the most alert of friends. The son of a Prime Minister endowed with a handsome sinecure, a position of some sort was assured him had he been both dunce and dullard. But Horace Walpole was not a dullard, and he was much more than the son of a Prime Minister. He stood out against his hereditary doom with a resolution which commands our respect, though it has caused him to be disparaged since, as no doubt it raised a laugh against him at the time. He would not drink; he would not dice; he would not be a country gentleman; he would not be a politician. He would, in short, be nothing save what it pleased him to be.

On the whole it pleased him best to be a gentleman, for

there is no reason why a gentleman should not write the wittiest letters in the world, provided that he does it carelessly, and has for correspondents the most exalted and the most accomplished of his time. The chief characteristic of this class he had acquired very young, perhaps at the cost of some labour—even, it is possible, of some renunciation. 'Good-night, child, I am in a violent hurry.' Whatever pains his letter had cost him, it was essential to pass it off as the merest trifle, something dashed down while he waited for the rain to stop—something, as the phrasing shows, spontaneous, careless, but spoken naturally in a tone of the highest breeding. He was careful to repeat the boast that he was in a violent hurry whenever he wrote anything. As for rhapsody of emotion or profundity of learning, those qualities he left to the professional writers who had only their brains to live by. Moreover, it is permissible for the amateur to spend his time over problems which fascinated Walpole, though no man of sense could waste a thought upon them. Since no one, himself least of all, took him seriously, he could devote several pages to the discussion of that difficult and vexed question—the age at which Lady Desmond died. Was she really 163, and could it be possible that she had danced with Richard the Third? For some reason these questions stirred his imagination. His eagerness to know the exact condition of Queen Catherine Parr's corpse, when it was dug up and examined, would seem excessive—save indeed that the lady was of the highest rank. For it is not possible to deny that he was a snob, and of the determined breed whose mothers have been Shorters while their fathers, though not of noble birth, have been exalted by their abilities to familiar converse with the great. Yet once that dart is levelled, no other can find a lodgment. It is not easy to call him dilettante or gossip, poetaster or dandy, when before these charges are out of your mouth the culprit has owned them of his own accord and gone out of his way to pronounce his sentence:

Good God! Sir, what am I that I should be offended at, or above, criticism or correction? I do not know who ought to be—I am sure no author. I am a private man of no consequence, and at best an author of very moderate abilities.

Even in matters of taste, upon which he had spent most of his life and a large part of his fortune, he was open to correction by people possessed of greater learning than he could claim. He was nothing but a private gentleman.

The reader will perceive that the habit of understatement is not only the essence of good breeding, but also a tool of great value in the hand of a writer. An author who knows no more than other people, who has no dignity to keep up, no convictions to enforce, no philosophy to expound, can say what he likes and think what he chooses. No one need attend to him. But if, in addition, by a mere stroke of luck, he possesses the wittiest of pens and the most observant of eyes, if he knows everybody worth knowing and sees everything worth seeing, we shall of course get every word he writes by heart. Since, however, writers should be serious, we shall in revenge allow him very little credit for his performance. It is the fashion to say that Walpole was so amusing because he was so frivolous, so witty because he was so heartless. He was certainly very much put out when old Madame du Deffand fell in love with him, and thought that at her age she could afford to talk about it openly. 'Dès le moment que je cessai d'être jeune, j'ai eu une peur horrible de devenir un vieillard ridicule', he wrote to her; and she replied, 'Vos craintes sur le ridicule sont des terreurs paniques, mais on ne guérit point de la peur; je n'ai point vu une semblable faiblesse'. He was terribly afraid of ridicule, and yet the old lady, whose passion he had snubbed, showed considerable penetration when she spoke of 'l'extrême vérité de votre caractère'. Understatement long persisted in, partly from motives of taste and propriety and partly from fear of ridicule, had disciplined Walpole's emotions so that they scarcely dared show themselves above ground; yet what there is of them, as sometimes happens with emotions repressed rather than exploited, rings startlingly true. '. . . he loved me and I did not think he did', he wrote of his quarrel

with Gray, when Gray was dead. But as for his heart, let
that rest in peace; there is some indecency in prying into it,
and he would certainly prefer that we should credit him
with none at all than allow him a grain too much. His brain
is our affair.

And yet here once more shall we not be guilty of some
credulity if we accept him entirely at his own estimate? The
affectation of indifference, the pose of amateurishness, were
common foibles at that time among men of birth whose
brains could not abstain altogether from the inkpot. But
perhaps there were moments when Walpole wished that
his father's name had been Shorter as well as his mother's,
and that fate had required him to use pen and paper in
earnest and not merely provide them, at a handsome salary,
for the use of the young men at the Treasury. At any rate
his warmest praises in the present volume are not for Lady
Di's illustrations in 'Sut water' to the Mysterious Mother,
nor even for Mrs. Damer's model of 'a shock dog in wax',
but for the plays of Shakespeare. 'Moi, je me ferais brûler
pour la primauté de Shakespeare.' Admiring the French and
owing much to them, still when it comes to tragedy what
are Voltaire and Racine and Corneille, compared with
Shakespeare? How did Voltaire dare criticize Shakespeare?
'Grossly ignorant and tasteless' was he not to see that the
phrase 'a bare bodkin' is as sublime in one way as the simplicity of Lady Percy's speech is sublime in another? 'I had
rather have written the two speeches of Lady Percy in the
second part of Henry IV than all Voltaire. . . . But my
enthusiasm for Shakespeare runs away with me.' That is,
indeed, an unwonted spectacle. But perhaps young Mr.
Jephson, the playwright, owed all this talk about Shakespeare and the English language 'far more energie, and
more sonorous too, than the French', and these interesting
speculations about 'a novel diction', 'a very new and
peculiar style' which might have amazing effect, 'by fixing
on some region of whose language we have little or no idea'
—perhaps Mr. Jephson drew all this down upon himself
because the old dandy and aristocrat did for the time being

envy young Mr. Jephson, who could set himself seriously to the task of writing and need not, since his name was Jephson, scribble off a tragedy 'in a violent hurry'.

A queer sort of imagination haunted the seemingly prosaic edifice of Walpole's mind. What but imagination gone astray and vagrant over pots and pans instead of firmly held in place was his love of knick-knacks and antiquities, Strawberry hills and decomposing royalties? And once at least Walpole made a little confession to Madame du Deffand. Of all his works he preferred *The Castle of Otranto*, for there he said 'j'ai laissé courir mon imagination; les visions et les passions m'échauffaient'. Vision and passion are not the gifts that we should ascribe offhand to Horace Walpole; and yet as we lose ourselves in the enormous variety and entertainment of his letters we must allow that somehow from his own angle he saw truly, he judged independently. Somehow he was not only the wittiest of men, but the most observant and not the least kindly. And among the writers of English prose he wears for ever and with a peculiar grace a coronet of his own earning.

A Friend of Johnson[1]

A GREAT book, like a great nature, may have disastrous effects upon other people. It robs them of their character and substitutes its own. No one, for instance, who has read what Carlyle has to say about Lamb ever rids his mind completely of the impression, in spite of the fact that we judge the writer of it far more than his victim. Some deposit remains with us. It is strange to reflect what numbers of men and women live in our minds merely because Boswell took a note of their talk. Two or three such lines have a generating power; a body grows from the seed. The ordinary English reader knows Baretti solely through Johnson. 'His account of Italy', said Johnson, 'is a very entertaining book; and, Sir, I know no man who carries his head higher in conversation than Baretti. There are strong powers in his mind. He has not, indeed, many hooks, but with what hooks he has he grapples very forcibly.' This may be, as Mr. Collison-Morley[2] says, 'a very good summary', and yet his character is scarcely to be summarized thus; his vitality is too great for that. Mr. Collison-Morley, further, has the advantage of knowing the Italian side of the story.

The Barettis came from Piedmont, and Giuseppe boasted romantically of his noble birth. He could not live at home, where they wished to train him for a lawyer, but ran away to see the world. He lived at Milan, Venice, and Turin by his pen, turning out ceremonial verses to order. His qualities, however, were not those that bring success. He was susceptible, but so importunate that a certain Mrs. Paradise had to snub him with boiling water from her tea urn. Great animal vigour and a powerful mind made him insolent and overbearing in manner before his fame authorized it. Thus

[1] *Times Literary Supplement*, July 29, 1909.
[2] *Giuseppe Baretti and his Friends*, by Lacy Collison-Morley.

187

he took it upon himself as a young writer to denounce
Goldoni, the Arcadians, and Italian blank verse, when they
were in fashion; later, when archaeology was the rage, he
declared that antiquaries should be clapped into lunatic
asylums, seeing merely the pedantic side of the pursuit and
failing from some lack of imagination to foretell its future.
To succeed in letters needed in that age the utmost tact.
Then as now France supplied Italy with her reading to a
great extent, for every province had its own dialect; authors
were miserably paid, and their manuscripts had to be passed
by two censors. Italy afforded no place for a man whose
intellect led him to despise mere grace and scholarship, and
whose temper urged him to speak out.

He decided to try his fortune in England. He was amazed
by London: Lincoln's Inn, he wrote home, was three times
the size of St. Mark's Square; 'a great street, hung with
painted signs and clamourous with droves of oxen and of
sheep, carriages and foot passengers, ran right through the
city; the wheels splash you with mud black as ink; there are
women of "perfect beauty" mixing with horrid cripples';
Fielding told him that a thousand or even two thousand die
every year from want and hunger, 'but London is so large
it is hardly noticed'; a din of whips and curses lasts all day
long, and at night the watchmen cry the hours hoarsely,
'vile hounds' ring bells as they collect the letters; sweeps,
milk-women, oyster-sellers vociferate perpetually. In spite
of this London gradually ousted all other places in his affections. To begin with he found that the Italian language was
in fashion, for an Italian tour was essential; and the Italian
opera was so popular that the audience followed the words
by the light of private candles. He could thus keep himself
by teaching—one of his pupils being the famous Mrs.
Lennox, by whom he was introduced to Johnson. The merits
of the society which Johnson ruled were precisely to the
taste of Baretti. He loved to stretch his legs, to talk enormously, to mix with men of all callings, to ramble the streets
at night with a companion, and the booksellers with their
vast and indiscriminate greed for copy suited his powers

admirably. His mind, we know, had strong hooks, and having set himself to learn English he made extraordinary progress in 'that strange and most irregular tongue'. He could speak street slang even, and soon could carry on a controversy in vigorous English prose. It is typical of him that he could acquire any living language with enthusiasm, but the dead languages bored him. He turned out dictionaries, and translations and travels, with the printer's devil waiting at the door, until a lump grew on his finger where the pen rested. His struggle to live by his brains is, for us, full of picturesque adventures. A dissertation upon the Italian poets introduced him to a wealthy English gentleman who had been engaged on a translation of Ariosto for twenty years. For the sake of Baretti's advice and conversation he offered him a house and garden in his park, a gold watch worth forty guineas, and a wife. But the friendship ended in bitterness; it was said that the watch was only lent. Whether it was that Baretti had a drop of hot Southern blood in him, or whether the society of scholars was in truth a rough and hasty world, we certainly find matter, even in a slight memoir like the present, for comparisons between that age and this. One cannot imagine, for instance, that writers then retired to their studies or worked by the clock. They seem to have learnt by talk; their friendships thus were important and outspoken. Conversation was a kind of strife, and the jealousies and contradictions which attended the display gave it at least an eager excitement. Goldsmith found Baretti 'insolent and overbearing', Baretti thought Goldsmith 'an unpolished man, and an absurd companion'. Mrs. Lennox, having complained that Baretti paid more attention to her child than to herself, he retorted: 'You are a child in stature and a child in understanding', being generally provoking, where opportunity offered. Indeed a society of clever people whose witticisms, jealousies, and emotions circulate is much like a society of children. Reticence and ceremony seem to mark middle age.

The life of Baretti reminds us, too, in a singular way of the rudeness that lay outside the coffee-houses and the clubs.

One afternoon in October, 1769, he walked from Soho to the Orange coffee-house in the Haymarket. On his way back a woman sitting on a doorstep jumped up and struck him. In the darkness he returned the blow, whereupon three bullies set upon him, and he was chased along Oxenden Street, shouting 'Murder' with a crowd at his heels, who reviled him for a Frenchman. One man made dashes for his pigtail, and to save himself Baretti drew a silver-bladed fruit knife, and stabbed him twice. As the only means of escape, for he was stout, near-sighted, and the road swam with puddles, he burst into a shop and gave himself up to the police. Goldsmith, we notice, drove with him to the prison and offered him 'every shilling' in his purse. The man died from the blow; Baretti was acquitted, and the fruit knife used to be shown at dessert. The same kind of roughness marks the famous friendship with the Thrales, of which Mr. Collison-Morley gives a very lively account. He lived in the family, not as a regular tutor with a salary, but as a hired friend who must talk in return for board and lodging, and might hope for an occasional present. The good-natured Mrs. Thrale stood it for nearly three years, and then, finding him intolerable with his airs and arrogances, treated him 'with some coldness'; whereupon he set down his dish of tea, 'not half drank', went 'for my hat and stick that lay in the corner of the room', and walked off to London without saying goodbye. Johnson pleaded for him. 'Forgive him, dearest lady, the rather because of his misbehaviour; I am afraid he has learned part of me.' It was true, no doubt, that he traded upon a certain likeness to the doctor, and expected the same consideration, but he learnt much from him that was wholly admirable. When he went back to Italy in 1763 he found that the old abuses at which he had tilted as a boy were still rampant. He decided to bring out a review, on the model of the *Rambler*, in which he could lash the Arcadians freely. In the person of Aristarco he delivered himself of his views upon the state of Italian literature, upon blank verse, Goldoni and the antiquaries, retailing at the same time some of Johnson's peculiarities—

that the Scotch are inferior, and that Milton is sometimes dull. Nevertheless, his satire told, and his controversies raised such an outcry that the *Frusta letteraria* was suspended. But 'no such criticism had as yet appeared in Italy' and it is to-day a classic among his countrymen. But he 'could not enjoy his own country'. England rewarded him with a Secretaryship at the Royal Academy, and added a pension in his later years. For, industrious as he was, and in receipt sometimes of huge profits, his earnings never stuck to him. A strange kind of clumsiness united to a passionate nature seemed to make a child of him. What, for instance, could be more childish than the quarrel with Johnson as to whether Omai, an Otaheitan, had beaten him at chess or not? 'Do you think I should be conquered at chess by a savage?' 'I know you were', says Johnson. The two men, who respected each other, parted and never met again. English people now scarcely read his books, unless it be the Italian dictionary, but his life is worth reading, because he exhibits so curious a mixture of power and weakness; he is in many ways so true a type of the man who lived by his pen in the eighteenth century; and Mr. Collison-Morley fills in the old story as Boswell and Mrs. Thrale told it with new matter from Italian sources. His life was full and vigorous; as for his works, he wished that every page lay at the bottom of the sea.

Fanny Burney's Half-Sister[1]

SINCE a copy of *Evelina* was lately sold for the enormous sum of four thousand pounds; since the Clarendon Press has lately bestowed the magnificent compliment of a new edition upon *Evelina*; since Maria Allen was the half-sister of the authoress of *Evelina*; since the story of Evelina owed much to the story of Maria Allen, it may not be impertinent to consider what is still to be collected of the history of that misguided and unfortunate girl.

As is well known, Dr. Burney was twice married. He took for his second wife a Mrs. Allen of Lynn, the widow of a substantial citizen who left her with a fortune which she promptly lost, and with three children, of whom one, Maria, was almost the same age as Fanny Burney when Dr. Burney's second marriage made them half-sisters. And half-sisters they might have remained with none but a formal tie between them, had not the differences between the two families brought about a much closer relationship. The Burneys were the gifted children of gifted parents. They had enjoyed all the stimulus that comes from running in and out of rooms where grown-up people are talking about books and music, where the piano is always open, and somebody —it may be David Garrick, it may be Mrs. Thrale—is always dropping in to dinner. Maria, on the other hand, had been bred in the provinces. The great figures of Lynn were well known to her, but the great figures of Lynn were merely Miss Dolly Young—who was so ugly—or Mr. Richard Warren, who was so handsome. The talk she heard was the talk of squires and merchants. Her greatest excitement was a dance at the Assembly Rooms or a scandal in the town.

Thus she was rustic and unsophisticated where the Burneys were metropolitan and cultivated. But she was bold

[1] *Times Literary Supplement*, August 28, 1930.

and dashing where they were timid and reserved. She was all agog for life and adventure where they were always running away in agonies of shyness to commit their innumerable observations to reams of paper. Unrefined, but generous and unaffected, she brought to Poland Street that whiff of fresh air, that contact with ordinary life and ease in the presence of ordinary things, which the precocious family lacked themselves and found most refreshing in others. Sometimes she visited them in London; sometimes they stayed with her at Lynn. Soon she came to feel for them all, but for Fanny in particular, a warm, a genuine, a surprised admiration. They were so learned and so innocent; they knew so many things, and yet they did not know half as much about life as she did. It was to them, naturally, that she confided her own peccadilloes and adventures, wishing perhaps for counsel, wishing perhaps to impress. Fanny was one of those shy people—'I am not near so squeamish as you are', Maria observed—who draw out the confidences of their bolder friends and delight in accounts of actions which they could not possibly commit themselves. Thus in 1770 Fanny was imparting to her diary certain confidences that Maria had made her of such a nature that when she read the book later she judged it best to tear out twelve pages and burn them. Happily, a packet of letters survives which, though rather meagrely doled out by an editor in the eighties, who thought them too full of dashes to be worthy of the dignity of print, allow us to guess pretty clearly what kind of secret Maria confided and Fanny recorded, and Fanny, grown mature, then tore up.

For example, there was an Assembly at Lynn some time in 1770 to which Maria did not want to go. Bet Dickens, however, overcame her scruples, and she went. However, she was determined not to dance. However, she did dance. Martin was there. She broke her earring. She danced a *minuet à quatre*. She got into the chariot to come home. She came home. 'Was I alone?—guess—well, all is vanity and vexations of spirit.' It needs little ingenuity to interpret these nods and winks and innuendoes. Maria danced with

Martin. She came home with Martin. She sat alone with Martin, and she had been strictly forbidden by her mother to meet Martin. That is obvious. But what is not, after all these years, quite so clear is for what reason Mrs. Allen disapproved. On the face of it Martin Rishton was a very good match for Maria Allen. He was well born, he had been educated at Oxford, he was the heir of his uncle Sir Richard Bettenson, and Sir Richard Bettenson had five thousand a year and no children. Nevertheless, Maria's mother warmly opposed the match. She said rather vaguely that Martin 'had been extravagant at Oxford, and that she had heard some story that he had done something unworthy of a gentleman'. But her ostensible objections were based perhaps upon others which were less easy to state. There was her daughter's character, for example. Maria was 'a droll girl with a very great love of sport and mirth'. Her temper was lively and warm. She was extremely outspoken. 'If possible,' Fanny said, 'she is too sincere. She pays too little regard to the world; and indulges herself with too much freedom of raillery and pride of disdain towards those whose vices and follies offend her.' When Mrs. Allen looked from Maria to Martin she saw, there can be no doubt, something that made her uneasy. But what? Perhaps it was nothing more than that Martin was particular about appearances and Maria rather slack; that Martin was conventional by nature and Maria the very opposite; that Martin liked dress and decorum and that Maria was one of those heedless girls who say the first thing that comes into their heads and never reflect, if they are amused themselves, what people will say if they have holes in their stockings. Whatever the reason, Mrs. Allen forbade the match; and Sir Richard Bettenson, whether to meet her views or for educational purposes, sent his nephew in the beginning of 1771 to travel for two years abroad. Maria remained at Lynn.

Five months, however, had not passed before Martin burst in unexpectedly at a dinner party of relations in Welbeck Street. He looked very well, but when he was asked why he had come back in such a hurry, 'he smiled,

but said nothing to the question'. Maria, although still at
Lynn, at once got wind of his arrival. Soon she saw him at a
dance, but she did not dance with him and the ban was
evidently enforced, for her letters become plaintive and
agitated and hint at secrets that she cannot reveal, even to
her dear toads the Burneys. It was now her turn to be sent
abroad, partly to be out of Martin's way, partly to finish her
education. She was dispatched to Geneva. But the Burneys
soon received a packet from her. In the first place, she had
some little commissions that she must ask them to discharge.
Would they send her a pianoforte, some music, Fordyce's
sermons, a tea cadet, an ebony inkstand with silver-plated
tops, and a very pretty naked wax doll with blue eyes to be
had in Fleet-street for half a crown—all of which, if well
wrapped up, could travel safely in the case of the pianoforte.
She had no money to pay with at the moment, for she had
been persuaded and indeed was sure that it was true economy if one passed through Paris to spend all one's money
on clothes. But she could always sell her diamonds or she
would give them 'a bill on somebody in London'. These
trifling matters dispatched, she turned to something of far
greater importance. Indeed, what she had to say was so
important that it must be burnt at once. Indeed, it was only
her great distress and being alone in a foreign land that led
her to tell them at all. But the truth was—so far as can now
be ascertained among the fragments and the dashes—the
truth was that she had gone much farther with Martin than
anybody knew. She had in fact confessed her love to him.
And he had proposed something which had made her very
angry. She had refused to do it. She had written him a very
angry letter. She had had indeed to write it three times over
before she got it right. When he read it he was furious. 'Did
my character', he wrote, 'ever give you reason to imagine
I should expose you because you loved me? 'Tis thoroughly
unnatural—I defy the world to bring an instance of my
behaving unworthy the Character of a Gentleman.' These
were his very words. And, Maria wrote, 'I think such the
sentiments of a Man of Honour, and such I hope to find

him', she concluded; for although she knew very well that Hetty Burney and Mr. Crisp disliked him, he was—here she came out with it—the man 'on whom all my happiness in this Life depends and in whom I *wish* to see no faults'. The Burneys hid the letters, breathed not a word to their parents, and waited in suspense. Nor did they have to wait long. Before the spring was over Maria was back again in Poland Street and in circumstances so romantic, so exciting and above all so secret that 'I dare not,' Fanny exclaimed, 'commit particulars to paper.' This much (and one would have thought it enough) only could be said: 'Miss Allen— for the last time I shall call her so,—came home on Monday last . . . she—was married last Saturday!' It was true. Martin Rishton had gone out secretly to join her abroad. They had been married at Ypres on May 16, 1772. On the 18th Maria reached England and confided the grand secret to Fanny and Susan Burney, but she told no one else. They were afraid to tell her mother. They were afraid to tell Dr. Burney. In their dilemma they turned to the strange man who was always their confidant—to Samuel Crisp of Chesington.

Many years before this Samuel Crisp had retired from the world. He had been a man of parts, a man of fashion, and a man of great social charm. But his fine friends had wasted his substance and his clever friends had damned his play. In disgust with the insincerity of fashionable life and the fickleness of fame he had withdrawn to a decayed manor house near London, which, however, was so far from the high road and so hidden from travellers in the waste of a common that no one could find it unless specially instructed. But Mr. Crisp was careful to issue no instructions. The Burneys were almost the only friends who knew the way across the fields to his door. But the Burneys could never come often enough. He depended upon the Burneys for life and society and for news of the great world which he despised and yet could not forget. The Burney children stood to him in the place of his own children. Upon them he lavished all the shrewdness and knowledge and disillusionment which he had won at such cost to himself and now found so useless in an old manor house on a wild common with only old Mrs. Hamilton and young Kitty Cook to bear him company.

It was, then, to Chesington and to Daddy Crisp that Maria Rishton and Susan Burney made their way on June 7 with their tremendous secret burning in their breasts. At first Maria was too nervous to tell him the plain truth. She tried to enlighten him with hints and hums and haws. But she succeeded only in rousing his wrath against Martin, which he expressed so strongly, 'almost calling him a Mahoon', that Maria began to kindle and ran off in a huff to her bedroom. Here she resolved to take the bull by the horns. She summoned Kitty Cook and sent her to Mr. Crisp with a saucy message: 'Mrs. Rishton sent compts. and hoped to see him at Stanhoe this summer'. Upon receiving the message Mr. Crisp came in haste to the girls' bedroom. An extraordinary scene then took place. Maria knelt on the floor and hid her face in the bedclothes. Mr. Crisp commanded her to tell the truth—was she indeed Mrs. Rishton? Maria could not speak. Kitty Cook 'claw'd hold of her left hand and shew'd him the ring'. Then Susan produced two letters from Martin which proved the fact beyond doubt. They had been married legally. They were man and wife. If that were so, there was only one thing to be done, Mr. Crisp declared—Mrs. Burney must be informed and the marriage must be made public at once. He behaved with all the sense and decision of a man of the world. He wrote to Maria's mother—he explained the whole situation. On getting the letter Mrs. Burney was extremely angry. She received the couple—she could do nothing else—but she never liked Martin and she never altogether forgave her daughter. However, the deed was done, and now the young couple had nothing to do but to settle down to enjoy the delights which they had snatched so impetuously.

All now depended, for those who loved Maria—and Fanny Burney loved her very dearly—upon the character of Martin Rishton. Was he, as Mr. Crisp almost said, a

Mahoon? Or was he, as his sister openly declared, a Bashaw?
Would he make her happy or would he not? The discerning
and affectionate eyes of Fanny were now turned observingly
upon Martin to find out. And yet it was very difficult to
find out anything for certain. He was a strange mixture. He
was high-spirited; he was 'prodigiously agreeable'. But he
was somehow, with his talk of vulgarity and distinction,
rather exacting—he liked his wife to do him credit. For
example, the Rishtons went on to take the waters at Bath,
and there were the usual gaieties in progress. Fischer was
giving a concert, and the eldest Miss Linley was singing,
perhaps for the last time. All Bath would be there. But poor
Maria sat alone in the lodgings writing to Fanny, and the
reason she gave was a strange one. Martin, 'who is rather
more exact about dress than I am, can't think of my
appearing' unless she bought a 'suit of mignionet linen
fringed for second mourning' to go in. She refused; the
dress was too expensive; 'and as he was unwilling I should
appear else, I gave up the dear Fischer—see what a cruel
thing to have a sposo who is rather a p-p-y in those sort of
things'. So there she sat alone; and she hated Bath; and
she found servants such a nuisance—she had had to dismiss
the butler already. At the same time, she was head over
heels in love with her Rishy, and one would like to suppose
that the tiff about the dress was made up by the present of
Romeo, the remarkably fine brown Pomeranian dog, which
Martin bought for a large sum at this time and gave her.
Martin himself had a passion for dogs.

It was no doubt in order to gratify his love of sport and
Maria's dislike of towns that they moved on later that
spring to Teignmouth, or as Maria calls it, to 'Tingmouth',
in Devon. The move was entirely to her liking. Her letters
gushed and burbled, had fewer stops and more dashes than
ever, as she endeavoured to describe the delights of Tingmouth to Fanny in London. Their cottage was 'one of the
neatest Thatch'd cottages you ever saw'. It belonged to a
sea captain. It was full of china glass flowers that he had
brought home from his voyages. It was hung with prints

from the Prayer-book and the Bible. There were also two pictures, one said to be by Raphael, the other by Correggio. The Miss Minifies might have described it as a retreat for a heroine. It looked on to a green. The fisher-people were simple and happy. Their cottages were clean and their children were healthy. The sea was full of whiting, salmon, and young mackerel. Martin had bought a brace of beautiful spaniels. It was a great diversion to make them go into the water. 'Indeed, we intend getting a very large Newfoundland dog before we leave this place.' And they intended to go for expeditions and take their dinner with them. And Fanny must come. Nothing could serve them but that Fanny should come and stay. It was monstrous for her to say that she must stop at home and copy her father's manuscripts. She must come at once; and if she came she need not spend a penny, for Maria wore nothing but a common linen gown and had not had her hair dressed once since she came here. In short, Fanny must come.

Thus solicited, Fanny arrived some time in July, 1773, and for almost two months lodged in the boxroom—the other rooms were so littered with dogs and poultry that they had to put her in the boxroom—and observed the humours of Tingmouth society and the moods of the lovers. There could be no doubt that they were still very much in love, but the truth was that Tingmouth was very gay. A great many families made it their summer resort; there were the Phippses and the Hurrels and the Westerns and the Colbournes; there was Mr. Crispen—perhaps the most distinguished man in Tingmouth—Mr. Green who lodged with Mr. Crispen and Miss Bowdler. Naturally, in so small a place, everybody knew everybody. The Phippses, the Hurrels, the Rishtons, the Colbournes, Mr. Crispen, Mr. Green and Miss Bowdler must meet incessantly. They must make up parties to go to the wrestling matches, and attend the races in their whiskeys, and see the country people run after a pig whose tail had been cut off. Much coming and going was inevitable; but, as Fanny soon observed, it was not altogether to Martin's liking. 'They will soon make this as errant a public place as Bristol Hotwells or any other place,' he grumbled. He had nothing whatever to say against the Phippses or the Westerns; he had the greatest respect for the Hurrels, which was odd, considering how very fat and greedy Mr. Hurrel was; Mr. Crispen, of course, who lived at Bath and spoke Italian perfectly, one must respect; but the fact was, Martin confided to Fanny, that he 'almost detested' Miss Bowdler. Miss Bowdler came of a respectable family. Her brother was destined to edit Shakespeare. Her family were old friends of the Allens. One could not forbid her the house; in fact she was always in and out of it; and yet, said Martin, 'he could not endure even the sight of her'. 'A woman', said Martin, 'who despises the customs and manners of the country she lives in, must, consequently, conduct herself with impropriety.' And, indeed, she did. For though she was only twenty-six she had come to Tingmouth alone; and then she made no secret of the fact, indeed she avowed it quite openly 'in the fair face of day', that she visited Mr. Crispen in his lodgings, and not merely paid a call but stayed to supper. Nobody had 'the most distant shadow of doubt of Miss Bowdler's being equally innocent with those who have more worldly prudence' but at the same time nobody could doubt that Miss Bowdler found the society of gentlemen more entertaining than that of ladies—or could deny that though Mr. Crispen was old, Mr. Green who lodged with him was young. Then, of course, she came on to the Rishtons and encouraged Maria in her least desirable attribute—her levity, her love of chaff, her carelessness of dress and deportment. It was deplorable.

Fanny Burney liked Martin very much and listened to his complaints with sympathy; but for all her charm and distinction, indeed because of them, she was destined unfortunately to make matters worse. Among her gifts she had the art of being extremely attractive to elderly gentlemen. Soon Mr. Crispen was paying her outrageous attentions. 'Little Burney' he said was irresistible; the name of Burney would be found—with many others, Miss Bowdler interjected—

cut upon his heart. Mr. Crispen must implore one kiss. It was said of course in jest, but Miss Bowdler took it of course in earnest. Had she not nursed Mr. Crispen through a dangerous illness? Had she not sacrificed her maidenly reputation by visiting him in his cottage? And then Martin, who had been perhaps already annoyed by Mr. Crispen's social predominance, found it galling in the extreme to have that gentleman always in the house, always paying out-rageous compliments to his guest. Anything that 'led to-wards flirtation' he disliked; and soon Mr. Crispen had become, Fanny observed, almost as odious as Miss Bowdler. He threw himself into the study of Italian grammar; he read aloud to Maria and Fanny from the *Faery Queen*, 'omitting whatever, to the poet's great disgrace, has crept in that is improper for a woman's ear'. But what with Miss Bowdler, Mr. Crispen, the Tingmothians and the influence of un-desirable acquaintances upon his wife, there can be no doubt that Martin was very uncomfortable at Tingmouth, and when the time came, on September 17, to say good-bye he appeared 'in monstrous spirits'. Perhaps everybody was glad that the summer was at an end. They were glad to say good-bye and glad to be able to say it in civil terms. Mr. Crispen left for Bath; and Miss Bowdler—there is no rash-ness in the assumption—left, for Bath also.

The Rishtons proceeded in their whiskey with all their dogs to visit the Westerns, one of the few families with whom Martin cared to associate. But the journey was unfortunate. They began by taking the wrong turning, then they ran over Tingmouth, the Newfoundland dog, who was running under the body of the whiskey. Then at Oxford Maria longed to see the colleges, but feeling sure that Martin's pride would be hurt at showing himself in a whiskey with a wife where in the old days he had 'shone forth a gay bachelor with a phaeton and four bays', she refused his offer to take her, and had her hair dressed, very badly, instead. Off they went again, and again they ran over two more dogs. Worst of all, when they arrived at the Westerns' they found the whole house shut up and the Westerns gone to Buckinghamshire. Altogether it was an unfortunate expedition. And it is impossible, as one reads Maria's breathless volubility to Fanny, to resist the conviction that the journey with its accidents and mistakes, with its troop of dogs, and Martin's pride, and Maria's fears and her recourse to the hairdresser and the hairdresser's ill success, and Martin's memories of gay bachelor days and phaetons and bay horses and his respect for the Westerns and his love of servants was typical of the obscure years of married life that were now to succeed each other at Stanhoe, in Norfolk.

At Stanhoe they lived the lives of country gentry. They repaired the ancient house, though they had but the lease of it. They planted and cleaned and cut new walks in the garden. They bought a cow and started a dairy for Maria. Dog was added to dog—rare dogs, wonderful dogs, spaniels, lurchers, Portugal pointers from the banks of the Dowrow. To keep up the establishment as establishments should be kept up, nine servants, in Martin's opinion, were none too many. And so, though she had no children, Maria found that all her time was occupied with her household and the care of her establishment. But how far better, she wrote, to be active like this instead of leading 'the loitering life' she had led at Tingmouth! Surely, Maria continued, scribbling her heart out ungrammatically to Fanny Burney, 'there are pleasures for every station and employment', and one cannot be bored if 'as I hope I am acting properly'; so that in sober truth she did not envy Fanny Lord Stanhope's *fête-champêtre*, since she had her chickens and her dairy, and Tingmouth, who had had the distemper, must be led out on a string. Why, then, regret Miss Bowdler and Mr. Crispen and the sport and gaiety of the old days at Tingmouth? Nevertheless, the old days kept coming back to her mind. At Tingmouth, she reflected, they had only kept a man and a maid. Here they had nine servants, and the more there are the more 'cabally and insolent' they become. And then relations came over from Lynn and pried into her kitchen and made her more 'bashful', as Martin would say, than ever. And then if she sat down to her tambour for half an hour Martin, 'who is I believe the Most Active Creature alive', would burst in and say. 'Come Maria, you must go with me and see how charmingly Damon hunts'—or he would say 'I know of a pheasant's nest about two miles off, you shall go and see it'.

'Then away we trail broiling over Cornfields—and when we come to the pit some Unlucky boy has Stole the Eggs . . . then I spend Whole Mornings seeing him Shoot Rooks— grub up trees—and at night for we never come in now till Nine o'clock—when tea is over and I have settled my accounts or done some company business—bed-time Comes.'

Bedtime had come; and the day had been somehow disappointing.

How could she mend matters? How could she save money so that Martin could buy the phaeton upon which his heart had been set ever since they were married? She might save on dress, for she did not mind what she wore; but alas; Martin was very particular still; he did not like her to dress in linen. So she must manage better in the house, and she was not formed to manage servants. Thus she began to dwell upon those happy days before she had gone to Tingmouth, before she had married, before she had nine servants and a phaeton and ever so many dogs. She began to brood over that still more distant time when she had first known the Burneys and they had sat 'browsing over my little [fire] and eating good things out of the closet by the fire side'. Her thoughts turned to all those friends whom she had lost, to that 'lovd society which I remember with the greatest pleasure'; and she could never forget in particular the paternal kindness of Dr. Burney. Oh, she sighed as she sat alone in Norfolk among the pheasants and the fields, how she wished that 'none of my family had ever quitted his sheltering roof till placed under the protection of a worthy husband'. For her own marriage—but enough; they had been very much in love; they had been very happy; she must go and do her hair; she must try to please her Rishy. And so the obscure history of the Rishtons fades away, save what is preserved by the sprightly pen of Maria's half-sister in the pages of *Evelina*. And yet—the reflection will occur—if Fanny had seen more of Maria, and more of Mr. Crispen and even more of Miss Bowdler and the Tingmouth set, her later books, had they been less refined, might have been as amusing as her first.

Money and Love[1]

STEEP though the ascent may be, the reward is ours when we stand on the top of the hill; stout though the biography undoubtedly is, the prospect falls into shape directly we have found the connecting word. The diligent reader of memoirs seeks it on every page—never rests until he has found it. Is it love or ambition, commerce, religion, or sport? It may be none of these, but something deep sunk beneath the surface, scattered in fragments, disguised behind frippery. Whatever it be, wherever it be, once found there is no biography without its form, no figure without its force. Stumbling and blundering in the first volume of Mr. Coleridge's life of Thomas Coutts,[2] we laid hands at length upon two words which between them licked rather a portly subject into shape, doing their work, as might be expected from their opposite natures, first this side, then that, until what with a blow here and a blow there poor Thomas Coutts was almost buffeted to death. Yet the friction kept him alive; he lived, in an emaciated condition, to the age of eighty-six. And of the two words one is money and the other is love.

Love in the first place had it all its own way. He married his brother's servant, Susannah Starkie, a woman older than himself. If he had been a poor man the marriage would have been thought sensible enough and the wife, one may be sure, would have come in for a word of praise from the biographers. But as he was always a rich man, and became eventually the richest man in the whole of England, it was incumbent on Thomas Coutts to prove that the Starkies, though now declined, were descended from the ancient family of the Starkies of Leigh and Pennington, and it is inevitable that we should inquire whether Mrs. Coutts broke

[1] *The Athenaeum*, March 12, 1920.
[2] *The Life of Thomas Coutts, Banker*, by Ernest Hartley Coleridge.

205

her heart and lost her wits 'beneath the burden of an honour
to which she was not born'. There is no doubt that she lost
her wits. Her heart, one must suppose, since no sound of
its breakage has escaped, was smothered to death. She is
scarcely mentioned. Perhaps she dropped her aitches. Perhaps it was as much as she could do to stand upright at the
top of the staircase in Stratton Street and shake hands with
the Royal Dukes without displaying her origin. She contrived never to give offence and never to attract attention;
and, from a housemaid, what more could be expected? Save
for one sinister gleam when she speaks a whole sentence in
her proper person, it is all dark and dim and decorous. She
had her children, it is true; of whom three daughters survived. But the children were heiresses, and must be sent to
fashionable schools, where Mr. Coutts, more ambitious for
them than for himself, hinted his wish that they should make
friends with the daughters of Lord George Sutton, 'as I
should like them to be acquainted with honest people'. They
had a French Countess of the old nobility for their governess.
From their birth onwards they were swathed and swaddled
in money.

In his office in the Strand, year in, year out, Thomas
Coutts made his fortune by methods which will be plain
enough to some readers and must remain a matter of mystery to others. He was a hard-headed man of business; he
was indefatigable; he 'knew how to be complaisant and how
and when to assert his independence'; he was judicious in
the floating of Government loans; and he lived within his
means. We may accept Mr. Coleridge's summary of his
business career, and take his word for it that the rolling up
of money went forward uneventfully enough. To the out-
sider there is a certain grimness in the spectacle. Who is
master and who is slave? The two seem mixed in bitter
conflict of some sort—such groans escape him now and then,
and the lean, wire-drawn face, with the tight-closed lips and
the anxious eyes, wears such an expression of nervous apprehension. Once, when he was driving with his old friend
Colonel Crawfurd, he sat silent hour after hour, and the

Colonel, reaching home, wrote in a fury to demand an explanation of 'this silent contempt', which in another would have demanded sword or pistol. 'It is too, too foolish', exclaimed poor Coutts; the truth was merely that 'my spirit's gone, and my mind worn and harras'd', and 'I am now rather an object of pity than resentment'.

But whatever secret anguish compelled the richest man in England to drive hour after hour in silence, there were also amenities and privileges attached to his state which lightened the office gloom and tinged the ledgers with radiance. The reader becomes aware of a curious note in the tone in which his correspondents address him. There is an intimate, agonized strain in all their voices. His correspondents were some of the greatest people in the land; yet they wrote generally with their own hands, and often added the injunction: 'Burn this Letter the moment it is read' . . . 'Name it not to my Lord', this particular document continues, 'or to any creature on earth'. For royal as they were, beautiful, highly gifted, they were all in straits for money; all came to Thomas Coutts; all approached him as suppliants and sinners beseeching his help and confessing their follies as if he were something between doctor and priest. He heard from Lady Chatham the story of her distress when the payment of Chatham's pension was delayed; he bestowed £10,000 upon Charles James Fox, and earned his effusive gratitude; the Royal Dukes laid their said circumstances before him; Georgiana, Duchess of Devonshire, confessed her gambling losses, called him her dear friend and died in his debt. Lady Hester Stanhope thundered and growled melodiously enough from the top of Mount Lebanon. Naturally, then, Thomas Coutts had only to say what he wanted, and some very powerful people bestirred themselves to get it for him. He wanted introductions for his daughters among the French nobility; he wanted George the Fourth to bank with him; he wanted the King's leave to drive his carriage through St. James's Park. But he wanted some things that not even the Duchess of Devonshire could procure. He wanted health; he wanted a son-in-law.

There was, Mr. Coleridge says, 'a singular dearth of suitors for his daughters and his ducats'. Was it that Mrs. Coutts had in her housemaid days thrown soapsuds over Lord Dundonald? Or was it that the presence of madness in the Coutts family showed itself unmistakably in the frequent 'nervous complaints' of the three sisters? At any rate, Sophia, the youngest, was nineteen when she became engaged to Francis Burdett; and heiresses presumably should be wearing their coronets years before that. Then her two elder sisters pledged their affections suitably enough. But love always came among the Couttses wearing the mask of tragedy or comedy, or both together in grotesque combination. The two young men, thus singled out, against all advice and entreaty rushed the Falls of Schaffhausen in an open punt. Both were drowned. Two years later Susan recovered sufficiently to marry Lord Guilford, and after mourning for seven years Fanny accepted Lord Bute; but Lord Bute was a widower of fifty-six with nine children, and Lord Guilford fell from his horse 'when in the act of presenting a basket of fruit to Miss Coutts', and so injured his spine that he languished in bodily suffering for years before, prematurely, he died.

But from all those impressions and turns of phrase which, more than any statement of facts, shape life in biographies as they do in reality, we are convinced that Thomas Coutts loved his daughters intensely and sincerely, pitying their sufferings, devising pleasures and comforts for them, and sometimes, perhaps, wishing to be assured that when all was said and done they were happy, which, upon the same evidence, it is easy to guess that they were not. Even in these days Sir Francis Burdett caused his father-in-law some anxiety. The following extract hints the reason of it:

Going to Piccadilly yesterday at two o'clock, I met Mr. Burdett. . . . I asked him where he was going . . . I asked him if he had been under any engagement to Mr. Whitefoord, upon which, to do him justice, he blushed—and, with great signs of astonishment, confessed that he had entirely forgot it, though he had particularly remembered it the day before . . . To us, *exact people*, these things seem strange.

Probably Mr. Coutts was not altogether surprised to find that a man who was capable of forgetting an enagement could defy the House of Commons, stand a siege in his house, be taken forth by Life Guards through a crowd shouting 'Burdett for ever!' and suffer imprisonment in the Tower. Later, Coutts had to insist that his son-in-law should leave his house; but on that occasion our sympathies are with the banker. Like most people, Sir Francis lost his temper, his manners, his humanity, and everything decent about him when he was in danger of losing a legacy. But for the present the legacies were secure, and the surface of life was splendid and serene. Mr. and Mrs. Coutts lived in the great house in Stratton Street; they travelled from one fine country seat to another, the guests of a Duke here, of an Earl there; their wealth increased and increased, and Thomas Coutts was consulted upon delicate matters by Prime Ministers and Kings. He acted as ambassador between the House of Hanover and the House of Stuart— almost equally to his delight, he transmitted winter petticoats from Paris to Devonshire House.

But the splendid surface had deep cracks in it, and when William the Fourth dined with the Couttses, Mrs. Coutts— so he declared—would always whisper to him on the way downstairs, 'Sir, are you not George the Third's *father?*' 'I always answered in the affirmative,' said the King . . . 'there's no use contradicting women, young or old, eh?' She was losing her wits. For the last ten years of her life she was out of her mind. But old Coutts would have her lead the King down to dinner, and would tend her faithfully himself when doctors and daughters besought him to put her under control. He was a devoted husband.

At the same time he was a devoted lover. During the ten years that Mrs. Coutts was going from bad to worse and being tenderly cared for by her husband, he was lavishing horses, carriages, villas, sums in the 'Long Annuities', upon a young actress in Little Russell Street. The paradox has disturbed his biographers. Leaving to others the task of determining how far the relation between the old banker and the young woman was immoral, we must admit that we like him all the better for it; more, it seems to prove that he loved his wife. For the first time he hears the birds at dawn and notices the spring leaves. Like his Harriot, birds and leaves seem to him innocent and fresh.

> You who can look to Heaven with so much pleasure and so pure a heart must have great pleasure in viewing such beautiful skies . . . eat light nourishing food—mutton roast and broiled is the best—porter is not good for you . . . I kiss the paper you are to look upon and beg you to kiss it just here. Your dear lips will then have touched what mine touch just now. . . . The estate of Otham, you see, I have enquired about. Your 3 p. ct. Consol and Long Annuity. . . .

So it goes on from birds to flannel night-caps, from eternal devotion to profitable investments; but the strain that links together all these diverse notes is his recurring and constant adoration for Harriot's 'pure, innocent, honest, kind, affectionate heart'. It was a terrible blow to his daughters and sons-in-law to find that at his age he was capable of entertaining such illusions. When it came out that, four days after Mrs. Coutts was buried, the old gentleman of seventy-nine had hurried off to St. Pancras Church and married himself (illegally, as it turned out, by one of those misadventures which always beset the Coutts family when they were in love) to an actress of no birth and robust physique, the lamentations that rent the family in twain were bitter in the extreme. What would become of his money? As they could not ask this openly, they took the more roundabout way of 'imputing to the servants' at Stratton Street that Mrs. Coutts was poisoning her husband and was in the habit of receiving men in her bedroom when half-undressed. Coutts replied to his daughters and his sons-in-law in bitter, agitated letters which make painful, though spirited, reading after a hundred years. How they tortured him! How they grudged him his happiness! How grateful he would have been for a word of sympathy! Still, he had his Harriot, and though she was only gone into the next room, he must write her a letter to say how he loves her and trusts her and begs her not to mind the spiteful things that his family say about her. 'Your constant, happy, and most affectionate husband' he signs himself, and she invokes 'My beloved Tom!' Indeed, Harriot deserved every penny she got, and we rejoice to think that she got them all. She was a generous woman. She was bountiful to her stepdaughters; she was always burying broken-down actors in luxury, and putting up marble tablets to their memories; and she married a Duke. But every year of her life she drove down to Little Russell Street, got out of her carriage, dismissed her servants, and walked along the dirty lane to have a look at the house where she had begun life as 'a poor little player child'. And once, long after Tom was dead, she dreamed of Tom, and noted on the flyleaf of her Prayer Book how he had come to her looking 'well, tranquil, and divine. He anxiously desired me to change my shoes', which was, no doubt, true to the life; but in the dream it was 'for fear of taking cold, as I had walked through waters to him', which somehow touches us as if Tom and Harriot had walked through bitter waters to rescue their little fragment of love from all that money.

The Dream[1]

THIS is a depressing book.[2] It leaves one with a feeling not of humiliation, that is too strong a word, nor of disgust, that is too strong also. It makes us feel—it is to Mr. Bullock's credit as a biographer—that we have been watching a stout white dog performing tricks in front of an audience which eggs it on, but at the same time jeers. There is nothing in the life and death of a best-seller that need cause us this queasiness. The lives of those glorious geese Florence Barclay and Ella Wheeler Wilcox can be read without a blush for them or for ourselves. They were performers too— conjurors who tumbled bank notes, billiard balls, fluttering pigeons out of very seedy hats. But they lived, and they lived with such gusto that no one can fail to share it. With Marie Corelli it was different.

Her life began with a trick and rather a shady trick. The editor of the *Illustrated London News*, a married man, 'wandering round Stratford-on-Avon church' fell in love with a woman. That bald statement must be draped. Dr. Mackay committed an immoral act with a female who was not of his own social standing. 'This unwelcome flowering of his lighter moments', as Mr. Bullock calls it—Corelliism is catching—was a child. But she was not called Marie and she was not called Corelli. Those were names that she invented later to drape the fact. Most of her childhood was spent draping facts in the 'Dream Hole', a mossy retreat in a dell at Box Hill. Sometimes George Meredith appeared for a moment among the tendrils. But she never saw him. Wrapped in what she called later 'the flitting phantasmagoria of the universal dream' she saw only one person— herself. And that self, sometimes called Thelma, sometimes

[1] *The Listener*, February 15, 1940.
[2] *Marie Corelli: The Life & Death of a Best-Seller*, by George Bullock.

Mavis Clare, draped in white satin, hung with pure lilies, and exhibited twice a year in stout volumes for which the public paid her ten thousand pounds apiece, is as damning an indictment of Victorian taste in one way as the Albert Memorial is in another. Of those two excrescences, perhaps that which we call Marie Corelli is the more painful. The Albert Memorial is empty; but within the other erection was a live human being. It was not her fault; society blew that golden bubble, as Miss Corelli herself might have written, from the black seed of shame. She was ashamed of her mother. She was ashamed of her birth. She was ashamed of her face, of her accent, of her poverty. Most girls, as empty-headed and commonplace as she was, would have shared her shame, but they would have hidden it—under the table-cloth, behind the chiffonier. But nature had endowed her with a prodigious power of making public confession of this small ignoble vice. Instead of hiding herself she exposed herself. From her earliest days she had a rage for publicity. 'I'll be "somebody"', she told her governess. 'I'll be as unlike anybody else as I can!' 'That would hardly be wise,' said Miss Knox placidly. 'You would then be called eccentric.' But Miss Knox need not have been afraid. Marie Corelli did not wish to be unlike anybody else; she wanted to be as like everybody else in general, and the British aristocracy in particular, as it was possible to be. But to attain that object she had only one weapon—the dream. Dreams, apparently, if made of the right material, can be astonishingly effective. She dreamt so hard, she dreamt so efficiently, that with two exceptions all her dreams came true. Not even Marie Corelli could dream her shifty half-brother into the greatest of English poets, though she worked hard to 'get him made Poet Laureate', or transform her very dubious father into an eminent Victorian man of letters. All that she could do for Dr. Mackay was to engage the Caledonian pipers to play at his funeral and to postpone that function from a foggy day to a fine one in order that his last appearance might be given full publicity. Otherwise all her dreams materialized. Ponies, motor-cars, dresses, houses furnished 'like the tea lounge at the Earl's Court Exhibition', gondolas, expensively-bound editions of Shakespeare —all were hers. Cheques accumulated. Invitations showered. The Prince of Wales held her hand in his. 'Out of small things what wonders rise', he murmured. Gladstone called on her and stayed for two hours. '*Ardath*', he is reported to have said, 'is a magnificent conception.' On Easter Sunday the Dean of Westminster quoted *Barabbas* from the pulpit. No words, the Dean said, could be more beautiful. Rostand translated her novels. The whole audience at Stratford-on-Avon rose to its feet when she came into the theatre.

All her dreams came true. But it was the dream that killed her. For inside that ever-thickening carapace of solid dream the commonplace vigorous little woman gradually ceased to live. She became harder, duller, more prudish, more conventional; and at the same time more envious and more uneasy. The only remedy that revived her was publicity. And like other drug-takers she could only live by increasing the dose. Her tricks became more and more extravagant. On May Day she drove through the streets behind ponies wreathed in flowers; she floated down the Avon in a gondola called *The Dream* with a real gondolier in a scarlet sash. The press resounded with her lawsuits, her angry letters, her speeches. And then even the Press turned nasty. They omitted to say that she had been present at the Braemar gathering. They gave full publicity to the fact that she had been caught hoarding sugar.

For her there is some excuse. But how are we to excuse the audience that applauded the exhibition. Queen Victoria and Mr. Gladstone can be excepted. The taste of the exalted is apt to become dropsical. And there is excuse for 'the million', as Marie Corelli called them—if her books saved one working-man from suicide, or allowed a dressmaker's drudge here and there to dream that she, too, was Thelma or Mavis Clare, there were not films then to sustain them with plush and glow and rapture after the day's work. But what are we to say of Oscar Wilde? His compliments may have been ambiguous; but he paid them, and he printed her stories. And what are we to say of the great ladies of her adored aristocracy? 'She is a common little thing', one of them remarked. But no lunch or dinner party was complete without her. And what are we to say of Mr. Arthur Severn? 'Pendennis' she called him. He accepted her hospitality, tolerated that effusion which she was pleased to call her passion, and then made fun of her accent. 'Ouwels', she said instead of 'owls', and he laughed at her. And what are we to say of the press that levelled all its cameras at the stout old woman who was ashamed of her birth, 'got busy' about her mother—was her name Cody or was it Kirtland? —was she a bricklayer's daughter or an Italian countess?— who had borne this illegitimate child?

But though it would be a relief to end in a burst of right-eous indignation, the worst of this book is that it provokes no such glow, but only the queasiness with which we watch a decked-up dog performing rather ordinary tricks. It is a relief when the performance is over. Only, unfortunately, that is not altogether the fact. For, still at Stratford-on-Avon, Mason Croft is kept precisely as it was when Marie Corelli lived there. There is the silver ink-pot still full of ink as she left it; the hands of the clock still point to 7.15 as they did when she died; all her manuscripts are carefully preserved under glass cases; and the 'large, empty bed, covered with a heavy white quilt, which is more awe-inspiring than a corpse, as a scarcely clothed dancer excites more than does a nude' awaits the dreamer. So Stratford-on-Avon, along with other relics, preserves a lasting monument to the taste of the Victorian Age.

The Fleeting Portrait

1. *Waxworks at the Abbey* [1]

NOBODY but a very great man could have worn the Duke of Wellington's top hat. It is as tall as a chimney, as straight as a ramrod, as black as a rock. One could have seen it a mile off advancing indomitably down the street. It must have been to this emblem of incorruptible dignity that the Duke raised his two fingers when passers-by respectfully saluted him. One is almost tempted to salute it now.

The connexion between the waxworks in the Abbey and the Duke of Wellington's top hat is one that the reader will discover if he goes to the Abbey when the waxworks are shut. The waxworks have their hours of audience like other potentates. And if that hour is four and it is now a trifle past two, one may spend the intervening moments profitably in the United Services Museum in Whitehall, among cannon and torpedos and gun-carriages and helmets and spurs and faded uniforms and the thousand other objects which piety and curiosity have saved from time and treasured and numbered and stuck in glass cases forever. When the time comes to go, indeed, there is not as much contrast as one would wish, perhaps, between the Museum at one end of Whitehall and the Abbey at the other. Too many monuments solicit attention with outstretched hands; too many placards explain this and forbid that; too many sightseers shuffle and stare for the past and the dead and the mystic nature of the place to have full sway. Solitude is impossible. Do we wish to see the Chapels? We are shepherded in flocks by gentlemen in black gowns who are for ever locking us in or locking us out; round whom we press and gape; from whom drop

[1] *The New Republic*, April 11, 1928.

raucously all kinds of dry unappetizing facts; how much beauty this tomb has; how much age that; when they were destroyed; by whom they were restored and what the cost was—until everybody longs to be let off a tomb or two and is thankful when the lesson hour is over. However, if one is very wicked, and very bored, and lags a little behind; if the key is left in the door and turns quite easily, so that after all it is an open question whether one has broken one's country's laws or not, then one can slip aside, run up a little dark stair-case and find oneself in a very small chamber alone with Queen Elizabeth.

The Queen dominates the room as she once dominated England. Leaning a little forward so that she seems to beckon you to come to her, she stands, holding her sceptre in one hand, her orb in the other. It is a drawn, anguished figure, with the pursed look of someone who goes in per-petual dread of poison or of trap; yet forever braces herself to meet the terror unflinchingly. Her eyes are wide and vigilant; her nose thin as the beak of a hawk; her lips shut tight; her eyebrows arched; only the jowl gives the fine drawn face its massiveness. The orb and the sceptre are held in the long thin hands of an artist, as if the fingers thrilled at the touch of them. She is immensely intellectual, suffering, and tyrannical. She will not allow one to look elsewhere.

Yet in fact the little room is crowded. There are many hands here holding other sceptres and orbs. It is only beside Queen Elizabeth that the rest of the company seems insig-nificant. Flowing in velvet they fill their glass cases, as they once filled their thrones, with dignity. William and Mary are an amiable pair of monarchs; bazaar-opening, hospital-inspecting, modern; though the King, unfortunately, is a little short in the legs. Queen Anne fondles her orb in her lap with plump womanly hands that should have held a baby there. It is only by accident that they have clapped a great crown on her hair and told her to rule a kingdom, when she would so much rather have flirted discreetly—she was a pretty woman; or run to greet her husband smiling—

she was a kindly one. Her type of beauty in its homeliness, its domesticity, comes down to us less impaired by time than the grander style. The Duchess of Richmond, who gave her face to Britannia on the coins, is out of fashion now. Only the carriage of the little head on the long neck, and the simper and the still look of one who has always stood still to be looked at assure us that she was beautiful once and had lovers beyond belief. The parrot sitting on its perch in the corner of the case seems to make its ironical comment on all that. Once only are we reminded of the fact that these effigies were moulded from the dead and that they were laid upon coffins and carried through the streets. The young Duke of Buckingham who died at Rome of consumption is the only one of them who has resigned himself to death. He lies very still with the ermine on his shoulders and the coronet on his brows, but his eyes are shut; his nose is a great peak between two sunk cheeks; he has succumbed to death and lies steeped in its calm. His aloofness compares strangely with the carnality of Charles the Second round the corner. King Charles still seems quivering with the passions and the greeds of life. The great lips are still pouting and watering and asking for more. The eyes are pouched and creased with all the long nights they have watched out—the torches, the dancing, and the women. In his dirty feathers and lace he is the very symbol of voluptuousness and dissipation, and his great blue-veined nose seems an irreverence on the part of the modeller, as if to set the crowd, as the procession comes by, nudging each other in the ribs and telling merry stories of the monarch.

And so from this garish bright assembly we run down-stairs again into the Abbey, and enter that strange muddle and miscellany of objects both hallowed and ridiculous. Yet now the impression is less tumultuous than before. Two presences seem to control its incoherence, as sometimes a chattering group of people is ordered and quieted by the entry of someone before whom, they know not why, they fall silent. One is Elizabeth, beckoning; the other is an old top-hat.

2. *The Royal Academy* [1]

'The motor-cars of Empire—the bodyguard of Europe—
the stainless knight of Belgium'—such is our English romance
that nine out of ten of those passing from the indiscriminate
variety of Piccadilly to the courtyard of Burlington House
do homage to the embattled tyres and the kingly presence of
Albert on his high-minded charger with some nonsense of
this sort. They are, of course, only the motor-cars of the
rich grouped round a statue; but whether the quadrangle in
which they stand radiates back the significance of everything
fourfold, so that King Albert and the motor-cars exude the
essence of kingliness and the soul of vehicular traffic, or
whether the crowd is the cause of it, or the ceremonious
steps leading up, the swing-doors admitting and the flunkeys
fawning, it is true that, once you are within the precincts,
everything appears symbolic, and the state of mind in which
you ascend the broad stairs to the picture galleries is both
heated and romantic.

Whatever visions we may have indulged, we find ourselves on entering confronted by a lady in full evening dress.
She stands at the top of a staircase, one hand loosely closed
round a sheaf of lilies, while the other is about to greet
someone of distinction who advances towards her up the
stairs. Not a hair is out of place. Her lips are just parted.
She is about to say, 'How nice of you to come!' But such is
the skill of the artist that one does not willingly cross the
range of her cordial and yet condescending eye. One prefers
to look at her obliquely. She said, 'How nice of you to
come!' so often and so graciously while I stood there that at
last my eye wandered off in search of people of sufficient
distinction for her to say it to. There was no difficulty in
finding them. Here was a nobleman in a kilt, the Duke of
R——; here a young officer in khaki, and, to keep him
company, the head and shoulders of a young girl, whose
upturned eyes and pouting lips appear to be entreating the

---

[1] *The Athenaeum*, August 22, 1919.

sky to be bluer, roses to be redder, ices to be sweeter, and men to be manlier for her sake. To do her justice, the gallant youth seemed to respond. As they stepped up the staircase to the lady in foaming white he vowed that come what might— the flag of England—sweet chimes of home—a woman's honour—an Englishman's word—only a scrap of paper— for your sake, Alice—God save the King—and all the rest of it. The range of her vocabulary was more limited. She kept her gaze upon the sky or the ice or whatever it might be with a simple sincerity which was enforced by a single row of pearls and a little drapery of white tulle about the shoulders. 'How nice of you to come!' said the hostess once more. But immediately behind them stumped the Duke, a bluff nobleman, 'more at home on the brae-side than among these kickshaws and knick-knacks, my lady. Splendid sport. Twenty antlers and Buck Royal. Clean between the eyes, eh what? Out all day. Never know when I'm done. Cold bath, hard bed, glass of whiskey. A mere nothing. Damned foreigners. Post of duty. The Guard dies, but never surrenders. The ladies of our family—Up, Guards, and at them! Gentlemen—' and, as he utters the last words in a voice choked with emotion, the entire company swing round upon their heels, displaying only a hind view of their perfectly fitting mess-jackets, since there are some sights that it is not good for man to look upon.

The scene, though not all the phrases, comes from a story by Rudyard Kipling. But scenes from Rudyard Kipling must take place with astonishing frequency at these parties in order that the English maidens and gallant officers may have occasion to insist upon their chastity on the one hand and protect it on the other, without which, so far as one can see, there would be no reason for their existence. Therefore it was natural to look about me, a little shyly, for the sinister person of the seducer. There is, I can truthfully say, no such cur in the whole of the Royal Academy; and it was only when I had gone through the rooms twice and was about to inform the maiden that her apprehensions, though highly creditable, were in no way necessary that my eye was caught by the white underside of an excessively fine fish. 'The Duke caught that!' I exclaimed, being still within the radius of the ducal glory. But I was wrong. Though fine enough, the fish, as a second glance put it beyond a doubt, was not ducal; its triangular shape, let alone the fact that a small urchin in corduroys held it suspended by the tail, was enough to start me in the right direction. Ah, yes—the harvest of the sea, toilers of the deep, a fisherman's home, nature's bounty—such phrases formed themselves with alarming rapidity—but to descend to details. The picture, No. 306, represents a young woman holding a baby on her knee. The child is playing with the rough model of a ship; the large fish is being dangled before his eyes by a brother a year or two older in a pair of corduroys which have been cut down from those worn by the fisherman engaged in cleaning cod on the edge of the waves. Judging from the superb rosiness, fatness, and blueness of every object depicted, even the sea itself wearing the look of a prize animal tricked out for a fair, it seemed certain that the artist intended a compliment in a general way to the island race. But something in the woman's eye arrested me. A veil of white dimmed the straightforward lustre. It is thus that painters represent the tears that do not fall. But what, we asked, had this great hulk of a matron surrounded by fish, any one of which was worth eighteenpence the pound, to cry for? Look at the little boy's breeches. They are not, if you look closely, of the same pattern as the fisherman's. Once that fact is grasped, the story reels itself out like a line with a salmon on the end of it. Don't the waves break with a sound of mockery on the beach? Don't her eyes cloud with memories at the sight of a toy boat? It is not always summer. The sea has another voice than this; and, since her husband will never want his breeches any more—but the story when written out is painful, and rather obvious into the bargain.

The point of a good Academy picture is that you can search the canvas for ten minutes or so and still be doubtful whether you have extracted the whole meaning. There is, for example, No. 248, 'Cocaine'. A young man in evening

dress lies, drugged, with his head upon the pink satin of a
woman's knee. The ornamental clock assures us that it is
exactly eleven minutes to five. The burning lamp proves
that it is dawn. He, then, has come home to find her waiting?
She has interrupted his debauch? For my part, I prefer to
imagine what in painters' language (a tongue well worth
separate study) would be called 'a dreary vigil'. There she
has sat since eight-thirty, alone, in pink satin. Once she rose
and pressed the photograph in the silver frame to her lips.
She might have married that man (unless it is her father,
of which one cannot be sure). She was a thoughtless girl,
and he left her to meet his death on the field of battle.
Through her tears she gazes at the next photograph—presumably that of a baby (again the painter has been content
with a suggestion). As she looks a hand fumbles at the door.
'Thank God!' she cries as her husband staggers in and falls
helpless across her knees, 'thank God our Teddy died!'
So there she sits, staring disillusionment in the eyes, and
whether she gives way to temptation, or breathes a vow to
the photographs, or gets him to bed before the maid comes
down, or sits there for ever, must be left to the imagination
of the onlooker.

But the queer thing is that one wants to be her. For a
moment one pretends that one sits alone, disillusioned, in
pink satin. And then people in the little group of gazers
begin to boast that they have known sadder cases themselves. Friends of theirs took cocaine. 'I myself as a boy for
a joke—' 'No, George—but how fearfully rash!' Everyone
wished to cap that story with a better, save for one lady
who, from her expression, was acting the part of consoler,
had got the poor thing to bed, undressed her, soothed her,
and even spoken with considerable sharpness to that unworthy brute, unfit to be a husband, before she moved on in
a pleasant glow of self-satisfaction. Every picture before
which one of these little groups had gathered seemed to
radiate the strange power to make the beholder more heroic
and more romantic; memories of childhood, visions of possibilities, illusions of all kinds poured down upon us from the

walls. In a cooler mood one might accuse the painters of some exaggeration. There must be well over ten thousand delphiniums in the Royal Academy, and not one is other than a perfect specimen. The condition of the turf is beyond praise. The sun is exquisitely adapted to the needs of the sundials. The yew hedges are irreproachable; the manor house a miracle of timeworn dignity; and as for the old man with a scythe, the girl at the well, the village donkey, the widow lady, the gipsies' caravan, the boy with a rod, each is not only the saddest, sweetest, quaintest, most picturesque, tenderest, jolliest of its kind, but has a symbolical meaning much to the credit of England. The geese are English geese, and even the polar bears, though they have not that advantage, seem, such is the persuasion of the atmosphere, to be turning to carriage rugs as we look at them.

It is indeed a very powerful atmosphere; so charged with manliness and womanliness, pathos and purity, sunsets and Union Jacks, that the shabbiest and most suburban catch a reflection of the rosy glow. 'This is England! these are the English!' one might exclaim if a foreigner were at hand. But one need not say that to one's compatriots. They are, perhaps, not quite up to the level of the pictures. Some are meagre; others obese; many have put on what is too obviously the only complete outfit that they possess. But the legend on the catalogue explains any such discrepancy in a convincing manner. 'To give unto them beauty for ashes. Isaiah lxi. 3'—that is the office of this exhibition. Our ashes will be transformed if only we expose them openly enough to the benignant influence of the canvas. So we look again at the Lord Chancellor and Mr. Balfour, at the Lady B., at the Duke of R., at Mr. Ennever of the Pelman Institute, at officers of all descriptions, architects, surgeons, peers, dentists, doctors, lawyers, archbishops, roses, sundials, battlefields, fish, and Skye terriers. From wall to wall, glowing with colour, glistening with oil, framed in gilt, and protected by glass, they ogle and elevate, inspire and command. But they overdo it. One is not altogether such a bundle of ashes as they suppose, or sometimes the magic fails to work.

A large picture by Mr. Sargent called 'Gassed' at last pricked some nerve of protest, or perhaps of humanity. In order to emphasize his point that the soldiers wearing bandages round their eyes cannot see, and therefore claim our compassion, he makes one of them raise his leg to the level of his elbow in order to mount a step an inch or two above the ground. This little piece of over-emphasis was the final scratch of the surgeon's knife which is said to hurt more than the whole operation. After all, one had been jabbed and stabbed, slashed and sliced for close on two hours. The lady began it, the Duke continued it; little children had wrung tears; great men extorted veneration. From first to last each canvas had rubbed in some emotion, and what the paint failed to say the catalogue had enforced in words. But Mr. Sargent was the last straw. Suddenly the great rooms rang like a parrot-house with the intolerable vociferations of gaudy and brainless birds. How they shrieked and gibbered! How they danced and sidled! Honour, patriotism, chastity, wealth, success, importance, position, patronage, power—their cries rang and echoed from all quarters. 'Anywhere, anywhere, out of this world!' was the only exclamation with which one could stave off the brazen din as one fled downstairs, out of doors, round the motor-cars, beneath the disdain of the horse and its rider, and so out into the comparative sobriety of Piccadilly. No doubt the reaction was excessive; and I must leave it to Mr. Roger Fry to decide whether the emotions here recorded are the proper result of one thousand six hundred and seventy-four works of art.

Poe's Helen[1]

THE real interest of Miss Ticknor's volume [2] lies in the figure of Mrs. Whitman, and not in the love letters from Poe, which have already been published. It is true that if it had not been for her connexion with Poe we should never have heard of Helen Whitman; but it is also true that Poe's connexion with Mrs. Whitman was neither much to his credit nor a matter of moment to the world at large. If it were our object to enhance the charm of 'the only true romantic figure in our literature', as Miss Ticknor calls him, we should have suppressed his love letters altogether. Mrs. Whitman, on the other hand, comes very well out of the ordeal, and was evidently, apart from Poe, a curious and interesting person.

She wrote poetry from her childhood, and when in early youth she was left a widow she settled down to lead a literary life in earnest. In those days and in America this was not so simple a proceeding as it has since become. If you wrote an essay upon Shelley, for example, the most influential family in Providence considered that you had fallen from grace. If, like Mr. Ellery Channing, you went to Europe and left your wife behind, this was sufficient proof that you were not a 'great perfect man', as the true poet is bound to be. Mrs. Whitman took her stand against such crudities, and, indeed, rather went out of her way to invite attack. Whatever the fashion and whatever the season she wore her 'floating veils' and her thin slippers, and carried a fan in her hand. By means of 'inverting her lampshades' and hanging up bits of drapery her sitting-room was kept in a perpetual twilight. It was the age of the Transcendentalists, and the fans and the veils and the twilight were, no doubt, intended to mitigate

---

[1] *Times Literary Supplement*, April 5, 1917.
[2] *Poe's Helen*, by Caroline Ticknor.

the solidity of matter, and entice the soul out of the body with as little friction as possible. Nature too had been kind in endowing her with a pale, eager face, a spiritual expression, and deep-set eyes that gazed 'beyond but never at you'.

Her house became a centre for the poets of the district, for she was witty and charming as well as enthusiastic. John Hay, G. W. Curtis, and the Hon. Wilkins Updike used to send her their works to criticize, or in very long and abstruse letters tried to define what they meant by poetry. The mark of that particular set, which was more or less connected with Emerson and Margaret Fuller, was an enthusiastic championship of the rights of the soul. They ventured into a sphere where words naturally were unable to support them. 'Poetry', as Mr. Curtis said, 'is the adaption of music to an intellectual sphere. But it must therefore be revealed through souls too fine to be measured justly by the intellect. . . . Music . . . is a womanly accomplishment, because it is sentiment, and the instinct declares its nature', etc. This exalted mood never quite deserted them when they were writing about matters of fact. When Mrs. Whitman forgot to answer a letter Mr. Curtis inquired whether she was ill 'or has the autumn which lies round the horizon like a beautifully hued serpent crushing the flower of summer fascinated you to silence with its soft, calm eyes?' Mrs. Whitman, it is clear, was the person who kept them all up to this very high standard. Thus things went on until Mrs. Whitman had reached the age of forty-two. One July night, in 1845, she happened to be wandering in her garden in the moonlight when Edgar Allan Poe passed by and saw her. 'From that hour I loved you', he wrote later. '. . . your unknown heart seemed to pass into my bosom—there to dwell for ever.' The immediate result was that he wrote the verses *To Helen* which he sent her. Three years later, when he was the famous poet of *The Raven*, Mrs. Whitman replied with a valentine, of which the last stanza runs—

> *Then, oh grim and ghastly Raven*
> *Wilt thou to my heart and ear*

Be a Raven true as ever
Flapped his wings and croaked 'Despair'?
Not a bird that roams the forest
Shall our lofty eyrie share.

For some time their meeting was postponed, and no word of prose passed between them. It might have been postponed for ever had it not been for another copy of verses which Mrs. Whitman ended with the line

I dwell with 'Beauty which is Hope'.

Upon receipt of these verses Poe immediately procured a letter of introduction and set off to Providence. His declaration of love took place in the course of the next fortnight during a walk in the cemetery. Mrs. Whitman would not consent to an engagement, but she agreed to write to him, and thus the famous correspondence began.

Professor Harrison can only compare Poe's letters to the letters of Abelard and Eloise or to the *Sonnets from the Portuguese*; Miss Ticknor says that they have won themselves a niche among the world's classic love letters. Professor Woodberry, on the other hand, thinks that they should never have been published. We agree with Professor Woodberry, not because they do damage to Poe's reputation, but because we find them very tedious compositions. Whether you are writing a review or a love letter the great thing is to be confronted with a very vivid idea of your subject. When Poe wrote to Mrs. Whitman he might have been addressing a fashion plate in a ladies' newspaper—a fashion plate which walks the cemetery by moonlight, for the atmosphere is one of withered roses and moonshine. The fact that he had buried Virginia a short time before, that he denied his love for her, that he was writing to Annie at the same time and in the same style, that he was about to propose to a widow for the sake of her money—all his perfidies and meannesses do not by themselves make it impossible that he loved Mrs. Whitman genuinely. Were it not for the letters we might accept the charitable view that this was his last effort at redemption. But when we read the letters we feel that the man who wrote them had no emotion left about anything; his world was a world of phantoms and fashion plates; his phrases are the cast-off phrases that were not quite good enough for a story. He could see neither himself nor others save through a mist of opium and alcohol. The engagement, which had been made conditional upon his reform, was broken off; Mrs. Whitman sank on to a sofa holding a handkerchief 'drenched in ether' to her face, and her old mother rather pointedly observed to Poe that the train was about to leave for New York.

Cynical though it sounds, we doubt whether Mrs. Whitman lost as much as she gained by the unfortunate end of her love affair. Her feeling for Poe was probably more that of a benefactress than of a lover; for she was one of those people who 'devoutly believe that serpents may be reclaimed. This is only effected by patience and prayer—but the results are wonderful.' This particular serpent was irreclaimable; he was picked up unconscious in the street and died a year later. But he left behind him a crop of reptiles who taxed Mrs. Whitman's patience and needed her prayers for the rest of her life. She became the recognized authority upon Poe, and whenever a biographer was in need of facts or old Mrs. Clemm was in need of money they applied to her. She had to decide the disputes of the different ladies as to which had been loved the most, and to keep the peace between the rival historians, for whether a woman is more vain of her love or an author of his work has yet to be decided. But the opportunities which such a position gave her of endless charity and literary discussion evidently suited her and the good sense and wit of the bird-like little woman, who was extremely poor and had an eccentric sister to provide for, seem to justify her statement that 'the results are wonderful'.

Visits to Walt Whitman [1]

THE great fires of intellectual life which burn at Oxford and at Cambridge are so well tended and long established that it is difficult to feel the wonder of this concentration upon immaterial things as one should. When, however, one stumbles by chance upon an isolated fire burning brightly without associations or encouragement to guard it, the flame of the spirit becomes a visible hearth where one may warm one's hands and utter one's thanksgiving. It is only by chance that one comes upon them; they burn in unlikely places. If asked to sketch the condition of Bolton about the year 1885 one's thoughts would certainly revolve round the cotton market, as if the true heart of Bolton's prosperity must lie there. No mention would be made of the group of young men—clergymen, manufacturers, artisans, and bank clerks by profession—who met on Monday evenings, made a point of talking about something serious, could broach the most intimate and controversial matters frankly and without fear of giving offence, and held in particular the view that Walt Whitman was 'the greatest epochal figure in all literature'. Yet who shall set a limit to the effect of such talking? In this instance, besides the invaluable spiritual service, it also had some surprisingly tangible results. As a consequence of those meetings two of the talkers crossed the Atlantic; a steady flow of presents and messages set in between Bolton and Camden; and Whitman as he lay dying had the thought of 'those good Lancashire chaps' in his mind. The book [2] recounting these events has been published before, but it is well worth reprinting for the light it sheds upon a new type of hero and the kind of worship which was acceptable to him.

[1] *Times Literary Supplement*, January 3, 1918.
[2] *Visits to Walt Whitman in 1890–91*, by J. Johnston and J. W. Wallace.

To Whitman there was nothing unbefitting the dignity of a human being in the acceptance either of money or of underwear, but he said that there is no need to speak of these things as gifts. On the other hand, he had no relish for a worship founded upon the illusion that he was somehow better or other than the mass of human beings. 'Well,' he said, stretching out his hand to greet Mr. Wallace, 'you've come to be disillusioned, have you?' And Mr. Wallace owned to himself that he was a little disillusioned. Nothing in Walt Whitman's appearance was out of keeping with the loftiest poetic tradition. He was a magnificent old man, massive, shapely, impressive by reason of his power, his delicacy, and his unfathomable depths of sympathy. The disillusionment lay in the fact that 'the greatest epochal figure in all literature' was 'simpler, homelier, and more intimately related to myself than I had imagined'. Indeed, the poet seems to have been at pains to bring his common humanity to the forefront. And everything about him was as rough as it could be. The floor, which was only half car- peted, was covered with masses of papers; eating and wash- ing things mixed themselves with proofs and newspaper cuttings in such ancient accumulations that a precious letter from Emerson dropped out accidentally from the mass after years of interment. In the midst of all this litter Walt Whitman sat spotlessly clean in his rough grey suit, with much more likeness to a retired farmer whose working days are over; it pleased him to talk of this man and of that, to ask questions about their children and their land; and, whether it was the result of thinking back over places and human beings rather than over books and thoughts, his mood was uniformly benignant. His temperament, and no sense of duty, led him to this point of view, for in his opinion it behoved him to 'give out or express what I really was, and, if I felt like the Devil, to say so!'

And then it appeared that this wise and free-thinking old farmer was getting letters from Symonds and sending mes- sages to Tennyson, and was indisputably, both in his opinion and in yours, of the same stature and importance as any of the heroic figures of the past or present. Their names dropped into his talk as the names of equals. Indeed, now and then something seemed 'to set him apart in spiritual isolation and to give him at times an air of wistful sadness', while into his free and easy gossip drifted without effort the phrases and ideas of his poems. Superiority and vitality lay not in a class but in the bulk; the average of the American people, he insisted, was immense, 'though no man can become truly heroic who is really poor'. And 'Shakespeare and such-like' come in of their own accord on the heels of other matters. 'Shakespeare is the poet of great personalities.' As for passion, 'I rather think Æschylus greater'. 'A ship in full sail is the grandest sight in the world, and it has never yet been put into a poem.' Or he would throw off comments as from an equal height upon his great English contemporaries. Carlyle, he said, 'lacked amorousness'. Carlyle was a growler. When the stars shone brightly—'I guess an exception in that country'—and some one said 'It's a beautiful sight', Carlyle said, 'It's a sad sight'. . . . 'What a growler he was!'

It is inevitable that one should compare the old age of two men who steered such different courses until one saw nothing but sadness in the shining of the stars and the other could sink into a reverie of bliss over the scent of an orange. In Whitman the capacity for pleasure seemed never to diminish, and the power to include grew greater and greater; so that although the authors of this book lament that they have only a trivial bunch of sayings to offer us, we are left with a sense of an 'immense background or vista' and stars shining more brightly than in our climate.

Oliver Wendell Holmes[1]

A HUNDRED years ago one might talk more glibly of American literature than it is safe to do at present. The ships that pass each other on the Atlantic do more than lift a handful of Americans and Englishmen from one shore to another; they have dulled our national self-consciousness. Save for the voice and certain small differences of manner which give them a flavour of their own, Americans sink into us, over here, like raindrops into the sea. On their side they have lost much of that nervous desire to assert their own independence and maturity in opposition to a mother country which was always reminding them of their tender age. Such questions as Lowell conceived—'A country of *parvenus*, with a horrible consciousness of shoddy running through politics, manners, art, literature, nay, religion itself?' and answered as we may guess, no longer fret them; the old adjectives which Hawthorne rapped out—'the boorishness, the stolidity, the self-sufficiency, the contemptuous jealousy, the half sagacity (etc., etc.) that characterize this strange people'—are left for their daily Press in moments of panic; for international criticism, as Mr. Henry James has proved, has become a very delicate and serious matter. The truth is that time and the steamboats have rubbed out these crudities; and if we wish to understand American art, or politics, or literature, we must look as closely as we look when blood and speech are strange to us.

The men who were most outspoken against us brought about this reasonable relationship partly because we read their books as our own, and partly because literature is able to suggest the surroundings in which it is produced. We are now able to think of Boston or Cambridge as places with a life of their own as distinct and as different from ours as the

[1] *Times Literary Supplement*, August 26, 1909.

London of Pope is different from the London of Edward VII. The man who contributed to this intimacy, which is founded upon an understanding that we differ in many ways, as much as any of the rest, was undoubtedly Oliver Wendell Holmes, although he did it by means that were very different from theirs. He was, in some respects, the most complete American of them all.

He was born in 1809 of the best blood in the country, for his father, the Rev. Abiel Holmes, came from an old Puritan stock which might be traced to a lawyer of Gray's Inn in the sixteenth century, and his mother, Sarah Wendell, had distinguished blood from many sources, Dutch and Norman and good American. His father was stern and handsome, and taught 'the old-fashioned Calvinism, with all its horrors'; his mother was a little sprightly woman, inquisitive and emotional. People who knew them said that the son inherited more from her than from his father. It was one of the charming characteristics of the mature man that he was always looking back to his childhood, and steeping it in such shade and quaintness as a 'gambrel-roofed house' built in 1730 will provide; like Hawthorne he had a pathetic desire to mix his childish memories with something old, mysterious, and beautiful in itself. There were dents in the floor where the soldiers had dropped their muskets during the Revolution; the family portraits had been slashed by British rapiers; and there was a chair where Lord Percy had sat to have his hair dressed. From the vague memories that hang about his early years, and inspire some of the pleasantest pages in his books, one may choose two for their importance. 'I might have been a minister myself, for aught I know, if —— had not looked and talked so like an undertaker.' It was not until much later that he could analyse what had happened to him as a child. When he could read he was taught that 'We were a set of little fallen wretches, exposed to the wrath of God by the fact of that existence which we could not help.' He was roused in revolt against what he called 'the inherited servitude of my ancestors', and not only decided against the ministry as a calling, but never ceased to preach the beliefs which his early revolt had taught him. These beliefs were started in him, or at any rate his old views were shaken for ever, by a peep through a telescope on the common at the transit of Venus. He looked, and the thought came to him, like a shock, that the earth too was no bigger than a marble; he went on to think how this planet is 'equipped and provisioned for a long voyage in space'. The shock seems to have shown him both that we are part of a great system, and also that our world will last for a period 'transcending all our ordinary measures of time'. If it is true that we are to continue indefinitely, then it is possible, he found, to consider that 'this colony of the universe is an educational institution' and this is 'the only theory which can "justify the way of God to man"'. We may disbelieve in the Garden of Eden and in the fall of man; and we may believe that 'this so-called evil to which I cannot close' is a passing condition from which we shall emerge. He had found a basis for that optimism which inspired his teaching, and, if the reasons which he gave seem insufficient, his conclusions and the way they came to him—looking through a telescope for ten cents at the transit of Venus—bear out much that we think when we know him better. The practical result of the conflict was that he became a doctor instead of a clergyman, spent two years in Paris studying his profession, visited England and Italy on his way, and returned to practise in Boston, living there and at Cambridge, with the exception of his hundred days in Europe, for the rest of his life.

The most diligent of biographers can find little to add to such a record, nor did Dr. Holmes come to the rescue. His letters are not intimate; like other people who write much about themselves in public, he has little to say in private. As a doctor he never won a large practice, for he not only collected a volume of poetry from time to time, but smiled when the door was opened and made jokes upon the staircase. When someone asked him what part of anatomy he liked best, he answered: 'The bones; they are cleanest'. The answer shows us the 'plain little dapper man', who could never bear the sights of a sick-room, who laughed to relieve the tension, who would run away when a rabbit was to be chloroformed, who was clean and scrupulous in all respects, and inclined, as a young man, to satirize the world with a somewhat acrid humour. Two friends have put together a picture of him. 'A small, compact, little man . . . buzzing about like a bee, or fluttering like a humming bird, exceedingly difficult to catch unless he be really wanted for some kind act, and then you are sure of him.' The other adds that he has a 'powerful jaw and a thick strong under-lip, that gives decision to his look, with a dash of pertness. In conversation he is animated and cordial—sharp, too, taking the words out of one's mouth.'

At this time, before the publication of the *Autocrat*, he was famous for his talk and for his verses. The verses were for the most part inspired by dinners and 'occasions'; they light up for us the circle of American men of letters who met and talked at Parker's Hotel, as men had talked at Will's Coffee House; they are addressed to people who know each other well. His reputation, therefore, independently of his medical works, was very intense, but very local. He was almost fifty when the first of the *Autocrat* papers 'came from my mind almost with an explosion'. *The Professor* and *The Poet* followed; then there were the two novels; he became, in short, a man of letters from whom the public expects a regular statement of opinion. Even at this distance it is easy to imagine the rush with which the *Autocrat* came into the world. Every breakfast-table in Boston knew the writer by repute, knew of his birth and traditions, and read his views in print with a kind of personal pride, as though he were the mouthpiece of a family. Those associations are no longer ours; but, as the manner of beauty clings when beauty is gone, so we can still relish the gusto with which Dr. Holmes addressed himself to his fellow-citizens.

This is true, and yet is it possible that we should not dwell upon such considerations if we were altogether beneath the *Autocrat's* spell? There is, we must own it, a little temptation to try to account for our ancestors' tastes, and so to avoid formulating our own. The chief interest, however, of these centenary celebrations is that they provide an opportunity for one generation to speak its mind of another with a candour and perhaps with an insight which contemporaries may hardly possess. The trial is sharp, for the books that live to such an age will live to a much greater age, and raise the standard of merit very high. Let us own at once that Dr. Holmes's works can hardly be said to survive in the sense that they still play any part in our lives; nor is he among the writers who live on without any message to deliver because of the sheer delight that we take in their art. The fact that there is someone who will write a centenary biography for a public that reads the *Autocrat* cannot be set down to either of these causes; and yet, if we seek it on a lower plane, we shall surely find reason enough. There is, to begin with, the reason that our own experience affords us. When we take it up at a tender age—for it is one of the first books that one reads for oneself—it tastes like champagne after breakfast cups of weak tea. The miraculous ease with which the talk flows on, the richness of simile and anecdote, the humour and the pathos, the astonishing maturity of the style, and, above all, some quality less easy to define, as though fruits just beyond our reach were being dropped plump into our hands and proving deliciously firm and bright—these sensations make it impossible to think of the *Autocrat* save as an elderly relative who has pressed half-sovereigns into one's palm and at the same time flattered one's self-esteem. Later, if some of the charm is gone, one is able to appraise these virtues more soberly. They have, curiously enough, far more of the useful than of the ornamental in their composition. We are more impressed, that is, by the honesty and the common sense of the *Autocrat's* remarks, and by the fact that they are the fruit of wide observation, than by the devices with which they are decked out.

The pages of the book abound with passages like the following:

Two men are walking by the polyphlœsbœan ocean, one of them having a small tin cup with which he can scoop up a gill of sea-water when he will, and the other nothing but his hands, which will hardly hold water at all—and you call the tin cup a miraculous possession! It is the ocean that is the miracle, my infant apostle! Nothing is clearer than that all things are in all things, and that just according to the intensity and extension of our mental being we shall see the many in the one and the one in the many. Did Sir Isaac think what he was saying when he made *his* speech about the ocean—the child and the pebbles, you know? Did he mean to speak slightingly of a pebble? Of a spherical solid which stood sentinel over its compartment of space before the stone that became the pyramids had grown solid, and has watched it until now! A body which knows all the currents of force that traverse the globe; which holds by invisible threads to the ring of Saturn and the belt of Orion! A body from the contemplation of which an archangel could infer the entire inorganic universe as the simplest of corollaries! A throne of the all-pervading Deity, who has guided its very atom since the rosary of heaven was strung with beaded stars!

This is sufficiently plausible and yet light in weight; the style shares what we are apt to think the typical American defect of over-ingenuity and an uneasy love of decoration; as though they had not yet learnt the art of sitting still. The universe to him, as he says, 'swam in an ocean of similitudes and analogies'; but the imaginative power which is thus implied is often more simply and more happily displayed. The sight of old things inspires him, or memories of boyhood.

Now, the sloop-of-war the Wasp, Captain Blakely, after gloriously capturing the Reindeer and the Avon, had disappeared from the face of the ocean, and was supposed to be lost. But there was no proof of it, and, of course, for a time, hopes were entertained that she might be heard from. Long after the last real chance had utterly vanished, I pleased myself with the fond illusion that somewhere on the waste of waters she was still floating, and there were *years* during which I never heard the sound of the great gun booming inland from the Navy-yard without saying to myself, 'The Wasp has come!' and almost thinking I could see her, as she rolled in, crumpling the water before her, weather-beaten, barnacled, with shattered spars and threadbare canvas, welcomed by the shouts and tears of thousands. This was one of those dreams that I nursed and never told. Let me make a clean breast of it now, and say that, so late as to have outgrown childhood, perhaps to have got far on towards manhood, when the roar of the cannon has struck suddenly on my ear, I have started with a thrill of vague expectation and tremulous delight, and the long-unspoken words have articulated themselves in the mind's dumb whisper, *The Wasp has come!*

The useful virtues are there, nevertheless. The love of joy, in the first place, which raced in his blood from the cradle was even more of a virtue when the *Autocrat* was published than it is now. There were strict parents who forbade their children to read the book because it made free with the gloomy morality of the time. His sincerity, too, which would show itself in an acrid humour as a young man, gives an air of pugnacity to the kindly pages of the *Autocrat*. He hated pomp, and stupidity, and disease. It may not be due to the presence of high virtues, and yet how briskly his writing moves along! We can almost hear him talk, 'taking the words out of one's mouth', in his eagerness to get them said. Much of this animation is due to the easy and almost incessant play of the *Autocrat*'s humour; and yet we doubt whether Dr. Holmes can be called a humourist in the true sense of the word. There is something that paralyses the will in humour, and Dr. Holmes was primarily a medical man who valued sanity above all things. Laughter is good, as fresh air is good, but he retracts instinctively if there is any fear that he has gone too deep:

> *I know it is a sin*
> *For me to sit and grin—*

that is the kindly spirit that gives his humour its lightness, and, it must be added, its shallowness. For, when the range is so scrupulously limited, only a superficial insight is possible; if the world is only moderately ridiculous it can never

be very sublime. But it is easy enough to account for the fact
that his characters have little hold upon our sympathies by
reflecting that Dr. Holmes did not write in order to create
men and women, but in order to state the opinions which a
lifetime of observation had taught him. We feel this even in
the book which has at least the form of a novel. In *Elsie
Venner* he wished to answer the question which he had asked
as a child; can we be justly punished for an hereditary sin?
The result is that we watch a skilful experiment; all Dr.
Holmes's humour and learning (he kept a live rattlesnake
for months, and read 'all printed knowledge' about poison)
play round the subject, and he makes us perceive how
curious and interesting the case is. But—for this is the sum
of our objections—we are not interested in the heroine; and
the novel so far as it seeks to convince us emotionally is a
failure. Even so, Dr. Holmes succeeds, as he nearly always
does succeed, in making us think; he presents so many facts
about rattlesnakes and provincial life, so many reflections
upon human life in general, with such briskness and such a
lively interest in his own ideas, that the portentous 'physio-
logical conception, fertilized by a theological idea', is as
fresh and almost as amusing as the *Autocrat* or *The Professor*.
The likeness to these works, which no disguise of fiction will
obscure, proves again that he could not, as he puts it, 'get
out of his personality', but by that we only mean to define
his powers in certain respects, for 'personality' limits
Shakespeare himself. We mean that he is one of those writers
who do not see much more than other people see, and yet
they see it with some indescribable turn of vision, which
reveals their own character and serves to form their views
into a coherent creed. Thus it is that his readers always talk
of their 'intimacy' with Dr. Holmes; they know what kind
of person he was as well as what he taught. They know that
he loved rowing and horses and great trees; that he was full
of sentiment for his childhood; that he liked men to be
strong and sanguine, and honoured the weakness of women;
that he loathed all gloom and unhealthiness; that charity
and tolerance were the virtues he loved, and if one could

combine them with wit it was so much to the good. Above all, one must enjoy life and live to the utmost of one's powers. It reads something like a medical prescription, and one does not want health alone. Nevertheless, when the obvious objections are made, we need not doubt that it will benefit thousands in the future, and they will love the man who lived as he wrote.